Making Decisions That Matter

How People Face Important Life Choices

Making Decisions That Matter

How People Face Important Life Choices

Kathleen M. Galotti
Carleton College

LEA LAWRENCE ERLBAUM ASSOCIATES, PUBLISHERS
2002   Mahwah, New Jersey   London

Lawrence Erlbaum Associates, Inc., Publishers
10 Industrial Avenue
Mahwah, NJ 07430

Cover design by Kathryn Houghtaling Lacey

Library of Congress Cataloging-in-Publication Data

Galotti, Kathleen M., 1957–
    Making decisions that matter : how people face important
life choices / Kathleen M. Galotti.
        p.   cm.
    Includes bibliographical references and indexes.
    ISBN 0–8058–3396–X (cloth) — ISBN 0–8058–3397–8 (pbk.)
    1. Decision making I. Title
    BF448 .G35 2002
    153.8'3—dc21   2001054527

Books published by Lawrence Erlbaum Associates are printed on acid-free paper,
and their bindings are chosen for strength and durability.

Printed in the United States of America
10 9 8 7 6 5 4 3 2 1

TO TIMOTHY AND KIMBERLYNN,
MY TWO MOST IMPORTANT DECISIONS

Contents

Preface

My PhD dissertation was on individual differences in syllogistic reasoning—the ways in which different people take premises such as "All astronomy books are large books" and "Some large books are red books" and try to see if any conclusion necessarily follows from them (e.g., "Some astronomy books are red books."). To say that a conclusion *necessarily* follows from premises is to say that it is impossible for the premises to be true and the conclusion to be false. (By the way, the example conclusion I provided does not necessarily follow from the premises I stated—even though most casual readers think that it does).

When you research peoples' syllogistic reasoning, it is easy to obtain statistically significant results. Change the wording, or change the order of terms, and you make a problem harder or easier. Another thing about studying syllogisms is that there are lots of practice effects, and a few shortcut tricks to solving them, so that with just a little practice, you can solve them much more rapidly than your research participants or students, which makes you look relatively gifted intellectually.

At my first job interview, an undergraduate student asked me what I thought syllogistic reasoning had to do with everyday reasoning and decision making—in other words, why it mattered. Cognitive psychologists have a standard, canned, and slightly superior response to this sort of question—we answer as follows: "So, basically you are saying that syllogisms are irrelevant to real life, right?" (Student nods). "And implicitly, you are saying that psychologists should only study relevant topics, am I correct?" (Student nods again). "Okay, then it follows, doesn't it, that psychologists should not study syllogisms." (Student, growing wary, nods a third time). "But ha ha—don't you see that that conclusion is reached through syllogistic reasoning?!" (Asked triumphantly. Student shrinks into seat, looks embarrassed. Psychologist wins.)

So, of course, I used this time-tested maneuver and finished the talk. But the question still haunted me. Just because the conclusion followed from the premises didn't mean that the student used syllogistic reasoning to arrive at it.

Since that time, I've been interested in the question of how well laboratory-derived models of reasoning and decision making apply to, and explain, real-world reasoning and decision making. It has seemed to me that we cannot take for granted that all of the findings that have been discovered in well-controlled experiments will occur in real life, for various reasons.

For one thing, real-life decisions are not self-contained—that is, all of the "given information" to be used is rarely, if ever, neatly typed and handed over to the decision maker the way it often is in typical research studies. A large part of real-world decision making probably involves seeking out this information and sifting through it.

Secondly, real-life decisions are often ones we care a lot about—we use our hearts and intuitions as well as our heads, and we're motivated to get them right. Not always so with the academic type of problems presented to research participants, who are typically given hypothetical scenarios divorced from their everyday experience (e.g., "Imagine you are the chief executive officer of a large metropolitan health care organization . . .).

In laboratory studies of decision making, there is often a single correct answer; in real life, many important decisions probably have no perfect outcome, but possibilities that vary in overall goodness. In laboratory studies, there may be formulas that apply to a problem that would lead a decision maker to choose that "correct" answer; very few real-life decisions possess this clear-cut structure.

I don't mean to claim that laboratory models of decision making are irrelevant —in some, perhaps many, cases I think they do illuminate basic principles of peoples' everyday cognitive functioning. What I do mean to do is to start raising the question of when and how laboratory-based phenomena apply.

As I began to research some real-life decision making, I found the literature much less extensive than I wished. Real-world decision making cannot be as easily controlled, and many findings are likely to be particular to a specific decision being studied. Nonetheless, to answer the question, "What do laboratory-derived models of decision making have to do with real-life decision making?," we have to know about real-life decision making. This book is an attempt to survey some of that literature, and to explicitly compare its major findings to existing models of decision making. I see it as a map of new territory, and hope it will be useful to others as they set out on a journey to study other examples of real-life decision making.

ACKNOWLEDGMENTS

This project was financially supported by Carleton College by a number of intramural grants. The first, which supported the initial stages of writing, was a Dean's Discretionary grant awarded in the summer of 1999. A second, larger grant, awarded by the Faculty Grants Committee, allowed me a term free of teaching obligations as I completed revisions to the manuscript during Spring term, 2001. I am very grateful to Dean Elizabeth McKinsey, President Stephen R. Lewis, and the other members of the Grants Committee for providing me the opportunity to pursue this extensive writing project.

Help and encouragement from my two editors, Judi Amsel and Bill Webber, must also be mentioned. Judi, who signed this project, and Bill, who inherited it, were both generous with their time and constructive in their feedback, and it was a pleasure to work with them. Debbie Ruel, my production editor, was likewise a gem to collaborate with.

Friends and former students uncomplainingly read through chapters, most notably Ann Lapeyre and Sara Voelz; also Annie Murray-Close and Kelly Carmichael. Helping me with the mundane and seemingly never-ending chores of reference-checking and correspondence were Carelton students (some of whom are now alumni): Sara Jane Olsen, Annie Murray-Close, and Laura Bloedorn. Hope Altenbaumer read through the entire manuscript and prepared the indices.

Ironically, the vast majority of this book was written at a time in my life when I needed to make many important personal decisions regarding family, career, and values. I thank many, many dear friends who encouraged me, argued with me, and believed in me as I traversed a rocky segment of my life's journey. For these untold and innumerable conversations, I thank (in alphabetical order): Nancy Ashmore, Linda Beckman, Marion Cass, Blythe Clinchy, Roy Elveton, Judy Fey, Angie Groth, Tracy Harris, Deanna Haunsperger, Will Hollingsworth, Anne Mullinax Jones, Steve Kennedy, Hope Langston, Ann and André Lapeyre, Beth Lavin, Bonnie Lovell, Carol and Art Nyberg, Lois Ornat, Deb Sackrison, Susan Singer, and Debby Wilkins. ⌐

Introduction
and Overview

Beth, an undergraduate psychology major at the college where I teach, is sitting in my office. We are having the 17th in what will turn out to be a long series of discussions on the topic, "What should Beth do after college?" Beth is pretty sure she wants to go to graduate school, but she's not 100% certain of her decision yet. Moreover, she has a million questions, doubts, and worries. Is she good enough to get in? Where should she go? In what area within psychology should she specialize? What are her job prospects when she gets out of school?

Over the years, I've worked with many students making this and other decisions: What to major in? How to find a summer internship? What kind of career? I've also discussed other important decisions with friends: What kind of day care provider should they have for their children? To which school should they send their children? Is it time to consider a career change? I've also sweated out a number of important decisions in my own life: Which job should I take (or should I have taken)? Is it time to change jobs? Should I consider adopting a child? These are just a few that come to mind. Because one of my research interests is decision making, I've felt both intrigued and privileged to have the opportunity to view these processes up close. This book describes what I've learned about applying the research findings from laboratory research in cognitive psychology to real-life decisions.

WHAT IS DECISION-MAKING?

Cognitive psychologists use the term *decision making* to refer to the mental activities that take place in choosing among alternatives. Let's consider this process with another perhaps familiar example: Choosing a new car. The decision about a new car may be part of a larger set of decisions about budgets and lifestyles. After all, sports cars and minivans have different characteristics, capabilities, and costs.

Typically, these decisions are made under conditions of some uncertainty. For example, people want a car that is very reliable, but they may not have good information about automobile reliability. And, even if there is reason to believe, for example, that Buicks are more reliable than Chevrolets, it does not follow that every Buick will be more reliable than every Chevy. So, the decision maker can almost never be absolutely certain that his or her decision will turn out exactly as planned. Dealing with this uncertainty appears to be a major factor in the way people approach decisions.

Car buyers also often have many goals in purchasing a car, and some of these goals may conflict. For example, people may want a car that has a powerful engine, has stylish looks, isn't terribly expensive, and has a good repair record. However, the cars that have powerful engines might not be the relatively inexpensive ones. Therefore, the car buyer may have to prioritize his or her goals—that is, decide which criteria matter most. Different people will attach different priorities to different goals at different times in their lives, of course, which is why, in most cases, there is no absolutely correct choice to make.

When I meet with students making important life decisions (e.g., choosing which college major to declare), they often show signs of agitation. They know that they need to make a decision but do not know how to do it. They wish the uncertainty over, but they don't want to close off options prematurely. They are aware that a lot of information relevant to the decision exists but don't know quite how to collect, organize, and use it all in the time allotted. They know there are no guarantees, but they don't want to make unfortunate choices.

Another source of difficulty in making this decision is the number of options available. My college has more than 30 majors available. In addition, there is an option for students to design their own interdisciplinary major. There are also options to double major, declare concentrations (sort of like minors), participate in off-campus study programs, and so on, adding complications to the process of making a final choice.

Between their goals and their potential options, students often seem to find the amount of potentially relevant information quickly becoming staggering. In these cases, the students seek help. Specifically, they often want to know what kind and how much information to gather. Is it enough, they wonder, to talk to one person majoring in each of the departments in which they are interested? Or should they try to survey two, or four? Depending on the number of majors they are considering, it is clear that the number of "interviews" could quickly become quite large.

Secondly, students wonder how to select among the various potential sources of information. For instance, how much should they rely on information from the different college departments, most of which either publish official handbooks or sponsor informational meetings? Which students should be interviewed, the top students in the department or the "average" students? The happy, enthusiastic students or the ones who are somewhat cynical?

Another issue is what to do with conflicting information. Say, for instance, that the department handbook describes the curriculum one way, but a friend who is a major reports that reality is at odds with the official description. Should one interrogate the department chair, conduct a written survey of all the majors, or believe one source and discount the other? And if so, which source?

Moreover, sophomore students I talk with often complain about the fact that they have to make this important decision while they are simultaneously leading their typically hurried lives. That is, they still have to study for tests, write papers, read assignments, meet their extracurricular commitments—in short, they have very little extra time to collect, sort through, weigh, and assess all the information they gather. Some of the students report feeling overwhelmed and joke about flipping coins or using dartboards to make the decision—figuring that "getting it over with" is well worth the possible costs of making an "irrational" decision. My surmise from these conversations is that the students simply don't know what it means to be rational when it comes to making an important real-life decision while living their lives in the real world. I argue in this book that there are ways of being rational that don't lead to endless deliberation or require the decision maker to spend a month sequestered in a log cabin without phones or electricity. To make that argument, I must first discuss the concept of rationality.

WHAT IS RATIONAL DECISION MAKING?

Sometimes decisions that are made carefully and well don't end up happily. Because decisions are often made under conditions of uncertainty, some do not yield the hoped-for results, even if made carefully and after thorough, unbiased consideration of the evidence. For this reason, psychologists generally argue that "goodness" of decision making cannot be measured by the success of individual decisions—luck, for instance, often plays too great a role. Instead, the yardstick of success is often taken to be the rationality of the decision.

So what exactly makes a decision a rational one? There are different definitions of rationality, of course. A typical definition comes from von Winterfeldt and Edwards (1986): rational decision making "has to do with selecting ways of thinking and acting to serve your ends or goals or moral imperatives, whatever they may be, as well as the environment permits" (p. 2). Let's translate this into a specific example. If you are trying to choose a new car, to choose "rationally" you need first to make sure that you are taking into consideration all of your relevant goals and objectives, not just the ones you think of first. If you walk onto a new car lot and pick out a car just because you think it looks "snazzy," then you probably aren't being rational. Why? Because you aren't taking into account all of your other goals and criteria, for example, a car that gets good gasoline mileage, a car that has up-to-date safety features, a car that has a certain amount of cargo space.

Rational decision making also requires that you gather information about your decision as carefully as possible under the circumstances. Rational decision making requires in particular that you look at not only evidence that supports your initial inclinations but also evidence that does not. (We will talk more about this counterintuitive point in chapter 3.) So, in the car example, rational decision making requires that you seek out unbiased information (e.g., you check out *Consumer Reports*, instead of relying only on the advice of a salesman, or even your uncle Fred).

PHASES OF DECISION MAKING

For most even minimally complex decisions, the decision maker has to engage in several tasks. These tasks might, in the typical case, be ordered so that one task is completed before the next one begins. In this case, we might refer to these tasks as stages of decision making. The term *stages* is meant to imply that the tasks have a predetermined order to them, that to accomplish stage 2, for example, one first must finish stage 1. This in turn implies that each stage is a prerequisite for the next, and that no skipping of stages can occur.

All of these are fairly stringent requirements, and the empirical evidence isn't clear enough to assert that typical decision-making processes meet them. As a consequence, I will use the term, *phases,* to refer to these tasks. The term *phases* is meant to imply that there may or may not be a set order to the tasks, that the performance of one task can overlap with the performance of another, that some tasks can be skipped, and that tasks can be done in different orders. I also want to allow for the possibility of a decision maker *cycling through* the different tasks, in other words, doing the first task, then the second, and then the third, then going back and revisiting the first, and so on.

For now, I'll just give a brief description of each of these phases of decision making. As you'll see in the table of contents, most of these phases are discussed in far more detail in chapters 2 through 5.

Setting Goals

When we try to understand why a person makes one decision rather than another, it often turns out that the reasons have to do with the decision maker's goals for the decision. Let's return to the example of choosing a college major. Many students I talk with describe their plan to declare an economics major, because their goal is to go into business after college. Others tell me they are thinking about biology because they want to get into medical school. (By the way, I'm just reporting what I've been told and am expressly not endorsing these views.) To the contrary, I've heard of medical schools that welcome a diversity of majors, and top CEOs often have very traditional "liberal-artsy" majors, such as classics or history.

The idea in setting goals is that the decision maker takes stock of his or her plans for the future, his or her principles and values, and his or her priorities. That is, the decision maker needs to develop answers to the question, "What am I trying to accomplish?" Those answers are the decision maker's goals, and they will influence decision making in various ways, as we will see.

Gathering Information

Before making a decision, the decision maker needs information. Specifically, she or he needs to know what the various options are. In some decisions (often called "go/no go" decisions), the options are two: take a particular course of action, or not. Even in this fairly simple case, however, the decision maker needs to gather information about the two options. For example, what are the likely consequences of each option, in both the short and long term? Who is affected in each option, and how? Do the effects change over time? Will taking or not taking a particular course of action obligate the decision maker to other decisions or plans? In other words, does each option open or close off other options?

Other decisions can be much more complex. For example, consider again the scenario of "purchasing a new car." In any given year, there are dozens of makes of different cars available. If you also consider all the different ways a given car can be customized, the options multiply rapidly. Somehow, the decision maker needs to gather some information about at least some of the options.

In addition to information about options, decision makers may need or want to gather information about possible criteria to use in making their choice. If you've never bought a car before, you might talk with experienced car buyers to get information about what things they consider. Or you might try to develop your own wish list of features your ideal car would have. Construction of this wish list might originate from the goals you've set.

Decision Structuring

For complex decisions, decision makers need a way of pulling together all of their information. This is especially true when there are a great number of options and when there are numerous points to be considered in making the decision.

Consider again the example of choosing a college major. In one of my studies, I surveyed 1st-year college students over a period of 1 year as they thought about this decision (Galotti, 1999a). Many of the students I surveyed (Galotti, 1999a) listed a wide variety of criteria they considered in making this decision. Among these were things like, "Do I enjoy the material?" "Will it lead to a career I am interested in?" "Does it have a lot of requirements?" "Do I like the faculty who teach the classes?" In my study, students listed about seven different criteria and about four different options, or possible majors. To really consider all these criteria and options, a decision maker will need to think about 28 different pieces of information (e.g., "Is biology a subject I enjoy?" "Is chemistry a subject I enjoy?" "Is psychology a subject I enjoy?" etc.)

Twenty-eight different things to think about is quite a lot. Somehow, the decision maker needs to determine or invent a way of managing this information. The way she or he does this comprises what is called the *decision structuring*.

Making a Final Choice

After gathering all the information, the decision maker needs to make a selection from the final set of options. This might involve a procedure as simple as flipping a coin or throwing a dart at a wall, or it might be a considerably more complex process. This process may involve other decisions, such as when to cease the information-gathering phase of the main decision or a decision about which information is more relevant or reliable.

Evaluating

A helpful (and probably often omitted) last phase of decision making is the evaluation of the entire process. What went well about the process? What didn't go so well? The aim here is to reflect and identify the areas of the process that can stand improvement as well as those that ought to be used again in future, similar decisions.

ISSUES IN THE STUDY OF DECISION MAKING

In the chapters to come, I'll be elaborating on most of the above phases, first from the point of view of theorists who have described ideal processes. I'll describe existing models of decision making that pertain to the different phases. I'll also present data from existing studies of real-life decision making to see how close reality comes to the ideal.

However, I will also be arguing that the way a decision is made depends heavily on a number of circumstances specific to that decision. To preview the conclusion, decision making processes and effectiveness vary, depending on a number of factors: the specific decision being made, and the characteristics of the individual or group making the decision being two of the most important. To understand real-life decision making, we'll need to think about each of these issues in turn.

What Counts as Decision Making?

One of the first issues we will need to confront is when people are actually making decisions. For example, suppose that every day at 9:30 A.M. you have a coffee break with your friends or co-workers. Is it accurate to say that last Tuesday you *decided* to take that coffee break? Or is it more accurate to exclude from decision making any of those actions a person takes out of habit? What about the following: Last week my veterinarian prescribed some medication for one of my dogs. Am I correctly described as having decided to give my dog this medication, even if my reason is simply that I typically follow my veterinarian's advice?

In both of these examples, a neutral observer could point out that there were alternatives available to the choice the decision maker ultimately made. After all, you could in theory choose to do something else at the normal coffee break time. But in practice, it might feel to you as though you were not making a conscious, reflective decision to take the coffee break but rather just going along and doing what you typically do.

In this book, we'll restrict our attention to those situations where the decision maker is explicitly aware of the alternatives and of the need to make a conscious selection of one over another. That means that choices that aren't perceived by the agent of the choice won't be discussed here. So actions taken without reflection, or carried out in blind adherence to someone else's instructions or orders, won't be considered here. As we'll see, restricting our discussion to this subset of instances will still leave us with a vast subject matter to consider.

Effects of Different Types of Decisions

I've already said that it's not a terribly rational procedure to walk onto a new car lot and choose the first car that appeals to you. And, anecdotally, it seems that few people do make this decision that way—there's at least some milling about the dealership, peering at the sticker, and climbing in and out of the front or rear seat, presumably to get information about comfort, roominess, or the like. However, it's easy to imagine other decisions that probably ought to be made quickly, and by what first appeals. Choosing a flavor of ice cream at your local Baskin Robbins 31 Flavors store comes to mind as just such an example. If you paused to gather complete information about ingredients or taste of each alternative (remember, there are 31!) and then attempted to systematically compare all your alternatives, you would surely annoy and irritate not only the store employee but also everyone behind you in line.

Similarly, some decisions seem to me to be very personal ones, ones that decision makers need to take the major responsibility for making. Job and career choices are two that immediately come to mind. Although it seemed appropriate to hear from significant others in my life (friends, parents, my spouse) when I made these decisions, it also seemed then and still seems as though these decisions had to be ones that, in the end, I chose.

Other types of decisions are ones in which I lean much more heavily on the advice of others. Medical decisions, for example, are ones in which I'll give much more weight to what my doctor, nurse practitioner, dentist, veterinarian, or pediatrician has to say than I will to my own opinions. Similarly, when working with a lawyer to structure my will, I'm apt to pay much more attention to his views about how courts are likely to interpret the wording of a document than I am to my own preferences for how a document ought to read.

All of these examples suggest that decisions will be made differently depending on what type of choice is at stake. No one has yet offered a complete categorization of decisions into types. However, it seems intuitive that certain classes of decisions can be identified. We will examine four different types of decision making in chapter 6—consumer (purchasing) decisions, legal decisions, medical decisions, and moral decisions—looking for similarities and differences in cognitive processes used across these four domains.

Individual Differences in Decision Making

Do people differ predictably in the way they approach decisions? Consider Anna and Sam. When confronted with a major decision, Anna places a premium on being logical and systematic, whereas Sam likes to "go with the flow." Psychologists use the term *individual differences* to refer to stable, enduring traits or characteristics that change the way a person approaches a task. With respect to decision making, some have suggested that there are real individual differences in the way people set goals, gather or organize information, make a final choice, and evaluate their performance. Some differences might stem from temperamental or personality differences. Psychologists investigating cognitive styles, learning styles, or thinking styles have described distinct approaches people take to other informational tasks, and some are beginning to apply concepts from that research specifically to the task of decision making. We'll look at some of these proposals in chapter 7.

A third way individuals differ in their decision making may be developmental. Children are often described as making quick, impulsive decisions, and adolescents are described as being extremely prone to take unwise risks. Developmental psychologists provide strong evidence that the way children and adolescents acquire and use information changes, depending on their developmental level and perhaps also on their participation in formal educational settings. Chapter 7 examines these ideas in greater detail.

People may also change the way they approach decisions as they acquire more practice in making those decisions. That is, experts in a domain probably do assess information and choose courses of action differently than do novices or beginners in that domain. Again, we'll look at this issue in chapter 7.

Making Decisions With Other People

The prototypical decision maker is the individual who sifts through information and compares alternatives. But, in real life, pairs or groups of people make many decisions. Spouses may make many major consumer decisions together (e.g., purchasing a car or house), teams of workers may decide whether and how to implement a new project, and juries determine the guilt or innocence of an alleged wrongdoer. How is it that decision making changes when there is more than one decision maker? Chapter 8 addresses this important question.

Improving Decision Making

Psychologists make distinctions between models of decision making that simply *describe* what it is that people do when they engage in a cognitive task and those that *prescribe*, or mandate, what people ought to do to be effective decision makers. In chapter 9, we'll consider the question of whether and how it is possible to influence peoples' decision making in such a way that it improves.

GOALS OF THE BOOK

I have three goals in writing this book. The first is to describe ongoing research that examines real people making real decisions, and compare it with theoretical predictions made from laboratory-based research. A second is to provide readers with some food for thought when it comes to their own decision making. A third goal is to point out questions and issues that await further research. As a cognitive and developmental psychologist, I believe in the importance of understanding contextual factors that support, frame, and constrain human behavior and cognition. I believe that the current state of the field of studies of decision making is exciting and rich, and I hope by the book's end I will have convinced you of that excitement and potential as well.

2

Setting Goals
and Making Plans

David, a sophomore geology major, rises late one Sunday morning and considers how to spend his day. There are several things he wants to accomplish—laundry, for starters, finishing his lab report that is due the next day, meeting his buddies for a quick game of basketball, calling home to wish his sister a happy birthday, and surfing the Web to get information on a company he hopes will respond favorably to his request to interview for a summer internship. Beyond those, David intends to do several other, routine, everyday things: take a shower, brush his teeth, get dressed, and eat brunch, to name just a few.

Psychologists would call many if not all of the items on the first list (and perhaps some on the second) David's *goals*. I mentioned in chapter 1 that goals often drive decisions; we will explore that idea here. We will also try to make clearer what makes something a goal.

GOAL SETTING

The processes by which people formulate and attempt to attain goals has received much attention in the psychological literature. Miller, Galanter, and Pribram (1960) created the widely regarded seminal work on goal-directed behavior, but the centrality of goals to other psychological constructs goes back much farther. William James (1890/1983) argued that "the pursuance of future ends and the choice of means for their attainment are thus the mark and criterion of the presence of mentality" (p. 21), thus thrusting the topic center stage in psychology, the science of the mind. Pinker (1997) argued that the presence of goals defines a person's (or animal's or extraterrestrial's) intelligence, arguing that "Intelligence . . . is the ability to attain goals in the face of obstacles by means of decisions based on rational . . . rules" (p. 62).

Kruglanski (1996) describes the importance of goals as follows:

Much human activity revolves around the pursuit of goals. Goals energize our behavior and guide our choices; they occupy our thoughts and dominate our reveries. Failure to attain them causes pain and suffering, whereas their successful attainment may bring about pleasure and satisfaction. Goals lend meaning and direction to our existence; a purposeless life, devoid of significant goals, is often decried as inferior and empty. (p. 599)

Little (1983, 1998) agreed that well-being and personal meaning come from both the setting and the accomplishment of personal goals, or as he calls them, "personal projects." He argues that personal projects "provide a sense of structure to human lives, a source of continuing personal identity, and a point of active interchange between people and their surrounding contexts" (p. 194).

What Is a Goal?

Goals have been defined as internal representations of desired states (Austin & Vancouver, 1996). You can think of a goal as a standard, as an ideal outcome that you would like to achieve in some realm of your life.

Goals are thought to be one energizer of people's behavior: When a discrepancy exists between a goal and the current state, people are often motivated to take actions to reduce that discrepancy. In this sense, goals regulate our behavior (Carroll, Durkin, Hattie, & Houghton, 1997). So, for instance, David, the college student in our opening example, completes his lab report on Sunday presumably because he has a goal to hand in completed work by the deadline, and he does not yet have completed work ready to hand in. That discrepancy causes him to take action to reduce it, namely, working on the lab report to complete it.

Goals do not need to be conscious or explicit. In fact, some have argued that physiological mechanisms of homeostasis, such as regulation of internal body temperature, function as goals that are nonconscious. If you are put in a very cold room, for instance, the discrepancy between your falling body temperature and your body's goal for your temperature motivates you to take action (e.g., shivering to restore equilibrium). This process can and will occur whether or not you are aware of it or intend for it to happen (Austin & Vancouver, 1996).

The more commonly thought of case, of course, involves goals that we have set intentionally. A student sets a goal, for example, of achieving an overall B grade point average. That student gets a C on a midterm in one course. This feedback, in light of her goal, might cause the student to redouble her efforts in the course, or to change courses, or to do things to improve her grades still more in other courses. The student's goals in this instance define an acceptable level of academic performance and inspire her to achieve in this realm (Carroll et al., 1997).

Carver (1996) sees peoples' goals as possessing internal structure. He argued that people pursue abstract, high-level goals by pursuing lower level activities. The novelist might address the broad, high-level goal of finishing her current book by committing to specific and smaller goals: clearing 3 hours a day from her schedule to write; going to a particular locale to do background research; editing a first draft.

Maslow (1954) argued that our goals are arranged hierarchically as well. His idea was that people have universal goals, starting with physiological needs (e.g., for food, water, oxygen), which must be fulfilled first. After these come safety needs, belongingness/love needs, esteem needs, cognitive needs, aesthetic needs, and the need for self-actualization. Maslow asserts that people can only start to address higher order needs when lower order needs are satisfied. For example, if a robber demands your wallet at knifepoint, that event challenges your safety needs, leaving you little energy or motivation to worry about your belongingness or esteem needs (e.g., whether you are loved by your siblings or held in high regard by your friends).

Dimensions of Goals

Goals differ in a number of other ways. They can be large (e.g., ensure the solvency of the Social Security program) or small (e.g., buy ground beef to make hamburgers). They can be for the next century or for the next 10 minutes. They can be about different things—chores, personal benchmarks in sports, or interpersonal relationships one wants to establish or improve. Some goals are quite complex, with several parts to them, which may require the establishment of subgoals; other goals may be quite simple. Here, I'll list a number of ways in which goals differ.

Content. Wadsworth and Ford (1983) divided personal goals into six different content areas, including work/school, family life, social life, leisure, personal growth and maintenance, and material/environmental. Williams and Long's (1991) taxonomy includes the following categories: academic achievement, personal health, friendships, job success, intimate relationships, and personal. Of course, these are not the only way to classify goals, but they do provide some useful ways of categorizing goals, pointing out major divisions of adults' lives that seem distinctly different.

Other researchers categorize goals broadly, according to the functions they are intended to fulfill. Some psychologists distinguish between *learning* or *mastery* goals, intended to help the individual gain a new skill or develop knowledge, and *performance* goals, intended to allow the individual to demonstrate her or his proficiency or talent, to receive praise, or to please others (Elliott & Dweck, 1988; Meece, Blumenfeld, & Hoyle, 1988). A performance goal, therefore, has as the central objective the "showing off" of an achievement, knowledge, or skill; a learning goal, in contrast, is aimed toward developing, extending, or deepening knowledge or a skill.

Another categorization of goals comes from the work of McGregor and Little (1998), who distinguish between goal efficacy and goal integrity. Efficacy has to do with people's attempts to shape their external environment (e.g., to achieve success, complete a task, receive a credential). Integrity, in contrast, has to do with the degree to which a person's various activities are consistent with his or her core or defining aspects (e.g., to define one's role, to express one's values or beliefs, to demonstrate one's commitments). Their research demonstrated that people's happiness was significantly correlated with their efficacy, whereas people's sense of meaning, which is separate from and independent of happiness, was correlated significantly with integrity.

Emmons (1996) studied categorized goals in 12 content areas and found that people who pursue intimacy goals (trying to establish deep and mutually gratifying relationships) reported greater subjective well-being, whereas people whose goals are dominated by themes of achievement or power have less.

Time Frame. The time frame of each goal also varies. Some goals span a lifetime ("have a rewarding life"), whereas others span only a day or even an hour. Time frame has to do with when the individual hopes to work toward the goal, accomplish the goal, or both. Zaleski (1987) reported that goals for longer time ranges tend to be ones rated by the goal setter as more important and are ones to which people devote more effort and persistence.

Complexity. Goals also differ in complexity. Some have one or very few parts that need to be coordinated (e.g., sweeping the floor). Some goals are broad and complex enough that they allow for subgoals (e.g., writing a book, mapping out a winning team strategy, reorganizing a department). Complexity concerns the number of distinct parts or subgoals a goal has.

Difficulty. Goals vary in difficulty. Some goals are relatively easy to achieve (e.g., weekly chores). When a person finishes folding laundry, for example, there may be a sense of accomplishment, but probably not as strong a sense as the individual would derive from, say, winning a marathon, or graduating summa cum laude from a very prestigious university or college. Goal difficulty has to do with the probability of success in attaining the goal.

Specificity. Consider two students, both working on a term paper. One sets a goal of "write a good paper," another, a goal of "write a 15-page paper, citing at least 25 articles from top psychology journals, with a clear thesis and transparent organization." The latter formulation exhibits much more specificity than the former. Much evidence in the industrial/organizational literature suggests that people who set more specific goals perform better and achieve more than do people who do not set any goals or people who set very general ("I'll just try to do my best") goals (Locke & Latham, 1990).

Some people describe their goals in broad, abstract ways (e.g., "acquire knowledge and education in my area of interest"), whereas others do so in more concrete, specific, and even superficial terms ("Pay attention in class"; Emmons, 1996). Findings were that anxiety and depression were significantly correlated with more abstract descriptions of goals, perhaps because more abstract goals are typically more difficult to accomplish.

Controllability.   Some goals are ones for which the individual has a great deal of control—it is largely up to them whether or not the goal is achieved. Other goals—for example, being on the basketball team that wins the state finals—are less under the control of any one individual. Controllability thus pertains to the degree to which the individual's own efforts ensure the completion of the goal.

Degree of Realism.   Some goals are long shots—fairly unlikely to be achieved by most people. An example might be "Win the Olympic gold medal in figure skating." Other goals are fairly likely to be achieved (e.g., "Accumulate enough credits to graduate" by a high school student). This dimension pertains to the statistical likelihood of achieving a goal.

Importance/Centrality.   Goals also differ in importance or centrality. Some goals seem to define who a person is—these goals are ones often called values or principles. Some popular press books for executives and professionals urge that they set aside time to intentionally and explicitly formulate a mission statement— a written philosophy that concisely expresses one's life goals (Covey, 1989). The mission statement is intended to help people realize, and keep in front of them, their own guiding principles for life, which helps them guide their decision making, their allocation of time and other resources, and even their sense of who they are. When central goals are thwarted, it is thought to produce stronger and more negative reactions than when less important goals are not achieved (Novacek & Lazarus, 1990).

Other goals are simply chores or tasks that need to be completed so that we can (in theory) get on with the business of fulfilling other higher level goals. Doing the laundry, paying the bills, making sure the car has enough fuel in it are all examples. These things that must be done aren't always very stimulating, but their completion enables the individual to pursue other more important goals.

Autonomy of the Goal.   Sheldon and Elliot (1998) argued that not all personal goals people set are personal, in the sense that they are well integrated with one's own values, principles, and core sense of who one is. Some personal goals, instead, are set because of external rewards and punishments—one completes their tax returns before April 15, for example, primarily because of the penalties that accrue for late payment. Even some goals without external payoffs are set, the authors argue, because people fear their own guilt or regret. So, for example, an overweight person might respond that they have a goal to lose weight, not because that goal is terribly important to their sense of who they are but rather because they believe that they ought to have that as a goal.

Setting and Revising Goals

How is it that goals come to be added to or subtracted from a person's list of goals? This important and intriguing question is one for which our answers are tentative at best.

First, it is worth noting that not all of a person's goals are ones that he or she has originated. On the job or at school, for instance, a supervisor or teacher often sets assignments, due dates, specifications, and so on. These goals are ones that the employee or student can embrace enthusiastically or assent to only grudgingly. These externally set goals might be internalized and redefined by the individual, but the point remains that these goals come into being from somewhere other than the individual.

Other goals are ones over which individuals appear to have greater control. How do these originate? One possibility is that as people periodically take stock of their lives and achievements, they notice some chronically unmet goal on their hierarchy (e.g., that they have not achieved a challenging job), which spurs them to think explicitly about how to remedy that situation (Austin & Vancouver, 1996). In so doing, the individual might develop new specific goals (e.g., "Meet with career counselor" or "Look at hiring ads in professional trade magazines").

Sheldon and Elliot (1998) made a distinction between *autonomous* goals that "are undertaken with a sense of full willingness and choice" versus *controlled* goals, "which are felt to be compelled by internal or external forces or pressures" (p. 546). Moreover, they describe two kinds of each type of goal. Autonomous goals can be either *intrinsic*, arising from a person's own interests, or *identified*, arising from a set of personal convictions. The distinction depends in part on whether the task is inherently enjoyable and autonomous (i.e., that one has the feeling throughout the pursuit of the goal that one is doing it because one wants to). Identified goals, in contrast, are goals a person pursues out of a sense of duty or obligation to one's values (e.g., a person might work at a homeless shelter not because she enjoys the environment but because she believes that such an action fulfills a higher purpose).

Likewise, controlled goals come in two flavors. The first contains *extrinsic* goals, ones that are motivated by external payoffs (e.g., money, awards, recognition). The second set of goals, *introjected*, is chosen because the person wishes to avoid internally imposed guilt or anxiety. For example, a student might spend an evening studying to avoid performing poorly on a test, not so much because he wants to perform well but because he does not want to feel guilty for wasting his and his instructor's time, his parents' tuition fees, and so on.

According to Sheldon and Elliot (1998), autonomous goals are more likely to receive sustained effort than are controlled goals. Presumably, controlled goals are not as fully owned by the person and, as a consequence, are likely to be less protected from competing goals. People appear to have trouble translating controlled goals into specific actions.

Individuals almost always have multiple goals. Thus, when a new goal is established, some integration of the new goal with existing goals is almost required. The individual is likely to have to figure out ways of striking a productive balance among all of her goals. As I talk with my college advisees, I am struck by how many of them take an overload of credits, engage in an intramural sport, take an important part in a campus musical or theatrical productions, volunteer for a local charitable organization, and try to maintain their health, all during the same 10-week period. For too many of them, health collapses first, forcing a reexamination of the relative importance of all of their goals, followed usually by some paring back of activities, or some respecification of the original goals, or some combination of the two.

Goal establishment is probably a cyclical activity. Once a goal is established, there will often need to be some means of assessing progress toward the goal. This assessment may require the establishment of yet more goals or subgoals, or a redefinition of the original goal.

For example, I've had a handful of students over the years who have come to my college as premed, certain as can be that their future involves medicine. To get into medical school, they know that they must take a number of science courses, and they must get good grades in them. As they take these courses, they discover to their great surprise, that they don't have interest in the subjects or the motivation to work as hard as they need to achieve the grades they desire. Often, this causes them to reevaluate the original, broader goal of a medical career.

What causes people to set different kinds of goals? One cause has to do with stable individual differences in personality. One trait along which people have been shown to differ is the degree of their self-efficacy (Bandura, 1989), roughly defined as the degree to which people believe in their own ability to achieve. People who are higher in self-efficacy have been shown to set goals that are more difficult to meet (Phillips & Gully, 1997). That is, a person who believes she is capable of doing well on an academic test and who is willing to study hard for it is a person more likely to be aiming for an "A." A competitive athlete is very likely to be a person who believes that, with sufficient practice and fine-tuning, she can win a class, or be ranked Number 1 in a particular year. Such people are very likely to set for themselves more difficult goals than people who are low in self-efficacy.

Dweck (1996, 1999) has examined the goals people set as a function of their broader frameworks or implicit theories of personality. The two implicit theories Dweck and her colleagues have studied are *entity* theories and *incremental* theories. The former theory is held when an individual believes that some trait, ability, or attribute is fixed; the latter is held when those same traits, abilities, or attributes are seen as malleable. For example, a person holding an entity theory of intelligence would see it as a fixed ability, whereas someone holding an incremental theory of intelligence would see it as more dynamic and capable of being cultivated and changed. Dweck's work shows that individuals with entity theories are oriented toward establishing goals that measure, judge, or evaluate the trait in question. In contrast, individuals with incremental goals attempt to develop the attribute and understand the dynamics behind it. The different goals they set leads to different reactions to setbacks and negative feedback:

> In overview, the model proposes that when individuals hold an entity theory of their intelligence and are oriented toward the goal of judging their intelligence, they are likely to view negative outcomes as reflections of their intelligence and will be vulnerable to a "helpless" reaction. In contrast, when individuals hold an incremental theory of their intelligence and are oriented toward developing their intelligence, they will be more likely to view setbacks as cues to focus on their effort or strategy . . . and will be more likely to display a more mastery-oriented reaction. Thus, in the domain of intelligence, I argue that the different theories create frameworks that foster different goals, impart different meanings to failure outcomes, and thus promote different reactions. (Dweck, 1996, p. 70)

Intelligence is not the only domain in which one can hold entity or incremental theories. Dweck and her colleagues have investigated other personality traits including moral character. Interestingly, theories have been shown to be domain specific, with people holding entity theories in some realms but incremental theories in others. Typically in any realm studied, close to 42.5% of the respondents seem to hold entity theories, another 42.5% hold incremental theories, and the remaining 15% have unclear theories (Dweck, 1996).

Dweck has shown that children classified as entity theorists select as goals things that would allow them to show off their talents and avoid negative judgments (performance goals), whereas children with incremental theories select goals that were harder but offered the opportunity to learn more (learning goals; Dweck, Chiu, & Hong, 1995; Dweck & Leggett, 1988). Other work of Dweck's suggests that adults, too, can be classified reliably as holding one or the other kind of goal within a domain and that the kind of theory one holds is unrelated to one's own ability, one's optimism, and one's self-confidence and self-esteem (Dweck, 1996, 1999). However, much of Dweck's work asks children and adults to select goals from a list provided or to set goals with respect to a specific experimental task. It remains to be seen whether her findings will replicate to the realm of self-set goals.

I see these different types of goals very clearly in my college students. Some really want to perform well. They care about their performance and about any measures of their performance. They study hard, work hard, and monitor their grades very carefully. If their grade point average is high (say, a 3.5 on a 4.0 scale), they become increasingly reluctant to risk harming that measure by, say, taking a course that is known to be hard, or taking a course in a new area that they aren't sure they'll master.

Other students act in very different ways. They also care a great deal about what they are doing in college, but they are much less interested in their grades than they are in what they are learning. They take more risks when they choose courses and are more willing to sign up for something completely different from any previous experience. When they receive a poor grade on a paper or an exam, they don't take it as a signal of their fixed intelligence but rather as a sign that they'll need to work harder or in a different way. A poor grade to this type of student isn't a failure—it's a temporary setback. That is, they treat a bad performance as feedback with which to improve on future performances.

Goal Commitment

At any given point in time, then, there are a variety of goals toward which a person is working. A person also has some, if not total, control over the amount of time, energy, and other resources he or she wants to commit to a particular goal. *Goal commitment* is the term used to describe how resistant a person is to changing a personal goal once it has been set (Donovan & Radosevich, 1998). Some goals are so important to us that we won't give up on them very easily; other goals seem much less important and are easily subject to revision or displacement.

Goals that we are committed to probably occupy a more central position in our goal hierarchy. An employee with a strong commitment to family, for example, might be expected to be less willing to let work-related issues divert her or him from spending evenings and weekends at home than might an employee with a more central goal for career advancement. Moreover, people are more likely to persist at goals for which they expect some success, relative to those that seem like long shots. Goals that people successfully meet are more likely to be attributed to their own efforts and abilities, relative to goals that are not met (Zaleski, 1988). These latter might be ones that become redefined over time.

Gollwitzer (1996) used the terms *wish* versus *binding goal* to describe the distinction between goals to which people are highly versus not so highly committed. Hollenbeck, Williams, and Klein (1989), studying undergraduate students setting goals about their grade point averages, found that commitment to difficult goals was higher when goals were public rather than private, when goals were self-set rather than assigned, when individuals had a stronger internal locus of control, and when they were high in need for achievement. A later meta-analysis of 83 independent samples also showed that goal commitment is strongly positively related to performance. The effects were especially pronounced for difficult as opposed to easy goals (Klein, Wesson, Hollenbeck, & Alge, 1999), although another meta-analysis suggested that the effects of goal commitment on the goal-performance relationship were small (Donovan & Radosevich, 1998).

Of course, the above discussion assumes that people are consciously aware of what their goals are and of the relative priority of each. This is simply fiction. Indeed, the point of many self-help/personal management books is to urge that people become more aware and more reflective of their goals so that they can then make conscious decisions about prioritization.

Covey, Merrill, and Merrill (1994) illustrated the problems that arise when people aren't aware of their own goals. They distinguished between *urgency*—the sense of something needing to be done right away—and *importance*—the sense of something needing to be done to fulfill an important objective. They argued that far too many of us allocate too much of our time, energy, and emotional reserves to activities that are urgent but not important (e.g., filing a report by a deadline) and not enough to goals that are important but not urgent (e.g., developing or maintaining quality relationships in one's family). In fact, their belief is that having a written mission statement helps people to decide the importance of every given goal or activity so that people can make enough time and space in their lives to address the important ones.

PLANNING

When a person has one or more goals, he or she often formulates a plan by which to achieve those goals. College students map out daily or weekly schedules, businesspeople formulate a strategy for attaining benchmarks, coaches and teams think about actions they can take to achieve a certain rank or standing.

Scholnick and Friedman (1987) defined planning as "a set of complex conceptual activities that anticipate and regulate behavior" (p. 3). As they described it, planning involves constructing a program or blueprint that specifies the relationships between objects and actions to be carried out on those objects on the one hand and various priorities and events on the other hand. Planning requires an orientation to future events (Nurmi, 1991), an ability to predict the consequences of various actions, and a willingness to prioritize one's goals. It may also require an ability to foresee likely obstacles or problems and to resist the construction of overly optimistic scenarios (Buehler, Griffin, & Ross, 1994). College students asked to provide definitions of what it means to plan, spoke in positive terms of anticipating the future, budgeting resources, scheduling and managing time, setting and prioritizing goals, organizing, achieving efficiency and satisfaction; and they spoke in negative terms of making predetermined decisions and responding automatically (Simons & Galotti, 1992).

Planning involves a number of components. It first requires an *object*—one or more of a person's goals. When time, money, and other resources are limited, as they often are, planning requires *prioritization*—the planner needs to decide on which goals to focus energy and which goals to postpone. Planning also requires *allocation of resources* to various goals—the planner needs to decide how much time, money, effort, and energy to spend on each of his or her goals. Plans often incorporate *mental simulations* of how to achieve a goal—mentally "running through" different scenarios and possibilities, imagining various consequences. This mental simulation can help in the identification of various conflicts (e.g., among different goals, between a goal and a value, or among different possible action sequences). Plans also frequently involve *monitoring* and *revision*, either of the goals themselves (some goals are maintained, some are dropped, and others are redefined) or to the plans, and new means of achieving a goal may need to be discovered or invented.

Scholnick, Friedman, and Wallner-Allen (1997) argued that many laboratory-based investigations of planning study "sequencing under constraints." For example, a task often used to study planning is the Tower of Hanoi task, depicted in Fig. 2.1. The Tower of Hanoi task requires the problem solver to move the disks from one peg to a second, under the constraints that only one disk can be moved each turn and that a larger disk may never be placed atop a smaller one. The task requires the planner to establish subgoals and to use a recursive procedure—first

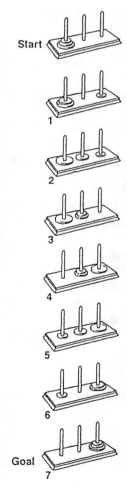

FIG. 2.1.   Optimal moves in the Tower of Hanoi task. From "What do they really measure? A comparative analysis of planning tasks," by E. K. Scholnick, S. L. Friedman, and K. E. Wallner-Allen, 1997, in *The Developmental Psychology of Planning: Why, How, and When Do We Plan?* S. L. Friedman and E. K. Scholnick (Eds.), pp. 127–156, Mahwah, NJ: Lawrence Erlbaum Associates. Copyright 1997 by Lawrence Erlbaum Associates. Reprinted with permission.

moving all but the last disk to the third, temporary storage peg, then moving the bottom disk to the second, destination peg, then figuring out a way of moving the all the disks but the last one back on top of the bottommost disk.

However, Scholnick et al. (1997) noted that this and other laboratory-based planning tasks omit important aspects of real-life planning. In particular, they fail to study the ways in which plans derive from, and in turn shape, goals.

One illustration of how planning and goals go together comes from Covey et al. (1994). Imagine a large jar, surrounded by several buckets containing large rocks, gravel, sand, and water, respectively. You could fit several large rocks in the jar. Some spaces will be left among those rocks. Some gravel can be poured into those spaces. Yet more, although smaller, spaces will be left, and sand that is poured from the next bucket could fill them. As you might have already guessed, there will again be small and hard-to-see spaces left that water can fill.

The above scenario is often demonstrated with the actual materials at executive seminars. The demonstrator, after finishing with the water, asks the audience what the point of the demonstration is. A frequent answer (given, no doubt, by someone who carries one of those thick day calendar books) is "There are always gaps, and if you work at it, you can always fit more in." But this answer misses another, perhaps more significant point entirely. The point, as Covey et al. (1994) put it, is that if you don't put the big rocks in first, you'll never be able to fit them in.

Goals are like the rocks and gravel and sand and water—with bigger objects corresponding to more important goals. The jar is analogous to all our resources: our time, our energy, our motivation. Our resources are not infinite, and what is taken up by some goals isn't available for others.

Plans and goals thus are heavily intertwined in our daily lives. Goals can form the impetus for the development of a plan. Plans arise in service of goals. Decision making is involved in the creation of both plans and goals, in ways we will see below.

GOALS AND DECISION-MAKING MODELS

Now that we have discussed what goals and plans are, we are ready to take up the question, what do they have to do with decision making? One theoretical model of decision making, image theory, focuses heavily on the decision maker's goals, principles, and values as driving decision making.

Image theory is described by its authors as seeing decision making:

> as guided by the beliefs and values that the decision maker, or a community of decision makers, holds to be relevant to the decision at hand. These beliefs and values dictate the goals of the decision. The point is to craft a course of action that will achieve these goals without interfering with the pursuit of other goals.

Image theory is driven by the concept of "fit" . . . the goal is to create a flow of activities that mutually support one another and that move the decision maker (or organization) in a desirable direction. (Beach, 1998, p. x)

Image theory posits that people have three mental representations, called images, that contain a person's principles and goals (Beach, 1993, 1998; Beach & Mitchell, 1987; Mitchell & Beach, 1990). Those images are the value image (containing the decision maker's values, morals, principles), the trajectory image (containing the decision maker's goals), and the strategic image (containing the decision maker's plans to attain her or his goals).

In making important decisions, the person is described as first doing a "quick and dirty" assessment of potential options, comparing each option to her three images. If the option violates one or more of the images, it is rejected from further consideration. This process is known as the prechoice screening of options (Beach & Potter, 1992). For example, suppose Rebecca is on a hunt for apartments. In theory, she'd like to have it all: a spacious apartment with lots of light, many closets, and a jacuzzi; in a beautiful clean building with laundry and recreational facilities; free underground parking; a fair landlord; and low, or at least very reasonable, rent. Sadly, when she looks, Rebecca never does find the apartment that meets all of these criteria. The beautiful ones are too expensive, the affordable ones are dark and small, and the ones with laundry facilities have no parking.

According to image theory, we make these kinds of decisions in two phases. In the first, we compare options (in this example, a specific apartment) to our three images and reject out of hand any that violate them. Remembering back to my own experience during graduate school, I recall refusing to even consider some apartments: those with broken or unsturdy locks, those with mice, or those in particularly seedy locales. In image theory terms, these rejected apartments could be described as violations of my strategic image (perhaps I figured if there were mice underfoot, I might have a heart attack, and thus not achieve my major goals).

According to image theory, options judged incompatible with one or more of these three images are dropped from any further consideration. This prechoice screening process does not allow trade-offs; that is, it is *noncompensatory*. Screening may result in a single option remaining active; in this case the decision maker's final choice is simply whether or not to accept the option. If he accepts the option, then his next task is to formulate a plan to achieve or implement it. If there is more than one survivor of the prechoice screening phase, then the decision maker may go on to make trade-offs or use other decision strategies to make the final choice. If there are no survivors, decision makers presumably attempt to discover new options.

Image theory recognizes two different kinds of decisions: *adoption* decisions and *progress* decisions. Adoption decisions are made about goals and plans. Adoption decisions (e.g., decisions to adopt a plan or goal) are the ones just described. As Beach and Mitchell (1998) described them:

An Adoption decision . . . is based, first of all, on whether the goal or plan is reasonable. That is, can it be done, does it cause trouble for other goals or plans, and does it conflict with relevant principles? If the answer to any of these is "yes," how unreasonable is it? If it is not too unreasonable, it might work out all right, but there is some point at which it simply is too unreasonable and must be rejected. (pp. 10–11)

A second kind of decision is a progress decision. These are used when plans for a decision are being implemented. Progress decisions assess

the compatibility between the forecasted future if implementation of the plan is continued . . . and the ideal future represented by the trajectory image. Incompatibility triggers rejection of the plan and adoption of a substitute. The substitute may be an entirely new plan, but more often it merely is a revision of the old plan that takes into consideration feedback about the environment. Failure to find a substitute plan that can generate a more promising forecast prompts revision or abandonment of the plan's goal. (Beach & Mitchell, 1998, p. 14)

Beach and Mitchell (1987; see also Beach, 1993, 1998; Mitchell & Beach, 1990) presented evidence from studies that support some different tenets of image theory. However, most of the studies involve simulations—for example, business students playing the role of CEOs and making decisions based on information provided about fictional companies. To date, only a few of the studies on image theory have encompassed the online processing of information during the course of a real-life decision.

Image theory has not made precise predictions of how many alternatives a decision maker will consider, nor of how this varies by the type of decision and the type of decision maker. We might expect that more important decisions will elicit the consideration of more alternatives, if in fact people spend more time thinking about important decisions than they do less important decisions. We might also speculate that well-educated decision makers might be more inclined to entertain more alternatives, perhaps because formal education helps people to develop strategies of managing more information. Image theory also suggests that people will describe important decisions as guided by values and their view of their future.

3

Gathering Information

In making any important decision, decision makers must acquire information—about options, about likelihood of outcomes, perhaps even about criteria to be used. The information can, and usually does, come from external sources—friends, reports, Web sites, magazine articles, professional recommendations, and so on. But information can also come from internal sources, as the decision maker reflects on her values and priorities.

Once information is gathered, of course, it needs to be processed. Some of the processing will involve interpretation; some of it might require that conflicts be resolved. Decision makers will also need to decide when they have gathered sufficient information on which to base their decision.

In the 1970s and 1980s, Kahneman and Tversky identified several implicit rules or shortcuts that people tended to use when processing information while making decisions. These rules or shortcuts have come to be known as heuristics and biases. We'll begin this chapter with a look at some of the major ones identified.

HEURISTICS AND BIASES IN INFORMATION USE

The first thing to say about the heuristics and biases that people have been shown to use frequently is that they have their place. Typically, they are ways of thinking that work well under many conditions but go drastically wrong in others. Von Winterfeldt and Edwards (1986) defined these heuristics and biases as "cognitive illusions"—discrepancies between an objectively correct answer or process and people's intuitions about the answer or process. These illusions tell us something about the ways in which people gather, sort, and integrate the information that goes into making a choice.

Availability

Sometimes, information that we use to make a decision comes not from external sources but instead from our own memory banks. For example, if you are a college student, you might consider the number of people you know in that major who are like you (in whatever relevant respects) as one factor in making a decision about what to major in. If you can think of more sociology majors that are like you (whatever that means!) than you can economics majors that are like you, you might lean more heavily toward sociology than economics.

But this assumes that you are equally able to think of people who are sociology majors and people who are economics majors. If you have taken roughly the same number of sociology and economics courses, and hang out with both kinds of people, this strategy might be a pretty good one to use.

There are other times, however, when judging how likely something is by how easy it is to think of examples from memory doesn't work so well. Here's a demonstration: Consider the problems in Table 3.1 and give your first intuitive response to each before reading further.

TABLE 3.1
Examples of Availability Usage

---

1. Consider the letter *l*. In the English language, is this letter more likely to appear in the first position of a word or the third position of a word? Give your intuition or "gut reaction."

2. Ten students from a nearby college have indicated a willingness to serve on a curriculum committee. Their names are Ann, Bob, Dan, Elizabeth, Gary, Heidi, Jennifer, Laura, Terri, and Valerie.

   a. The dean wants to form a two-person committee. What is your estimate of the number of distinct committees that could be formed? (Don't use formulas; just respond intuitively.)

   b. The dean wants to form an eight-person committee. What is your estimate of the number of distinct committees that could be formed? (Don't use formulas; just respond intuitively.)

3. Consider the two structures shown below:

   A

   x x x x x x x x x x
   x x x x x x x x x x
   x x x x x x x x x x

   B

   x x
   x x
   x x
   x x
   x x
   x x

   A path in a structure is a line that connects one "x" from each row, starting with the top row and finishing at the bottom row. How many paths do you think each structure has? (Again, give an intuitive estimate.)

Note. From "Availability: A Heuristic for Judging Frequency and Probability," by A. Tversky and D. Kahneman, 1973, *Cognitive Psychology, 5,* 212–213. Copyright © 1973 by Academic Press. Reprinted by permission.

Tversky and Kahneman (1973) presented problems such as these to under-graduate students and found that their intuitions were systematically wrong. In Problem 1, for instance, the letter *l* occurs more frequently in the third than in the initial position. In Problems 2 and 3, the answers for options A and B are the same.

What accounts for the errors? Tversky and Kahneman (1973) argued that when faced with the task of estimating the likelihood of something, people rely on the *availability heuristic*—"assessing the ease with which the relevant mental operation of retrieval, construction, or association can be carried out" (p. 208). In other words, examples that are easier to think of, to remember, or to see or calcu-late stand out more in our mind. Because of the salience of those examples, we judge them to be more frequent or probable than instances or examples that are harder to think of, remember, or compute.

In Problem 1, it turns out to be easier to think of words that begin with *l* (for example, *lesson, lift, likely*) than it is to think of words that have *l* as the third let-ter (*ball, welcome, bulb*). The reason for this may have to do with the way our lexi-cons, or mental dictionaries, are organized—alphabetically by the first letter. As with paper or electronic dictionaries, it's relatively easy to search for words by initial letter than by interior letters.

In Problem 2, the number of distinct committees that can be formed is exactly equal to the number of possible eight-person committees that can be formed (45, for those who have to know). Two-person committees seem more numerous, Tversky and Kahneman (1973) argued, because they are more distinct. There are five two-person committees, with no overlap in membership, but any two eight-person committees will have at least some overlap. Distinctiveness makes differ-ent committees easier to think of and, hence, more available. You can easily see, however, that two-person and eight-person committees have to be equally nu-merous. Consider that every two-person committee defines an eight-person non-committee, and vice versa.

The same kind of analysis applies to Problem 3. The number of paths in either structure is given by the formula x^y, where x is the number of xs in a row, and y is the number of rows. The number of paths in Structure A, then, is $8^3 = 512$. The number of paths in Structure B is 2^9, also equal to 512. Paths in A are shorter and therefore easier to visualize than those in B. The ease of visualization makes paths more available and, hence, deemed more numerous in A than in B.

Availability is not always a bad heuristic to use. If we can be sure that ease of constructing or calling instances to mind is unbiased, then it may be the best, or even only, tool to use when judging frequency or probability. In our earlier exam-ple, if you are using your memory of sociology and economics majors to decide which is more like you, and if you can be sure that you are equally likely to have met and gotten to know both types of people, then there is no obvious problem in using this heuristic. If, on the other hand, there is reason to believe that your experience has been biased (you live on a dorm floor with 20 economics majors and no sociology majors, for instance), then the use of this heuristic is probably not a fair one.

Representativeness

Trick question: Rob flipped a coin six times and obtained the following results: heads, heads, heads, tails, tails, tails. Hope flipped a second coin and obtained the following results: tails, tails, heads, tails, heads, heads. Which of the two students was more likely to have been using a fair, balanced coin?

Most people who respond to this question intuitively believe that Hope was. After all, her sequence of responses are less patterned, and more random looking. In fact, however, both outcomes are equally likely, according to the laws of probability. (I warned you it was a trick!)

People generally expect that a random process, such as a coin flip, will always produce results that are random looking. That is, they expect the results to be representative of the process that generated them. People who make judgments this way are said to be using the representativeness heuristic.

Here's a way, from the laboratory of Kahneman and Tversky (1973), in which use of the representativeness heuristic can cause decision making to go awry. In one study, undergraduate subjects were assigned to three conditions. Base-rate-condition subjects were instructed, "Consider all first-year graduate students in the United States today. Please write down your best guesses about the percentage now enrolled in each of the following nine fields of specialization." The nine fields are shown in Table 3.2. Similarity-condition subjects were presented with the personality sketch shown in Table 3.2(a) and asked to rank the nine fields in terms of "how similar is Tom W. to the typical graduate student in each of the following nine fields of graduate specialization." Prediction-condition subjects were also given the personality sketch but told that it was written several years ago, during Tom W.'s senior year of high school, and based on his response to projective tests (for example, a Rorschach test). They were then asked to predict the likelihood that Tom W. was currently a graduate student in each of the nine fields.

Table 3.2(b) shows that the research participants apparently used the representativeness heuristic. That is, students estimated the likelihood that Tom W. is a graduate student in field X by comparing his personality description to their beliefs about what typical graduate students in field X are like, ignoring base rates. Base rates are important information, however. The failure to include base rate information in estimates of probability can lead to answers that are in error, often by an order of magnitude or more.

A related bias described by Tversky and Kahneman (1971) is the (mistaken) belief in the law of small numbers. The idea is that people expect small samples (of people, of coin flips, of trials in an experiment) to resemble in every respect the populations from which they are drawn. In actuality, small samples are much more likely to deviate from the population and are therefore a less reliable basis from

TABLE 3.2
Stimuli From a Study of the Representativeness Heuristic

(A) Personality sketch of Tom W.

Tom W. is of high intelligence, although lacking in true creativity. He has a need for order and clarity, and for neat and tidy systems in which every detail finds it appropriate place. His writing is rather dull and mechanical, occasionally enlivened by somewhat corny puns and by flashes of imagination of the sci-fi type. He has a strong drive for competence. He seems to have little feel and little sympathy for other people and does not enjoy interacting with others. Self-centered, he nonetheless has a deep moral sense.

(B) Estimated base rates of nine areas of graduate specialization, and summary of similarity and prediction data for Tom W.

Graduate Specialization Area	Mean Judged Base Rate (in %)	Mean Similarity Rank	Mean Likelihood Rank
Business administration	15	3.9	4.3
Computer science	7	2.1	2.5
Engineering	9	2.9	2.6
Humanities and education	20	7.2	7.6
Law	9	5.9	5.2
Library science	3	4.2	4.7
Medicine	8	5.9	5.8
Physical and life sciences	12	4.5	4.3
Social science and social work	17	8.2	8.0

Note. From "On the Psychology of Prediction," by D. Kahneman and A. Tversky, 1973, *Psychological Review, 80*, 237–251. Copyright © by American Psychological Association. Reprinted by permission.

which to draw a conclusion. Said another way, only very large samples can be expected to be representative of the population from which they come.

Man-who arguments are another example of the misuse of the representativeness heuristic (Nisbett & Ross, 1980). A *man-who argument* is usually advanced by someone who has just confronted, for instance, a statistical summary of a number of cases reporting that lung cancer rates are significantly higher among smokers than nonsmokers. The reply "I know a man who smoked three packs a day and lived to be 110" is a particularly vivid example of ignoring base-rate information and instead paying as much attention to small sample sizes (the individual man who was known; $N = 1$) as to large ones (those cases summarized, where N may be 10,000).

How might the representativeness heuristic be used in making everyday decisions? Consider the following problem given to undergraduates by Nisbett, Krantz, Jepson, and Kunda (1983):

David L. was a senior in high school on the East Coast who was planning to go to college. He had compiled an excellent record in high school and had been admitted to his two top choices: a small liberal arts college and an Ivy League university. David had several older friends who were attending the liberal arts college and several who were attending the Ivy League university. They were all excellent students like himself and had interests similar to his. The friends at the liberal arts college all reported that they liked the place very much and that they found it very stimulating. The friends at the Ivy League university reported that they had many complaints on both personal and social grounds and on educational grounds.

David initially thought that he would go to the smaller college. However, he decided to visit both schools himself for a day.

He did not like what he saw at the private liberal arts college: Several people whom he met seemed cold and unpleasant; a professor he met with briefly seemed abrupt and uninterested in him; and he did not like the "feel" of the campus. He did like what he saw at the Ivy League university: Several of the people he met seemed like vital, enthusiastic, pleasant people; he met with two different professors who took a personal interest in him; and he came away with a very pleasant feeling about the campus. (p. 353)

Undergraduates reading this passage were then asked to say which school they thought David should attend and how strong their feelings were about their judgements (e.g., he should *definitely* go to the liberal arts college; he should *probably* go to the liberal arts college; it's a toss-up; he should *probably* go to the Ivy League university; he should *definitely* go to the Ivy League University). Of the approximately 75 research participants, 74% recommended that David go to the Ivy League university, despite his friends' complaints. Presumably, they based their decision on David's own experience.

A second group of research participants read the above passage with the following paragraph added to the second paragraph:

He proceeded systematically to draw up a long list, for both colleges, of all the classes which might interest him and all the places and activities on campus that he wanted to see. From each list, he randomly selected several classes and activities to visit, and several spots to look at (by blindly dropping a pencil on each list of alternatives and seeing where the point landed). (p. 353).

Given this additional information, only 56% of these research participants recommended that David L. go to the Ivy League institution. The researchers argued that the additional information served to cue the research participants to think about the fact that his visit could only gather a small sample of life at each institution. The cue further highlighted the idea that there was a much larger possibility of error in the small sample of information gathered (from the campus visit) relative to the much smaller possibility of error in the large sample (gathered from friends who spend every day at the institution).

Anchoring

Suppose I ask you to answer a numerical question with an estimate (assuming that you don't know the exactly correct value): As of April 2001, what percentage of

African countries are members of the United Nations? (I'll give you the correct answer below). Suppose I pose this question to two people, Rebecca and Will, and I spin a "wheel of fortune" to give each one a starting value, from which to begin their estimating. Now, Will and Rebecca watch me spin this wheel, and they know that the value the wheel stops at is chosen by chance. Rebecca's starting value is 10; Will's is 65. If they are like most research participants in Tversky and Kahneman's (1974) study, Rebecca will arrive at an estimate of around 25; Will, around 45. In other words, their initial starting point will have huge effects on their final estimates. (By the way, when I checked the 2000 *World Almanac* I found that 100% of the 54 African nations were members of the United Nations).

Likewise, consider two groups of high school students, each given 5 seconds to estimate a complex expression. Group 1 estimates

$8 \times 7 \times 6 \times 5 \times 4 \times 3 \times 2 \times 1$, reporting a mean estimate of 2250;

Group 2 estimates

$1 \times 2 \times 3 \times 4 \times 5 \times 6 \times 7 \times 8$, reporting a mean product of 512.

As you can tell, both problems are identical, and (as you might not be able to tell quickly), both estimates are too small: The correct value is 40,320. Tversky and Kahneman (2000) explain these results this way: People tend to perform the first few steps of multiplication, then extrapolate. The extrapolation tends to be too little rather than too much. This explains that both groups of participants underestimated the answer. In addition, those who started with $1 \times 2 \times 3$ begin with a smaller value than do those who begin with $8 \times 7 \times 6$, so the first group more significantly underestimates the result.

Sunk Cost Effects

Consider the following hypothetical decision, offered to research participants by Arkes and Blumer (1985, p. 126):

> Assume that you have spent $100 on a ticket for a weekend trip to Michigan. Several weeks later you buy a $50 ticket for a weekend ski trip to Wisconsin. You think you will enjoy the Wisconsin ski trip more than the Michigan ski trip. As you are putting your just-purchased Wisconsin ski trip ticket in your wallet, you notice that the Michigan ski trip and the Wisconsin ski trip are for the same weekend! It's too late to sell either ticket, and you cannot return either one. You must use one ticket and not the other. Which ski trip will you go on?
>
> $100 ski trip to Michigan
>
> $50 ski trip to Wisconsin

Arkes and Blumer (1985) found that about 54% of the participants chose the more expensive, but expected-to-be-less-enjoyable, trip. They point out that this violates one of the axioms of rational economic theory, which states that decisions ought to be based on the future costs and benefits estimated for each option. Instead, most research participants seemed to be influenced by the amount of money already spent and unable to be recovered—the so-called sunk costs.

The sunk cost effect is shown as "a greater tendency to continue an endeavor once an investment in money, effort, or time has been made" (Arkes & Blumer, 1985, p. 124). As the authors note, sunk costs are not limited to monetary expenditures:

> Should I continue this unhappy relationship? I have already put so much into it. Should I continue with this terrible job? I spent a year in training to get this position. We suspect that many bad movies are seen to their completion simply because once the viewer realizes how poor the movie is, several minutes and dollars have already been invested. This sunk costs promotes lingering until the bitter end. During the Viet Nam War some people counseled against ending the hostilities before total victory had been achieved because to do so would have meant the waste of those lives already lost. (p. 126)

The explanation offered for the sunk cost effect is that people desire to not be or appear to be wasteful (Arkes, 1996). Referring to the ski trip example, it seems to waste more money to not go on the more expensive Michigan trip than the less expensive Wisconsin trip. The problem with this logic is that, for both ski trips, the nonrefundable fee has already been paid and will not be refunded, regardless of what you do. Therefore, those nonrecoverable costs should have no effect on your plans. In fact, in studies of the sunk cost effect (Arkes & Ayton, 1999), children appear less likely to fall prey to this error than adults! These authors explain this paradox by supposing that as children get older and come to rely more on rules, they overgeneralize a "don't waste resources" rule.

A study by Staw, Barsade, and Koput (1997) demonstrated evidence of the use of the sunk cost bias in real-life decision making. These authors studied data collected from 132 California banks over a 9-year period. They looked specifically at when banks were likely to write off bad loans. They found that this was especially likely if the senior management of the bank had recently changed. In other words, if a senior bank executive made a loan that turned out to be bad, it was far more likely that he or she would continue the loan than would a new person in that same position. Making a bad loan, it seems, invited bank executives to "remain committed to [a] losing course of action, sometimes to the extent of 'throwing good money after bad'" (p. 130).

Illusory Correlation

At the school where I teach, different dorms have acquired stereotypes about the kinds of students they attract. One dorm, Goodhue, is said to house the more unconventional students; another, Burton, attracts the more "with-it" or "cool" students. Frequently when my students do research projects involving surveys, they ask the respondents to indicate which dorm they live in because my students are convinced that there are large personality differences between groups of students housed in different dorms. Invariably, however, the data don't bear out those student intuitions—there is little to no evidence of systematic personality differences as a function of dorm.

How can my students see such an association so strongly, when it apparently isn't there? My best guess is that they are falling prey to the bias of illusory correlation. Chapman and Chapman (1967, 1969; Chapman, 1967) presented an even more compelling demonstration of this phenomenon. They were puzzled by a controversy within the field of clinical psychology over the use of the draw-a-person test. This is a psychodiagnostic test in which the client is asked to draw a person, and the drawings are scored according to a number of dimensions (e.g., whether the figure drawn is muscular, has atypical eyes, is childlike, is fat). Clinicians had reported strong correlations between some of the features of drawings and particular symptoms and behavioral characteristics (e.g., atypical eyes are drawn by suspicious clients; big heads are drawn by intelligent clients). However, these reports were never confirmed by researchers studying the test itself.

In one study, Chapman and Chapman (1967) gave undergraduates who were unfamiliar with the draw-a-person test a series of 45 drawings that they randomly paired with symptoms allegedly displayed by the people who drew them. These undergraduates "discovered" the same correlations that clinicians had been reporting. Because the drawings and symptoms were randomly paired, it appeared that the undergraduates shared with the clinicians a preexisting bias as to what relationships would be found in the data. That is, they "discovered" relationships they expected to find, even when those relationships really were not there.

Variables that tend to be falsely associated are typically ones that seem to have some prior association in the minds of people (Chapman & Chapman, 1967). On the surface, it seems to make sense that suspicious clients might draw wide-eyed figures—the wide eyes might be an artistic or symbolic representation of their suspiciousness. The point here is that the associations people bring to a situation often color their judgment to the point where they see relationships that are not really there.

Confirmation Bias

Eight years ago we had a new house built. Given my research focus, I of course did not want to make the decision carelessly, impulsively, or irrationally, so it took a long time to choose a design and a builder. My spouse and I walked through at least 100 model homes (I stopped counting after awhile); oddly enough, we built a replica (of sorts) of the very first model we saw.

The process we used to choose a builder was equally complex. We met scores of builders during our trips to model homes. We found one builder whom we liked a lot. However, we wanted to base our decision on something more solid than the fact that he seemed nice. We asked him for a list of previous customers. He gave us a list of about 12 names. I phoned each one in turn. Each one gave the man glowing references, and I became more and more confident that we had found our dream builder.

Now, the story has a very happy ending. We did hire him, he did build our house, and it was done on time and for the price he quoted us. In 8 years, there have been no structural problems. I'd recommend him enthusiastically in a heartbeat.

However, the fact that I grew more confident after talking to his previous satisfied customers was, in retrospect, an example of biased information searching. Specifically, I was falling prey to something called *confirmation bias*. This bias is the tendency to search only for information that will confirm one's initial hunch or hypothesis and to overlook or ignore any other information.

This bias was experimentally demonstrated by Wason (1960, 1977). He used the following task: You are given the numbers 2, 4, and 6 and told that this triplet of numbers follows a rule. Your job is to determine what the rule is, but to do so you need to observe certain guidelines. You may not ask direct questions about the rule. Instead, you have to offer your own examples of triplets and for each one you give, you'll be told whether or not it follows the rule. Also, you should try not to guess—announce a rule only when you are confident that you know what it is.

When I do this demonstration in class, it often goes something like the following:

Student: 6–8–10.
Me: Yes, that follows the rule.
Student: 10–12–14.
Me: Yes, that follows the rule.
Student: 100–102–104.
Me: Yes, that follows the rule.
Student: Is the rule any three even sequential integers?
Me: No.
Student (looking puzzled): Are you *sure?*
Me: Yes.

Of Wason's 29 original subjects, only 6 discovered the correct rule without first making incorrect guesses. Of the others, 13 made one wrong guess, 9 reached two or more incorrect conclusions, and 1 reached no conclusion at all (Wason, 1960). These results suggest, first, that this task is deceptively difficult. The manner in which most people go wrong seems to be as follows: They develop a general idea of the rule, then construct examples that follow that rule. What they fail to do is to test their rule by constructing a counterexample—a triplet that, if their rule is correct, won't receive a "yes" answer from the experimenter.

To explain why this approach is problematic, Wason points out a feature of the task that mirrors the situation facing any scientist testing other scientific hypotheses: An infinite number of hypotheses can be constructed that are consistent with any set of data (in this case, the triplets that are judged by the experimenter to follow the rule). For instance, suppose at a certain point in the experiment, you've found out that all of the following triplets follow the rule (whatever that rule is): 2, 4, 6; 8, 10, 12; 20, 22, 24; 100, 102, 104. What rules are consistent with this set? Here are just a few: Any three even numbers that increase by two; any three even numbers that increase by two but the last number is not greater than 500; any three even numbers where the second is the arithmetic average of the first and third; any three even numbers where the second is the arithmetic average of the first and third, but the last number is not greater than 500; any three even numbers that increase; any three increasing numbers; any three numbers. The above list suggests that it's very easy, with a little thought, to generate hundreds of rules for any given set of numbers.

There simply is no pattern of results (even from hundreds of experiments) that can prove a theory *true,* just as no rule about three numbers can be proven true, even by a large number of examples that apparently follow it. Instead, the best one can do is to try to disprove as many incorrect rules (or, if you are a scientist, as many alternative hypotheses) as possible. So, if you think the correct rule is any three increasing even numbers, you are better off testing the rule with a triplet that is a counterexample to the rule (e.g., 3, 5, 7). Why? If this triplet follows the rule, then you know immediately that your hypothesis is wrong. Suppose you instead generate another example of the rule (e.g., 14, 16, 18). If you're told that it does follow the rule, you won't be able to use it to prove your hypothesis true (because no hypothesis can ever be proven true), and you haven't managed to rule anything out.

In my house builder example, I went wrong by only seeking information that would potentially confirm my hunch that the builder was reputable. Obviously, he would give me names only of people he believed were satisfied with his work. Families with whom he'd had disputes (if in fact he'd ever had any) wouldn't make it onto the list of previous contacts he gave out.

Actually, I did do one thing right in making this decision—I did call both the Better Business Bureau and the local builder's association. He checked out just fine with both groups—neither had record of a single complaint against him. To be honest, though, I paid a lot more attention to the glowing reports of satisfied customers (that were very salient and available to me) than I did to the rather unexciting news that no complaints had ever been lodged.

All of this goes to show that even when the study of decision making is your professional center, you aren't immune from the biases and heuristics that can and do affect the ways in which you search for relevant information.

PROSPECT THEORY
AND FRAMING EFFECTS

One way of explaining many of the above heuristics and biases comes from a theory developed by Kahneman and Tversky (1979), called *prospect theory*. It was originally conceived as an alternative to economic models of decision making, which started from the assumption that people try to behave rationally and to maximize their satisfaction. To do this, people need to behave with some consistency because the values that define a person's satisfaction are assumed to be rather stable. If, for example, you make a career choice on Day 1, choosing to become an investment banker, but in exactly the same circumstances on Day 2 choose instead to become a missionary, it would appear as if you are acting inconsistently and, thus, irrationally. (Note: If you want to claim that your values changed between the 2 days, fine, but then the premise of the problem, that you were acting under identical circumstances, is not fulfilled.)

Tversky and Kahneman (1981; Kahneman & Tversky, 1979) noted that people's hypothetical decision making could often show these apparently irrational inconsistencies. One way they demonstrated this was through the use of the now-famous Asian flu problem, which goes as follows (Tversky & Kahneman, 1981):

> Imagine that the U.S. is preparing for the outbreak of an unusual Asian disease, which is expected to kill 600 people. Two alternative programs to combat the disease have been proposed. Assume that the exact scientific consequences of the program are as follows:
>   If Program A is adopted 200 people will be saved.
>   If Program B is adopted, there is a ⅓ probability that 600 people will be saved, and a ⅔ probability that no people will be saved.
>   Which of the two programs would you favor? (p. 453)

Of the 152 university students responding to this question, 72% percent chose Program A over Program B.

One hundred and fifty-five other university students read the identical problem, but were offered the following choices: (1) If Program C is adopted, 400 people will die; (2) If Program D is adopted, there is a ⅓ probability that nobody will die, and a ⅔ probability that 600 people will die. Faced with these alternatives, 78% of the students chose Program D over Program C.

Do you notice a problem? If you go back and read the pairs of options carefully, you'll see that Program C has exactly the same effect as Program A, and Program B and Program D likewise are exactly alike, simply described in different words. What then, does it mean for the majority of people to prefer one program over another when the two are described in one set of terms but to reverse these preferences when other descriptions are given?

Tversky and Kahneman (1981) referred to this as the *framing effect*, a major feature of prospect theory. Basically, the idea is that the way the decision maker conceives of the options, outcomes, and probabilities varies as a function of the way the option is described, in part, and also as a function of the decision maker's values, characteristics, and habits. In particular, people are much more willing to gamble on possible future winnings or gains and much less likely to gamble on possible future losses. Consequently, when future outcomes are described in terms of possible gains, people are more likely to gamble than they are when those very same outcomes are described in terms of possible losses.

Kahneman and Tversky (1984) explained people's appraisal of gains and losses by means of the value function presented in Fig. 3.1. Imagine yourself at Point A on the function, evaluating whether or not to enter a gamble in which you will either win $5 or lose $5. The function shows that your value for gains is less steep

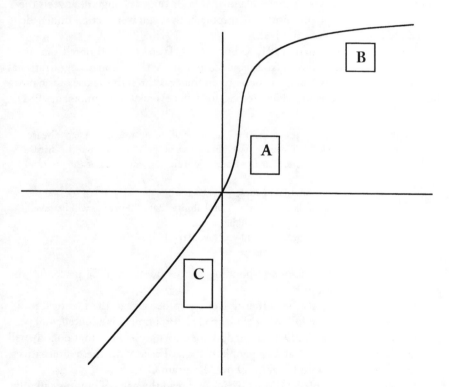

FIG. 3.1.   A hypothetical value function. From "The Framing of Decisions and the Psychology of Choice" by A. Tversky and D. Kahneman, 1981, *Science, 222,* pp. 453–458. Copyright 1981 by the American Association for the Advancement of Science. Adapted by permission.

than your value for loss. Put another way, the extra satisfaction you'd get from winning $5 is less than the amount of satisfaction you would lose if you were to forfeit the $5.

Framing, then, changes the point on the graph from which you see yourself starting. If I can describe a situation to you that makes you feel that your current position is Point B, you will evaluate the effects of a proposed change differently than if my description causes you to think of yourself at Point C.

Here's another example of a framing effect: Driving on the road, you notice your car is running low on gasoline, and you see two service stations, both of which are advertising gasoline. Station A's price is $1.00 per gallon; Station B's price is $0.95. Station A's sign also announces "5 cents/gallon discount for cash!" Station B's sign announces "5 cents/gallon surcharge for credit cards." All other factors (e.g., cleanliness of the stations, whether you like the brand of gasoline carried, number of cars waiting at each) being equal, to which station would you choose to go? Many people report a preference for Station A, the one that offers a cash discount (Thaler, 1980). It is interesting that people have this preference because both stations are actually offering the same deal: a price of $.95 per gallon if you use cash, and $1.00 per gallon if you use credit cards.

When described as a "cash discount," the price at the first gas station seems to be a bargain—people assume that they are starting from a reference point of $1 a gallon and then saving or gaining a nickel. In the case of Station B, however, people describe the situation to themselves as a surcharge just for the privilege of using a credit card. The owners of Station B then seem to be rip-off artists, and in a huff people drive into Station A, where they will be paying exactly the same price!

Kahneman and Tversky (1979) argued that we treat losses more seriously than we treat gains of an equivalent amount (whether it be of money or some other measure of satisfaction). That is, we care more about losing a dime than we do about gaining a dime, or more about losing a dollar than gaining a dollar. The problem is that simply changing the description of a situation can cause us to adopt different reference points and, therefore, to see the same outcome as a gain in one situation and a loss in the other. That in turn might cause us to change our decision making, not because anything in the problem has changed but simply because the way we describe the situation to ourselves has.

By the way, some recent research by Fagley and Miller (1997) has suggested that framing effects differ depending on whether the content of the problem is about saving human lives or saving money and that women show more of a framing effect than men. It has also been suggested that positive frames encourage people to process information less thoroughly and more automatically, whereas negative frames encourage more comprehensive, thorough, and deliberate analysis (Dunegan, 1993).

LABORATORY MODELS
OF INFORMATION SEARCH

Decision-making researchers have created a task specifically to study the way in which people gather information when making complex decisions. This task makes use of something called an information board (Payne, 1976; Senter & Wedell, 1999). The typical decision studied with this technique is one of a hypothetical search for an apartment.

The board has several rows and columns of cards on it, providing information about several different apartments. Each apartment is represented in a specific column. Each row depicts information about a particular aspect of each apartment. For example, the top row gives information about the rent of each apartment; the second row, the size of the apartment (in square feet); the third, the number of closets, and so on. One side of the card describes what the aspect of the information is (e.g., rent or number of closets); the reverse side shows the actual value of that aspect for that apartment (e.g., $550 per month or four closets).

The purpose of using this means of displaying information is for a researcher to examine how much information people seek before making a final decision and in what order they seek the information. The research participant can only turn over one card at a time and may or may not be allowed to leave the information displayed.

Payne's (1976) study showed that the amount of information people seek before making a final decision varies a great deal, depending on how many alternatives they have to choose among. His research participants had either 2, 6, or 12 alternatives (apartments) to choose from. There were also either 4, 8, or 12 dimensions (e.g., rent, number of closets) presented for each decision. Participants were told to take as much time as they wanted to make a decision, that is, to choose which of the apartments presented they would prefer for themselves, given the information available. Participants were not instructed to use all of the information, and if they asked, they were told to feel free to use as little or as much information as they wanted.

Payne (1976) found that as the number of alternatives (apartments) went up, people sought a lower fraction of the available information. When only two apartments were presented, the majority of research participants looked at all the available information, whether that was 4, 8, or 12 aspects of each apartment. On average, participants examined about 80% of the available information when there were two alternatives. As the number of alternatives increased, the percentage of available information examined dropped. With six alternatives, the participants chose to examine only 58% of the available information; with 12 alternatives they examined only 51%.

Similarly, as the number of dimensions went up, participants used a lower fraction of the available information. When four dimensions were presented (e.g., rent, size, cleanliness, distance from campus), participants examined about 75% of the available information. With eight dimensions (all of the previous plus noise level, closet space, parking availability, kitchen facilities), participants examined 63% of the available information. With 12 dimensions, participants looked at 51% of the information.

Even more interesting was the pattern people used to acquire information. When given just two apartments from which to make a selection, participants always turned over the same number of cards for both alternatives, often turning over all the cards. However, with 6 or 12 apartments, participants tended to search for information dimension by dimension, quickly ruling out alternatives.

Payne (1976) had participants think aloud as they did this task, and those data support this interpretation. For example, one participant, considering one apartment, said:

> The rent for apartment E is $140. Which is a good note. The noise level for this apartment is high. That would almost deter me right there. Ah, I don't like a lot of noise. And if it's high, it must be pretty bad. Which means, you couldn't sleep. I would just put that one aside right there. I wouldn't look any further than that. Even though, the rent is good. (p. 375)

Another participant said:

> Since we have a whole bunch [of alternatives] here, I'm going to go across the top and see which noise levels are high. If there are any high ones, I'll reject them immediately. . . . Go to [apartment] D. It has a high noise level. So we'll automatically eliminate D. (p. 375)

Senter and Wedell (1999) described the way people search for information in this task as being alternativewise with few alternatives (i.e., people turn over cards column by column). When there are more alternatives, people search dimensionwise (by rows). Presumably, in the latter case, people are making quicker rule-out decisions, possibly to keep to a manageable level the amount of information that needs to be actively considered. You might note that this description is very consistent with image theory (Beach, 1993; Mitchell & Beach, 1990), which holds that people quickly winnow down the number of alternatives that they will devote energy to consider. People will reduce the alternatives to a manageable number by eliminating those which violate a value, strategic, or trajectory image.

Nichols-Hoppe and Beach (1990) described the two different information search strategies as compensatory and noncompensatory. A compensatory search is one in which the individual seeks to make trade-offs among different dimensions. For example, a person might be willing to pay higher rent for a larger, quieter apartment. Alternatively, he might put up with more noise and a less desirable neighborhood if the rent was at a bargain level. In these examples, high values on one or more aspects of the decision compensate for low values on others—the decision maker is willing to make trade-offs.

In contrast, a noncompensatory procedure is one in which there are no trade-offs. For example, if you were looking for an apartment and rejected out of hand any option with a rent higher than some value (say, $500 a month), regardless of how nice, or big, or quiet, or desirable on any other dimension it was, you'd be engaging in noncompensatory decision making.

Nichols-Hoppe and Beach (1990) looked at the way in which people searched for information in the information-board task. They counted a search as compensatory when the person sought the same number (plus or minus 1) of pieces of information for all alternatives. For example, if a research participant looked at information on rent, size, number of closets, noise level, and so on for all apartments on the board, he or she was described as having performed a compensatory search. If, on the other hand, they looked at an unequal number of pieces of information, they were counted as having used a noncompensatory search. One way this could happen is if, for example, they stopped looking at information on a given apartment if it had too high a rent or was too noisy.

Nichols-Hoppe and Beach (1990) found that what seemed to govern whether a person would use compensatory or noncompensatory search most was the number of alternatives being considered. With only two apartments to choose from, people tended to gather more information and to use compensatory procedures. Otherwise, with more alternatives (e.g., 6 or 12), people tended to use noncompensatory procedures.

Another factor that affected how much information people sought was their level of anxiety. Those participants who received higher scores on a measure of test anxiety examined more pieces of information about the apartments than did participants who had not scored highly on the anxiety measure. In addition, some research participants experienced pressure to make a good decision. They were (falsely) told the following by the experimenter:

> Being able to make good decisions is obviously very important, and we believe that the ability to make good decisions is significantly related to intelligence . . . we intend to let you make some decisions and then to give you a standard IQ test . . . we are going to compare the results of your IQ test with judgments of your decision making capabilities and we will evaluate your decisions in three ways. First, of course, we will look at what you actually decide, how good your decisions are. Second, the experimenter will evaluate the manner in which you go about making your decision. Third, after all your decisions are made, you will be asked to explain and defend all of your decisions; your defense will be tape recorded for later review by a panel of judges. (Nichols-Hoppe & Beach, 1990, pp. 165–166)

Pretty scary instructions! Luckily, the investigators never made good on these promises. However, research participants given these instructions did inspect more pieces of information, perhaps because the pressure made them feel more cautious about their decision making. Low-pressure instructions, in contrast, were as follows:

There seems to be no single right or wrong way to go about making decisions . . . in many circumstances, such as the situations you'll face here, there are really no definitely "right" or "wrong" decisions either . . . so just use your natural decision-making style to select whatever options you feel are best. (Nichols-Hoppe & Beach, 1990, p. 166)

People receiving these instructions inspected about 11% fewer pieces of information. When people were told that the decision was an unimportant one, they were also less likely to inspect more pieces of information, relative to when they were told the decision was important.

PURSUING USELESS INFORMATION

Sometimes in our zeal for pursuing information, we start gathering data that ultimately turns out to be of little use, either because we don't have time to process it or because it isn't relevant to making the decision in the first place. Bastardi and Shafir (1998) demonstrated this phenomenon in a controlled study. Undergraduate volunteers were presented with problems such as the following:

You are considering registering for a course in your major that has very interesting subject matter and will not be offered again before you graduate. While the course is reputed to be taught by an excellent professor, you have just discovered that he may be on leave. It will not be known until tomorrow if the regular professor will teach the course or if a less popular professor will. Do you:
   [a] Decide to register for the course?
   [b] Decide not to register for the course?
   [c] Wait until tomorrow (after finding out if the regular professor will be teaching) to decide about registering for the course? (pp. 20–21)

In this version of the problem, 42% of the respondents chose Option A, 2% chose Option B, and 56% chose Option C. This latter group was then given the following scenario:

It is the next day, and you find out that the less popular professor will be teaching the course. Do you:
   [a] Decide to register for the course?
   [b] Decide not to register for the course? (p. 21)

This time 29% of the original set of respondents chose Option A, whereas 27% chose Option B. These two percentages, by the way, sum to the 56% of the respondents who chose the original Option C.

Those respondents who originally chose either Option A or Option B aren't acting in a surprising way. Neither are the respondents who initially chose Option C, then chose Option B. We could describe this latter group as waiting to see if the popular professor will teach the course. When that outcome doesn't happen, they decide not to take the course.

The surprising findings come from that group of participants who chose Option C initially—that is, to wait to gather more information before making a decision. The surprising thing is that when they receive information that points in the direction of their not taking the course, they choose to take it anyway! In essence, it's not clear why this group of respondents didn't just choose to enroll in the course in the first place, in other words, why they didn't initially choose Option A.

Especially interesting are the findings from another group of college students, who were given a simpler version of the decision to make. They were told that the less popular professor was going to teach the course and were asked whether or not they would enroll in it. Eighty-two percent said they would, 18% said they would not.

Notice the discrepancy between the two sets of students. Those told up front about a less popular professor teaching a course are overwhelmingly likely to choose to take the course. Those who wait to gather information to see if the less popular professor will in fact teach the course are ultimately less likely to take it. Many of these (29% of the students) chose to wait for information that turns out to be useless.

Bastardi and Shafir (1998) used the term *noninstrumental information* to refer to information people think will be relevant to their decision but turns out not to be. The problem with the pursuit of this information is twofold. First, people waste time waiting for information that doesn't bear on their decision. This time could be allocated to other relevant activities—assessing the value of other, presumably useful, information; reflecting on one's goals and priorities; or making the final selection.

But that's not all. According to Bastardi and Shafir (1998), once people pursue useless information, they often go on to use it, making it part of their decision when it really shouldn't be. Notice that in the simple version of the problem described above, when the less popular professor is certain to teach the course, 82% of students say they'll take it anyway. However, when it isn't certain who will teach the course, 56% choose to wait. When the information is finally made available, and is exactly the same as the information offered to people in the simple version, only 71% end up choosing to take the course. In other words, waiting for the information apparently caused 11% of people to change the decision they would have made had they been in the simple version condition.

You might be wondering how relevant the above results are to a real-life decision. After all, hypothetical situations might not elicit what people's real responses would be if they were actually faced with the situation. Bastardi and Shafir (1998) addressed just this question in another study with 45 Princeton undergraduates. Students participated in small groups of 8 to 10. When they arrived, they were shown a Panasonic dual-cassette player, still in its original wrapping, and presented with the following entry form:

> As part of our study of people's tastes and preferences, we are currently raffling some prizes. You will now be given the opportunity to participate in a raffle for the dual-cassette player on display (list price: $99.99). Each cassette player will be raffled among 50 participants, and there will be no fee for entering the raffle. However, if you win, you will be required to pay a small amount for the prize. Unfortunately, the dean's office has not yet indicated if they will help fund this research. If the dean's funding is awarded, winners will have to pay $10.00 to receive the cassette player. If the funding is not awarded, we will have to charge $30.00. We apologize for not knowing yet whether the price will be $10 or $30.
>
> If you would like to participate in the raffle, please fill in your name and phone number below. If you would rather not participate, please hand in this form blank: signing your name indicates a commitment to pay for the prize if you win the raffle. (p. 26)

As in the hypothetical case, Bastardi and Shafir (1998) had two conditions in their study. In the simple condition, "the experimenter explained that, after the forms had been printed, it was found that the grant had not been awarded, and that the winner of the raffle would have to pay $30 for the tape player" (p. 26). In this condition, 57% of the undergraduates chose to participate in the raffle and committed themselves to paying $30 if they were chosen the winner.

Also as in the hypothetical case, there was an uncertain condition. In this one, the uncertain condition was as follows:

> the experimenter explained that he was on his way to a meeting and that he would announce before the end of class (the students were all enrolled in an introductory psychology course) whether the price was $10 or $30. Participants had the option to make their decision and turn in their forms immediately, or they could keep their forms until the end of class, when the exact price would be announced. Approximately 45 min later the experimenter returned with the news that the grant had not been awarded and that the fee would be $30. Thus, participants in the uncertain condition now faced the same decision as those in the simple condition. Those who had deferred then indicated their choice and the forms were collected. (Bastardi & Shafir, 1998, p. 26).

Of those in the uncertain condition, 32% chose to wait for information. Ultimately, only 23% of students in this condition chose to enter the raffle, compared with 57% of students in the simple condition, facing exactly the same decision.

Bastardi and Shafir (2001) concluded that in decision making it is not always the case that the more information the better: "The pursuit of information may lead it to have greater weight in ensuing decisions. Important decisions—especially those that affect other people or for which one feels accountable—may exacerbate both the tendency to pursue missing information and the reliance on such information once obtained" (p. 218).

Bastardi and Shafir (2001) raised the possibility that one explanation for the phenomenon of the pursuit of useless information is that during the course of making an important decision, people need to discover and construct their own values. As they discover or clarify these values, their decision making is affected. Presumably, this implies that decision makers with more articulated values and goals will be at an advantage in making better decisions.

THE PROBLEM OF INFORMATION OVERLOAD

One of my studies of real-life decision making was of high school students choosing a college (Galotti, 1995a; Galotti & Mark, 1994). When we asked students what made this decision so difficult, an interesting complaint arose among some of the research participants: The sheer amount of information available to them was overwhelming. One respondent commiserated:

> The process of decision making has been, well, unpleasant to say the least. O.K., I hate it. First of [sic] there are 6 billion (or so) colleges out there, and for some reason they all have access to lots and lots of glossy paper on which they print that which they feel will make me want to attend. At least 3 thousand of these arrive a day. These I now believe are completely useless. Well, maybe not completely. But most of what they say has nothing to do with anything important. Very, very few list their price, which is a major factor for me, some list majors, but some do not, and even after sifting through this plethora of propaganda, I feel like I have accomplished nothing.

This student is voicing a complaint I often hear when I'm talking to students about important decisions—the information available to them can be overwhelming.

In my study of college students choosing a major, I found a similar lament from another student:

> To make a *good* choice about a major to declare I would like to take a class in each area a student could major in. . . . Then I would like a past student from each of the major areas to come back to college so I could talk with him or her and see what they're doing or planning on doing with their major. Then I would also do many things I had already done, things like going to the career research center to evaluate your interests.

There certainly doesn't seem much to argue with here, does there? When facing an important decision, it only makes sense to gather lots of information about all the alternatives. What better way than taking a class in each major offered and in talking to an alumnus/alumna from each major?

Well, maybe there is one problem with this advice. After all, taking one class might not give you a very true picture of what all the other classes in that major would be like. Maybe you'd like a particular class only because the professor was entertaining, or a particular topic captured your interests, or you liked the other students in that particular class. So it would probably be a better strategy to take two or three classes in each possible major.

But here's the catch. At my college, there are about 25 different regular majors, not to mention a few special majors that students can petition for. If a student took even just two courses per possible major, that would be 50 courses, at least. At my school, it would take you about 5 or 6 years of exploring, plus 1 or 2 more to complete the major!

Similar problems arise with the strategy of talking to one alum from each major—the number of conversations this would necessitate (25–30) would be almost prohibitive. When you think about how long each conversation would have to be to make it useful, it seems that at least 1 hour would be required. And, once again, you'd need to worry about how typical a single alum from each major would be, and might need or want to make sure you interviewed a minimum of two to three or more alums per major. Now you're up to 50–75 conversations. Realistically, the chances of arranging, scheduling, and holding that many conversations is slim.

Similar problems apply to the strategies of interviewing current majors in every discipline or to reading through materials academic departments and programs prepare for their majors. Many departments issue handbooks that present requirements, career information, and describe opportunities available. However, many of these booklets are 20–30 pages long.

Moreover, even if you had time to gather all that information, it's not clear how you would integrate and process it. Lacking some systematic means of keeping track of it all, it is likely that much of the gathered information would be ignored. In fact, the high school research participants reported just this occurrence when they talked about large stacks of unread college catalogs and brochures. They started out excited to receive these catalogs and pored conscientiously over the first few that arrived. However, as the stacks of paper grew high, time grew short, and deadlines for decisions loomed, much of that gathered information went unread and unprocessed. But some information would be used. Unfortunately, our best guess, given all the work on heuristics and biases described above, is that the information that was used may well have been processed incompletely or incorrectly.

In short, I've tried to show you in this chapter that gathering lots of information is not, by itself, sufficient to ensure a good decision. First, safeguards have to be put in place to reduce bias in the acquisition of information. Next, the reliability of the information needs to be assessed explicitly. Then, the information gathered has to be put together in some way as to allow major themes and trends to be noticed and the implications thought about. As I hope the information in this chapter makes clear, our everyday or natural approach to gathering information can be problematic. One possible impediment to making effective decisions in everyday life may be figuring out more systematic strategies to gather and manage information. In chapter 4, we'll take a look at some of these.

4

Structuring the Decision

So far we've seen that goals and values can, and probably should, drive decisions, at least important decisions. We've also seen that although it is good to gather information, doing so by itself doesn't guarantee that the information will be processed or used appropriately, or even at all.

Good decision making requires making use of information, somehow relating it back to one's goals, values, and principles. In this chapter, we will take a look at possible ways of doing this. This process of decision making is called structuring the decision.

Slovic, Lichtenstein, and Fischoff (1988) equated decision structuring with "all the options, consequences, and uncertainties considered in the course of reaching a decision" (p. 675). To structure a decision explicitly (which is what I'll be discussing from here on) means to devise some system by which the information gathered about the decision can be processed. One thing decision structuring accomplishes, therefore, is keeping track of the information, making sure it doesn't get lost or forgotten. Decision structuring also helps set up the information in some kind of format that will be useful in making the final selection. Finally, decision structuring relates the information to the goals or values driving the decision.

Decision structuring need not be a very complicated or elaborate procedure. A simple way to structure a decision is to follow the suggestion of Benjamin Franklin, in a treatise on what he called Moral Algebra:

> When . . . difficult Cases occur, they are difficult, chiefly because while we have them under Consideration, all the Reasons *pro* and con are not present to the Mind at the same time; but sometimes one Set present themselves, and at other times another, the first being out of Sight. Hence the various Purposes or Inclinations that alternately prevail, and the Uncertainty that perplexes us.
>
> To get over this, My Way is, to divide half a Sheet of Paper by a Line into two Columns; writing over the one *Pro*, and over the other *Con.* Then during three or four Days consideration, I put down under the different Heads short Hints of the different Motives, that at different Times occur to me, *for* or *against* the Measure. When I have thus got them all together in one View, I endeavor to estimate their respective Weights; and where I find two, one on each side, that seem equal, I strike

them both out. If I find a Reason *pro* equal to some *two* Reasons *con,* I strike out the three. If I judge some two Reasons *con,* equal to some three reasons *pro,* I strike out the five; and thus proceeding I find at length where the Balance lies; and after a Day or two of farther Consideration, nothing new that is of Importance occurs on either side, I come to a Determination accordingly. And, tho' the Weight of Reasons cannot be taken with the Precision of Algebraic Quantities, yet, when each is thus considered separately and comparatively, and the whole lies before me, I think I can judge better, and am less liable to make a rash Step; and in fact I have found great Advantage from this kind of Equation, in what may be called *Moral* or *Prudential Algebra.* (from letter to Joseph Priestly, September 19, 1772; Silverman, 1986, pp. 254–255)

There are a number of ideas in Franklin's method that are well supported by studies in cognitive psychology that were conducted many years after he reported his intuitions. First, Franklin is noting the fact that people can only keep in mind so many things at once. Cognitive psychologists speak of *working memory* as that part of memory in which we actively process information (Baddeley, 1993). That the space available in working memory is severely limited is well-known to psychologists, from the time of George Miller's paper "The Magical Number Seven, Plus or Minus Two" (Miller, 1956). Miller reported that the number of unrelated pieces of information the average adult person can retain is about seven, although the number can vary from five to nine.

To make effective decisions, people need to find ways to overcome these inherent limitations. One way is simple: write down ideas and possibilities to help keep better track of them. It is also useful to allow time for reflection in decision making. The ideas or possibilities that occur to you at one moment may be dependent on your mood, your immediate situation or context, or the task or conversation in which you are currently immersed (Eich, 1995; Roediger & Guynn, 1996). By keeping track of possibilities over a number of days, you allow for the chance that as your context or mood changes, other ideas might occur to you.

It helps, too, to have some system for organizing the ideas; Franklin suggests a very simple one, dividing ideas into pro and cons. He further describes a system of weighting the importance of various ideas, rather than simply counting up the number of reasons pro and the number of reasons con. It's easy to see why this is important. Imagine a list of 20 rather trivial reasons on one side of a decision and a corresponding list of one very important reason on the other. Simply counting ignores the fact that some reasons are more significant than others and, hence, must be accorded more weight.

But a simple pro/con list is not the only way of organizing information and ideas. Fig. 4.1 presents another one from a home builder's association. They presented it in an advertisement to try to help potential home buyers think about different aspects of new homes. They divide these aspects into general categories (e.g., price and location, exterior, interior) and within those general categories, more specific ones. For example, in the category Interior, this checklist reminds

	Model #	Model #	Model #	Model #	Model #	Model #
	Builder	Builder	Builder	Builder	Builder	Builder
Price and Location						
Price Range						
Location Preference						
Exterior and Lot						
Architectural Style (2-story, rambler etc.)						
Siding (wood, stucco, brick, etc.)						
Driveway (asphalt, concrete						
Deck/Patio						
Lot Size and Location						
Landscaping Allowance						
Interior						
Floor plan						
Total square footage						
Number of bedrooms						
Size of bedrooms						
Number of bathrooms						
Master bedroom suite						
Styles/size of kitchen						
Kitchen features(center island, dinette etc.						
Living room						
Family room						
Dining room						
Finished lower level						
Three-season porch						
Four-season porch						
Deck						
Screened porch						
Overall closet space						
Garage size						
Windows/doors (style, location)						
Flooring (carpets, tile etc.)						
Gas or Electric						
Exterior and Lot						
Decorating Allowance						
Vaulted ceilings						
Fireplaces						
Appliances						
Whirlpool tub						
Central air						
Security System						
Overall construction quality						
Overall energy efficiency						
Overall rating						

FIG. 4.1. A checklist for home buyers. *Note.* From *Homes on Parade* (pp. 30–31), by South Central Builders Association, 1999. Copyright 1999 by South Central Builders Association. Reprinted with permission.

the prospective buyer to consider not only the number of bedrooms and number of bathrooms but also the overall floor plan, the inclusion of a deck or porch, closet space, flooring, and others. The checklist has several blank columns to allow the home buyer to rate different possible models on each of the listed aspects.

This figure illustrates a more complete and complex way of structuring a decision than does Franklin's. It encompasses a written list of the criteria or factors a decision maker should consider, space for the decision maker to consider one or more alternative options, and space to record the decision maker's assessment of each option on each criterion (e.g., House Model #3 rates poorly on the factor of Size of bedrooms).

One thing missing in this checklist, however, is space for the decision maker to weigh the importance of various factors or criteria. For example, it's pretty easy, I would imagine, for most people to find their dream house when money is no object. For many of us, though, that factor or criteria sets an absolute limit (i.e., I cannot spend $4 million on any home, no matter how terrifically it meets all my criteria). In structuring a decision, there needs to be a means for decision makers to indicate the importance of each aspect or factor.

DECISION MAPS

Table 4.1 presents another decision map, as I've called it (Galotti, 1995a, 1995b). This one was generated a year ago by one of my undergraduate research assistants and advisee, the summer before her senior year of college. This student, whom I'll

TABLE 4.1
Barbara's Structuring of Her Decision to Keep or Drop a Second Major

Factor/Criterion	Importance Weight	Alternatives/Options		
		Keep 2nd Major	Drop 2nd Major	Drop Out of School & Be a Bum
Not being a quitter/looking cool for graduate school	7	10	0	0
Interacting with weird students in the major	7	2	7	10
Avoiding a required course I don't want to take	7	0	10	10
Taking fun courses	8	4	8	0
Getting a degree in 2nd major	3	10	0	0
Taking cool courses in first major	9	2	8	0

call Barbara, had a double major—psychology and another discipline (names and disciplines have been changed to protect the innocent!). She was considering whether or not to drop the second major and convert to being just a psychology major. Because we were working on a study of people's real-life decision making at the time, I asked her to use one of the decision-making sheets we were giving to research participants, wherein she would list the factors or criteria, the importance weights of those options, and her options as she saw them.

The table shows that Barbara saw three distinct options for herself. The first was to keep the second major, the second was to drop it, the third was to drop out of school altogether. Barbara also listed six criteria. The most important one for her, as indicated by the importance weights (on a scale from 0–10, where 10 represents maximal importance), was whether she would have time to take "cool" classes in psychology her next and final year of college.

This map, too, lacks certain information. Specifically, there is no indication of how uncertainty enters into this decision. Take the criterion, Taking fun courses. Whether or not a course is fun, as you might recall, isn't always guaranteeable. Certain topics are more or less interesting, of course, but even then there can be some surprises. I picked up my second college major—economics—after signing up for an intro course to knock off a distribution requirement, never expecting to find it engaging! But sometimes, even with the most engaging material and the most talented professor, things don't always live up to their billing. The chemistry among the students in the class can be off, the professor can be dealing with unexpected personal crises, or issues can crop up at the school or college that take everyone's attention off of academics. Thus, Barbara couldn't know for certain whether she would actually get fun courses.

Decision maps usually are incomplete. People can overlook options, overlook criteria, give the wrong weights to their criteria, or ignore probability information. And they can do any combination of these.

Listing Criteria

In any decision, some sort of criteria have to be used to select among the options. As we noted earlier, these criteria optimally are derived from peoples' values and goals. That is, if people were extremely reflective about their own principles, and about what they wanted from life, this would enhance their ability to make the best decisions.

In different studies of real-life decision making, people involved in the process of making a decision list only a handful of factors or criteria. For example, high school students choosing a college listed approximately 8 to 10 factors, or criteria (Galotti, 1995a; Galotti & Mark, 1994). College students in the process of choosing a major list about seven criteria (Galotti, 1999a). Pregnant women considering which type of birth attendant (e.g., midwife, family practioner, obstetrician) listed only about 3.5 (Galotti, 1998).

There were some slight, but statistically significant, differences in the number of factors listed as a function of both educational level and academic ability. In the pregnancy study, women with graduate education (e.g., a master's, doctoral, or comparable professional degree) listed more factors than did women with only a high school education. However, the differences were small (about one factor, on average), suggesting that years of schooling have only a modest effect on performance on higher order thinking tasks (see also Perkins, 1985). Likewise, in the high school study, students with greater academic ability (as measured by class rank, grade point average, and standardized test scores) listed more criteria than did students of average or lower academic ability. However, again, the absolute size of the difference in performance between high- and lower ability students was small.

It is interesting that people seem to keep the number of factors or criteria to about Miller's magical number seven. It may be that this is the largest number of factors or criteria that they can keep track of. This possibility is consistent with the finding that, over the course of a year, the same individual is likely to keep the same number of criteria, even though about half of the specific criteria listed change (Galotti, 1995b; Galotti, 1999a). That is, a student who listed six factors in April of his or her junior year of high school might list six factors again a year later, but only about three of the original factors would reappear on the second list.

Weighting Criteria

Return for a moment to the quotation from Benjamin Franklin, presented at the beginning of this chapter. Franklin made a very important point: Not all reasons (or factors) carry equal importance. He spoke of estimating the weights of reasons, stating, "and where I find two, one on each side, that seem equal, I strike them both out. If I find a Reason *pro* equal to some *two* Reasons *con*, I strike out the three. If I judge some two Reasons *con*, equal to some three reasons *pro*, I strike out the five."

Of course, this method assumes that people can accurately quantify the importance of two factors. That is, they can know and state how important one factor is with respect to a combination of other factors. We don't know how true this is, although research from decision making experiments suggests that people are not very accurate at providing weights of the different factors they use (Reilly & Doherty, 1989).

In fact, in the research I've described previously, we looked at whether including people's importance weights led to better predictions of their final choices than did ignoring their importance weights. In most cases, using the participants' own importance weights made little difference.

Fischhoff (1991) talked about those instances in which people hold *articulated values*, that is, where they have clear ideas about their own values. For example, if I ask you to rate the importance of ketchup on a hot dog on a scale of 100 (*maximum*) to 0 (*none*), the issue is whether whatever response you make (be it 57, or

22, or 13.8) has much meaning. Sometimes, Fischhoff argued, people will cheerfully provide numerical ratings, but the ratings themselves reflect very little.

Fischhoff (1991) suggested that people are likely to have articulated values only in very specific circumstances: for example, when they have a great deal of time to think about their values, when they are motivated to clarify their values, when they have an opportunity to discuss their values and hear about others, when they do not feel under pressure to provide justification for these values. We don't know yet how many real-life decision-making situations this list (and other items on the list) apply to, but there is reason to be skeptical that people often have enough direct access to their values to put Ben Franklin's procedure into meaningful practice (Seidl & Traub, 1998).

Listing Options

Another aspect of a decision map is the number of alternatives under active consideration at any given point in time. Sometimes a decision has just two options: do something, or don't (these are sometimes called go/no-go decisions). Other times, the decision framework limits the number of options available.

Other decisions allow a much wider set of possible options. When high school students choose colleges, they have hundreds of possibilities in the United States alone. If a person goes to buy a new car, there are dozens of models available at any given time. In these kinds of decisions, the question is how the decision maker decides which options to consider.

One thing that is clear is that not all theoretical options or possibilities receive serious consideration. Instead, many people seem to construct a short list of possibilities. I'm borrowing this short list terminology from hiring processes typical at many institutions. The process goes like this: A job is advertised, and applications are sent in; let's say there are 200. Those 200 individuals are on the long list of applicants—just by applying, they've made the list. Now a folder is set up for each applicant. In each folder, typically, is the following: a resumé (we call it a curriculum vita in academia), a statement of teaching philosophy (usually one to two pages); a statement of research interests (usually two to three pages); a cover letter describing how the candidate sees herself or himself fitting into the position; any reprints of published articles (typically four to five, 10 pages each); and three to five letters of recommendation from professors that know of the candidates' teaching or scholarship.

That's a lot of information for everyone on the hiring committee to process, especially when there are 200 candidates. So, typically, the members of the committee first cull the long list into one of about 10 to 20 of the more promising candidates. This would be called a medium list. Then, everyone on the committee would take a closer look at those 10 to 20 files. Eventually, a short list is constructed of the three or four most promising candidates. Those candidates (the finalists) are the ones that are typically brought to the campus for an interview.

Beach and Mitchell, creators of image theory, take the position that the real work of decision making is done not during the final selection, but rather during this early screening phase, which they call the prechoice screening of options (Beach, 1993). For it is here that most logically possible options get weeded out. Their theory suggests that in all decisions people would at any time only be considering a handful of options.

Data from studies of people making decisions support the idea that people winnow down alternatives to a short list. For the high school students choosing a college, the average number of different schools under active consideration at any one time was between four and five (Galotti, 1995a). For the college students choosing a major, the average number of majors considered was about four (Galotti, 1999a). For the pregnant women considering birth attendants, the average was three or four. Very few individuals in either study listed more than five options at a time, and several listed just one or two. These data don't prove image theory, of course, because there could be many other reasons why people limit the amount of information to consider. But it is interesting, and very consistent with the predictions of image theory, that the limitations would be more severe for the number of options under consideration than for the number of criteria being used to make the decision.

Dealing With Uncertainty

We have not yet dealt with the topic of uncertainty; but uncertainty can and often does play a major role in real-life decision making. Take the example of pregnant women choosing a birth attendant for their upcoming deliveries: Whether or not a woman wants a home birth with a lay midwife or a hospital birth with an obstetrician will depend on many factors (e.g., her philosophy of birth, her insurance, her proximity to various caregivers), but a very important and frequently mentioned one was the safety of the baby. All mothers (I assume) hope and pray (and the optimists may even expect) an uncomplicated delivery. But such events are not absolutely guaranteed. Though the statistical likelihood of a routine delivery may be very high in a particular case, there are no guarantees.

The decision making literature is replete with examples of peoples' inability to use probability information correctly (see some of the following textbooks for reviews: Baron, 1994; Hogarth, 1980; Plous, 1993; Rachlin, 1989). That is, even when explicitly given information about the specific probability of occurrence of some event, people don't use the information correctly. Some of the heuristics and biases described in chapter 3 make this point very clear.

A very striking bias we haven't yet reviewed comes from the work of Fischhoff and his associates (Lichtenstein, Fischhoff, & Phillips, 1982), showing people's overconfidence in their own judgment. Specifically, people's assessment of the chances of their having answered correctly outstrips their actual performance. This is demonstrated most clearly with calibration curves.

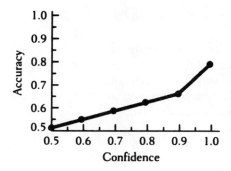

FIG. 4.2. Example of a calibration curve. *Note.* From *Cognitive Psychology In and Out of the Laboratory* (2nd ed., p. 452), by K. M. Galotti, 1999, Pacific Grove, CA: Brooks/Cole Wadsworth. Copyright 1999 by Wadsworth Publishing Co. Reprinted with permission.

Imagine answering a series of trivia questions, each of which has two choices (e.g., the film *The Big Chill* was first released in [a] 1983 or [b] 1984). For each question, you pick either answer A or answer B, then you provide a confidence rating of your answer. If you are just making a guess, your confidence should be 50% (any number lower than this means that you think you are more likely to be wrong than right, so you should have chosen the other answer). A confidence rating of 100% means, not surprisingly, that you are 100% certain that your answer is correct. Values between 50% and 100% indicate intermediate levels of confidence, with higher numbers reflecting higher confidence.

Your overall accuracy on the set of questions is irrelevant for our present purposes. What matters here is the relationship between your accuracy and your confidence rating. In several studies (reviewed by Lichtenstein et al., 1982), research participants were given a long list of questions similar to the one I gave previously. A plot of their accuracy as a function of their confidence ratings was made. For example, the experimenters looked at all of the questions for which a subject rated his or her confidence as 60% and calculated the proportion of those questions the subjects answered correctly. Typical findings are shown in Fig. 4.2. Notice that the 45-degree line would indicate that confidence and accuracy were perfectly synchronized: Questions for which a subject had a confidence rating of 0.6 would actually be answered accurately 60% of the time. This kind of finding is rarely, if ever, found. Instead, typical curves are bowed out from the 45-degree line, as shown in the figure.

This kind of curve—plotting confidence against accuracy—is called a calibration curve. The closer the curve is to the 45-degree line, the better the calibration, or fit, between confidence and accuracy. Deviations from the curve below this line are said to indicate overconfidence, where confidence ratings are higher than actual accuracy. Deviations above the line would indicate underconfidence, a phenomenon that rarely occurs. The general idea is this: For all of the response to which participants give an 80% confidence rating (presumably, meaning that they estimate the probability of their answering correctly as 80%), they are correct only about 60% of the time. Further, when subjects say they are 100% certain of the answer, they are correct only about 75–80% of the time. In short, people's impressions of their own accuracy are inflated.

The point of all this is to suggest that people's intuitions about probability are not closely aligned with mathematical probability theory. Left to our own intuitions, we are likely to go astray. When we speak casually of an 85% chance of some event occurring, no matter how emphatically we speak, it is not terribly likely that the few numbers being used are being used correctly.

LIMITING INFORMATION UNDER CONSIDERATION

We've seen repeatedly that when making decisions, people appear to limit the amount of information they actively consider at any given time. Why might this be? A number of related possibilities exist. The first I've already described: people's working memory capacity and possibly other features of our cognitive architecture make it necessary to limit the number of pieces of unrelated information we can consider at any given time.

Another explanation comes from the work of Perkins (1985; Perkins, Allen, & Hafner, 1983), who studied people's critical thinking. They asked their research participants to think aloud as they considered various policy issues and questions, such as "Would restoring the military draft significantly increase America's ability to influence world events?" or "Would a 5-cent deposit on bottles and cans significantly reduce litter?" Among other things, Perkins scored each person's response for the number of different lines of argument they advanced as well as the number of objections they raised to their own previous thinking.

The issues the researchers chose were, by design, those that had a number of arguments on both sides. However, the authors found that none of the research participants, not even the graduate students, explored the issues in very much depth. In general, the graduate students mentioned slightly more than three different arguments, and only gave one objection to their own previous thinking; the high school students in the sample described only two different arguments and averaged about 0.6 of an argument (Perkins, 1985). Perkins described this performance as significant underexploration of the issues at hand.

One reason for the underexploration was advanced by Perkins et al. (1983). They described many people as having a "makes-sense" epistemology—that is, they describe many people as reasoning about an issue just until they are able to mentally construct a scenario that, at least superficially, makes sense. Then they stop. What they don't do is actively interrogate or question their assumptions. They don't think critically. They don't go beneath the surface of their intuitive model of the situation.

How does this apply to real-life decision making? It may be that people only consider a few options or a few criteria for the same reason they only consider a few lines of argument in everyday reasoning—they don't question themselves enough. That is, they don't stop to think, "Have I really thoroughly listed all of the important factors I should be using in this situation?" and "Is my list of options really complete?"

In a sense, people may simply be mentally lazy. Or, to put it in slightly less unflattering terms, they may be *satisficing*—a term coined by Simon several decades ago (e.g., Simon, 1956). Simon's idea was that people don't usually try to maximize the outcomes of the decisions they make in a perfectly rational way (as decades of economic models had assumed). Instead, he held, people (and other organisms) use an approximate rationality—they search until they find an option that satisfies their needs and suffices to meet their criteria. Put another way, people don't search for the very best option they can find, only the first one that will satisfy and suffice (hence, *satisfice*) their needs.

One benefit of satisficing, or in general of keeping the amount of information to be considered in a decision limited, may be the reduction of stress. Anecdotally, some of my friends and students seem to assume that when they are in the middle of the decision-making process, still unsure of their final choice, they are somehow not performing well. They apologize, they shrug, they explain and try to justify themselves far more than do friends or students who have come to a final conclusion. Considering more alternatives, or using more criteria to decide among alternatives, increases the amount of information to be gathered, evaluated, and integrated. That in turn can prolong the decision-making process. Then, the delay could make people feel as though they are not going about the process correctly.

In this chapter, we've looked at how people organize the information they have gathered and reflected on their values to produce criteria. The studies reviewed have typically forced research participants to do these things explicitly. However, it may be that when left to their own devices, people don't always or ever lay out their criteria and options in any systematic way. They may do many of these things implicitly, intuitively, or maybe even not at all. We'll return to this theme in chapter 5, as we examine how people make a final selection.

5

Making a Final Choice

In the previous chapters, I outlined the chronology of decision making processes, at least as they are conceived in the abstract. I also discussed how people might clarify their values, goals, and strategies and how they might begin to refine their ideas about their options and the factors or criteria to be used to choose among those options. Now we come to a look at how people make a final choice—that is, how they select from all the options available the one they wish to have or implement.

CHOOSING FROM AMONG MULTIPLE OPTIONS

Of course, this assumes that people always have multiple options, and, as we will soon see, this isn't the case, at least in many of the real-life decision making scenarios studied to date. Some decisions come down to one option: Should I do something or shouldn't I? Should I accept this offer or not? To begin, though, I'll concentrate on decisions with multiple (e.g, two or more) options.

Satisficing

One way to cut down on the amount of work in choosing among multiple options is to use a strategy called satisficing (Simon, 1955). The idea is to find an option that suffices to meet your needs and that at least minimally satisfies your criteria. It does not mean searching for the best option or the optimal alternative. To the contrary, to satisfice means to find the first acceptable alternative. So, if you want a house with four bedrooms and a large yard for under $150,000, you search until you find the first alternative that meets all these criteria. Then you select it. You don't look at other options that might also meet all your criteria to choose among them (i.e., other houses costing under $150,000 that have four bedrooms and large yards). Of course, if none of the houses you see meets all of your important criteria, then you have to rethink your criteria and decide if some of them can be broadened a bit, or else you can think of some means of generating new options.

Elimination by Aspects

Another strategy people have been observed to use is called elimination by aspects (Tversky, 1972). Imagine yourself entering a realtor's office and expressing interest in buying a house. That realtor very well might start you out at a computer that will assess the aspects of a house that are important to you, so as to construct a list of homes you should visit. The computer program might start out by asking you to select a price range. You might select, say, a range of $100,000 to $149,999. The computer program will then eliminate from further consideration any house with a price range outside these limits. Even if a house were priced at $150,000, just $1 more than the upper limit of the range you specify, the program would never show it to you, even if that house met all of your other criteria perfectly. In other words, it will have eliminated, by the aspect of price, all options that don't exactly fit.

The elimination by aspects strategy is a favorite, apparently, of some television commercial producers. My favorite example comes from an ad for breakfast cereals. It begins with what appears to be every conceivable type of boxed breakfast cereal sitting on a rather large table. The announcer asks a question along the lines of "Which of these cereals have eight essential vitamins and minerals? These don't." (He knocks about one third of the cereal boxes off the table.) "And which are high in fiber? Not these." (Another bunch of boxes sails into the air.) "And which are low in sugar?" (More boxes careening to the floor.) "If you want a healthy choice for your breakfast cereal, there really is only one choice, and it's . . ." (OK, I forget which one it is. The point is, aspect by aspect, all the other cereals are eliminated.)

Now, you might ask, what's wrong with this approach? Well, the problem is it doesn't allow for any trade-offs. Imagine in the house example that although price was very important to you, also important were closets, a big kitchen, and a location in a town with great schools. You prefer, strongly, not to spend more than $150,000. So you refuse to go see any houses with an asking price of more than that. However, there is what turns out to be your dream house—in a perfect town, tons of closets, a cavernous kitchen, even an in-ground swimming pool—with a list price of $150,001. Had you stuck strictly to your policy of not considering any alternative above $150,000, you would have missed out.

Trade-offs are tricky things. They make decision making much more gray instead of black and white. Decision makers who allow for making trade-offs set themselves up for more work. It's quicker and easier to eliminate many options with one fell swoop. But easier does not always mean optimal.

NORMATIVE MODELS OF CHOICE

So how should a decision maker optimally select a final choice among options? We've discussed already in chapters 2 and 3 that the decision ought to be grounded in the decision makers' values and goals. But is there any more specific advice that can be offered?

Some social scientists believe there is. Economists and psychologists distinguish between *normative* and *descriptive* models (Baron, 1994). Normative models define ideal performance under ideal circumstances. Descriptive models, in contrast, simply detail what it is that people actually do when they make decisions.

Linear Models

One set of normative models that can be used to select among options goes by the name of linear models (Dawes, 1982; Dawes & Corrigan, 1974). In such models, decision makers are asked to (a) break a decision down into independent criteria (e.g., asking price, number of square feet); (b) determine the relative importance weights of each criterion; (c) list all alternatives (e.g., different possible houses to buy); and (d) rate the alternatives on each criterion.

Different linear models can be applied to the data generated in the process above. For example, one model might weight each criterion equally. Another might use information only from the criterion the decision maker regards as most important. A third might make use of the individually-generated importance weights, multiplying the ratings by the weightings and summing. For example, the weighting for Four Bedrooms might be equal to that for Price, but higher than that for Large Yard. Therefore, houses with four bedrooms and a good price but a small yard would receive a higher score than would houses with three bedrooms and a good price but a large yard. Linear models would result in a predicted value for each alternative, given the criteria and the importance weights. Such values could be used to rank order the alternatives in terms of their overall goodness to the decision maker, given that person's own values and perceptions.

Linear models involve a weighted combination of numerical information (e.g., predicting a college student's probability of graduating by using some sort of equation to combine various predictor variables, such as high school grade point average, standardized test scores, family income, and level of motivation). If the weights are chosen so that they optimize the relationship between the set of predictor variables and the outcome variable, then the model is said to be a proper linear model (Dawes, 1982). Depending on the particular linear model under discussion, different criteria can be weighted differentially or equally. Kleinmuntz (1990) and Dawes (1982) have presented elaborate arguments to the effect that the use of linear models, even improper ones (i.e., ones with weights assigned randomly), almost always leads to better decisions than does the exclusive use of intuitions.

Let's take a specific example of how linear models could be used in real-life decision making. I'm going to present a fictional but plausible decision map for a high school senior deciding on a college. Let's call him Tim. Table 5.1 presents his criteria, the importance weights he attaches to those criteria, the current options

TABLE 5.1
Tim's Structuring of His Decision About Which College to Attend

		Alternatives/Options		
Factor/Criterion	Importance Weight	Carleton College	Pomona College	Harvard University
Small college (size of class)	9	10	8	1
Reputation	5	5	7	10
Near a city; public transportation	4	0	8	10
Cost (after financial aid)	8	5	7	8
Offers lots of majors	5	9	6	10
Will I know high school friends who go there?	3	9	2	5

he is considering, and his perceptions of how well those options stack up on each criterion.

As you can see, Tim is currently deliberating among three schools: Carleton, Pomona, and Harvard. Tim has listed six criteria and has attached different importance weights to each criterion. He cares most about the size of the college, preferring a smaller institution to a larger one. He also cares a lot about cost. He'd also like it if the school were to attract some known friends from high school and if it were near a city with public transportation, but these factors carry much less weight.

We can also see what Tim's perceptions are of each school for each criterion. For example, on the factor of reputation, Tim perceives Harvard to have the best reputation (so he gives that option a 10 on that criterion); Pomona a good one, and Carleton an "OK" one. (The dean and president at Carleton, where I work, would no doubt welcome my reminding you at this point that the example is fictional and that Tim's perceptions may well be incorrect, or biased. In any case, Tim's perceptions are his perceptions, and other people may well have a very different set of perceptions.)

Now, given this decision structure, how might Tim go about making a final selection, according to a linear model? The answer depends on the specific linear model chosen, of course. In the following sections, I present three examples of models.

The Top Criterion Model. In this model, Tim pays attention only to how the options stack up on the criterion he thinks is the most important. In this example, Tim has rated Small college as most important (that criterion has the highest importance weight). Given only this criterion, Tim should choose Carleton College, which scores a 10 on this factor; Pomona is a fairly close second, with a score of 8, and Harvard lags far behind with a 1. (If my dean or president are still reading, that example was for them!)

But this model forces Tim to ignore a lot more information. Tim has indicated that he doesn't just care about size; he cares about other aspects of the colleges as well.

The Equally Weighted Criteria Model.   In this model, Tim treats all the criteria as equally important. He takes into consideration all of his criteria, summing up for each alternative his perceptions of it as measured against each criterion. So, for Carleton, he adds $10 + 5 + 0 + 5 + 9 + 9$ to obtain 38. The values for Pomona and Harvard, computed similarly, are 38 and 44, respectively. These values tell Tim that when all of his criteria carry equal weight, Harvard is the best choice. Carleton and Pomona are distinct second choices, and they are tied.

The equally weighted criteria model takes more information into account than does the top criterion model. And yet, it still leaves out possibly important data. Simply put, some criteria are more important to Tim than others, but the equally weighted criteria model doesn't take this into account.

The MAUT Model.   To discuss this model, I first need to talk about expected utility theory, or EU, as it is commonly known to economists and other decision-making researchers.

Utility models are based on the economic concept of *utility*, which roughly translates into *satisfaction*. Utility models are ones in which the decision maker is assumed to be trying to maximize her or his overall satisfaction. Such models assume that if a decision maker has two options, A and B, and expects option A to lead to greater satisfaction than option B, that the decision maker will unquestionably opt for A.

Making a decision can be compared to a gamble. In most gambles, you win (or lose) particular amounts of money depending on certain outcomes. Probability theory tells us (assuming fair coins, decks of cards, and the like), what the odds are of any outcome. The dollar amount won or lost tells us the monetary worth of each outcome.

It would be nice if we could somehow combine information about probabilities and amounts that can be won or lost. In fact, one way of doing so is to calculate the *expected value* of each outcome. Expected values are calculated by multiplying the probability of each outcome by the amount of money won or lost for that outcome and summing these values over all possible outcomes. The resulting value is the overall amount of money we can expect to win or lose.

As an example, imagine a lottery with 10 tickets, numbered 1 through 10. If the ticket drawn is numbered 1, you win $100. If the ticket drawn is numbered 2, 3, 4, or 5, you win $50. Any other numbers drawn are worth nothing. The expected value of this lottery, then, is

$$.1 * \$100 + .1 * \$50 + .1 * \$50 + .1 * \$50 + .1 * \$50 + (5 * [.1 * 0]) = \$30.$$

Thirty dollars, then, is the amount of money I expect to win or lose if I were to take the gamble an infinite number of times.

We can express this idea algebraically,

$$EV = \Sigma i[p(i) * v(i)], \tag{1}$$

where *EV* is the expected value of the gamble, *p(i)* is the probability of the *i*th outcome, and *v(i)* is the monetary value of that outcome.

So what? you might be thinking. Well, for one thing, the expected value tells you how much money (if any) you should be willing to spend for a given gamble. If you are making rational decisions, you should not spend more for the ticket than the expected value of the lottery. (In some lotteries for charity, of course, you may want to donate more money simply to support the cause. In that case, you would need to add the expected value of the lottery and the amount of money you are willing to donate.)

Expected value calculations are useful, then, when the outcomes at stake can be measured in monetary units. But, of course, not every decision involves monetary outcomes. We often care about other aspects of possible outcomes: our chances for happiness, success, or fulfillment of goals. Here's where the idea of utility comes in. Recall that psychologists, economists, and others use this term to refer to such things as pleasure, fulfillment, and the satisfaction that comes from achieving goals. A choice that fulfills one goal will have less utility than a choice that fulfills that same goal plus another.

We can adapt the procedure for calculating expected values to use this concept of utility as follows:

$$EU = \Sigma i \, [p(i) * u(i)], \tag{2}$$

where *EU* stands for the expected utility of a decision, and *u(i)* is the utility of the *i*th outcome. The summation is again over all the possible outcomes.

How exactly are peoples' utilities assessed? It turns out that the measurement of utilities is fairly straightforward. If you select one outcome and assign it the value of 0, then you can assign other values using this as the reference point. It does not matter which outcome is chosen as the 0 point because the final decision depends on differences in expected utilities, not on the absolute value of the utilities (see Baron, 1994, for more on this process).

Expected utility theory is seen by many as a normative model of decision making. It can be shown (see Baron, 1994) that if you always choose so as to maximize expected utility, then over a sufficiently large number of decisions, your own satisfaction will be highest. In other words, there is no better way of choosing among options that in the long run will increase overall satisfaction than using expected utility.

One problem in applying expected utility to a real-life decision is that decisions are often multifaceted. So, your utility for a given option might be high in some respects, low in others, and middling on others. This might stem from your having several goals, not just one, and finding it hard to figure out how they all fit together. Fortunately, there is a model that provides a means of integrating different dimensions and goals of a complex decision. It is called multiattribute utility theory (MAUT, for short).

Multiattribute Utility Theory.   To illustrate a MAUT calculation, let's go back to Tim, the high school student choosing among Carleton, Harvard, and Pomona. In the current example, Tim could use MAUT to calculate overall values for each school based on all the information found in Table 5.1. To do this, he would first multiply the importance weights by the ratings and sum over all the criteria. So, for Carleton, the value would be $(9 * 10) + (5 * 5) + (4 * 0) + (8 * 5) + (5 * 9) + (3 * 9) = 227$. For Harvard, the corresponding values would be $(9 * 1) + (5 * 10) + (4 * 10) + (8 * 8) + (5 * 10) + (3 * 5) = 228$. For Pomona, the corresponding values are be $(9 * 8) + (5 * 7) + (4 * 8) + (8 * 7) + (5 * 6) + (3 * 2) = 231$. Thus, using a MAUT model, Tim would find his best choice to be Pomona, with Harvard as a second choice and Carleton just a hair below it, in terms of Tim's overall values.

The MAUT model takes into account much more information and thus is a more complex and more complete model than either of the two presented earlier. However, it does rest on the assumption that people can realistically assign importance weights that truly reflect their values. Many psychologists are skeptical of this idea, especially if a person has not thought much about the issue ahead of time—that is, if a person's values are not well articulated, then the way he or she assigns importance weights may well be arbitrary (Fischhoff, 1991).

How well do these models do in predicting people's actual decision making? I've been asking just this question in my own research. I've been having research participants fill out instruments similar to that shown in Table 5.1. Later, I remove that sheet and ask the participant to rate each alternative on an overall scale of "goodness." This allows me to see how well their overall ratings correlate with the expected values for each alternative calculated from the three linear models previously described: top criterion, equally weighted criteria, and MAUT.

In the choosing a college study, I found that the latter two models better fit the students' data than did the top criterion model (Galotti, 1995a). Fig. 5.1 shows the relevant data. Correlations were at about the .70 level between the predicted value of both the MAUT and the equally weighted criteria models, both for higher ability and average ability high school students. They were at about the .60 level for lower ability (but still college-bound) students. For this group only, the simpler top criterion model seemed to do as well in predicting students' overall impressions.

Notice that the MAUT model did not outperform the equally weighted criteria model, for any group of students. This suggests that students aren't really using the importance weights in coming to a final rating of each alternative.

The general order of magnitude (i.e., correlations of around .6 or .7) persisted in the studies of college students choosing a major (Galotti, 1999a) and pregnant women choosing a birth attendant (Galotti, 1998). However, there were fluctu-

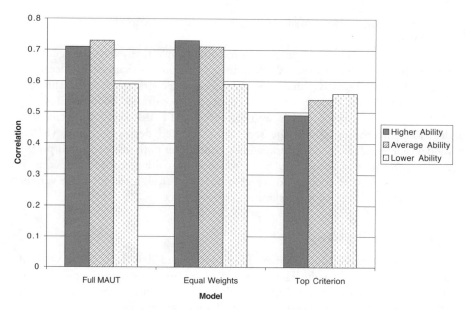

FIG. 5.1.   Correlation of overall impressions with expected values calculated from linear models. Choosing a College Study (based on data from Galotti, 1995a).

ations in which specific model was most highly correlated, which seemed to depend in part on the educational level of the research participant as well as on the specific decision being studied.

Of course, these results do not necessarily mean that people actually used linear models in integrating information. That is, the analytic procedure I required of research participants (i.e., listing criteria, listing options, rating options on criteria) may or may not have mirrored the cognitive processing they naturally do in these kinds of decisions. No research participant ever claimed to have spontaneously used this procedure in his or her own decision making. In fact, there is reason to wonder whether people's natural decision making ever is as analytical as a linear model. We'll return to this theme at the end of the chapter.

DECISIONS WITH A SINGLE OPTION

Not all researchers agree with the premises of linear models in general, and utility models in particular. Some have argued against the idea that people ever or often use analytical procedures, such as those involved with linear models, when making important decisions (Frisch & Clemen, 1994). These proposals would suggest that linear models do not capture the actual cognitive processes used in real-life decision making. Some have offered alternative descriptive models of what people actually do.

Some of these models argue that in real life, people rarely have a large set of options from which to make a selection. Instead, the idea is that real-life decisions frequently come down to taking or not taking a single course of action. In this section, we'll look at models that often focus on single-option decision making.

Two such descriptive models are image theory (IT; Beach, 1998), which was described in chapter 2, and the recognition primed decision-making (RPD) model (Klein, 1998). The fundamental assumption of both models is that people rarely go through a formal structuring process in making real-life decisions in which they lay out all their options and criteria, then weigh and integrate various pieces of information, as various linear models predict.

Image Theory, Revisited

As we've seen in previous chapters, IT posits instead that most of the work of decision making is done during a phase called the prechoice screening of options (Beach, 1993). In this phase, decision makers typically pare down the number of options under active consideration to a small number, sometimes one or two. They do this by asking themselves whether a new goal, plan, or alternative is compatible with three images: the value image (containing the decision maker's values, morals, principles); the trajectory image (containing the decision maker's goals and aspirations for the future); and the strategic image (the way in which the decision maker plans to attain her or his goals). Options judged incompatible with one or more of these three images are screened out. The process is noncompensatory: Violations of any image are enough to rule out that option.

For example, suppose you're a high school student choosing a college. You have decided that you want a small college, at least 100 miles from home (to discourage surprise visits from Mom or Dad), that offers a program that will lead to a physical therapy career. You visit many places, falling in love with the campus of Morris College, a fictional but idyllic place in a lovely setting. Morris College has a faculty that you find engaging and caring when you talk to them on a visit; its dorms are new and sparkling clean; the computer facilities are new and gleaming; and the food in the dorms is actually tasty. Morris is just the right size for you and in a perfect location. But it's a liberal arts college and so doesn't offer any preprofessional programs, such as one in physical therapy.

If a physical therapy program is indeed part of your trajectory image, and if part of your strategic image is the belief that your college course work must include work in physical therapy, you'll reject Morris College as an option, regardless of the fact that it has so many other attractive aspects. If it violates one or more of your images, you won't make trade-offs between those aspects (in this case, program offerings at the college) and other aspects (e.g., facilities, food, size, location) that are very attractive to you. Instead, Morris College will be screened out, or dropped, from your list.

Screening may result in a single option remaining active; in this case, the decision maker's final choice is simply whether or not to accept the option. If there is more than one survivor of the prechoice screening phase, then the decision maker may go on to use compensatory or other decision strategies to make the final choice. If there are no survivors, decision makers presumably attempt to discover new options.

In one study testing the predictions of IT (Potter & Beach, 1994a), undergraduate research participants were asked to imagine that they were helping a friend find a room to rent. They were given five criteria for the rooms and then a description of five different rooms. The rooms violated either none of the criteria, one of the criteria, or three of the criteria. The room described as violating three criteria was rejected as an option by all participants. Of the rooms described as violating none of the criteria, 97% of the participants said they would put them on a short list from which their friend could choose. Rooms described as violating only one of the five criteria were added to the short list by slightly more than one third of the participants. When asked what they would do if all the rooms on the short list turned out to be unavailable, 89% of the study participants answered that they would look for new rooms rather than reconsider the old ones that did not make the short list.

Potter and Beach (1994b) argued that decision making is a two-stage process — first, screening out weak or unacceptable alternatives, followed by choice. They further conclude that the screening stage is probably the more important of the two. Evidence from a variety of studies supporting image theory (Beach, 1993, 1998; Beach & Mitchell, 1987; Beach & Potter, 1992; Mitchell & Beach, 1990; Potter & Beach, 1994a, 1994b) has involved simulated and hypothetical decisions. Thus, less is known about how well it predicts real-life decision behavior. Although the intuitive appeal of the theory is quite strong, it will take further investigation to figure out how to implement a rigorous test of the theory in real-life contexts.

The Recognition Primed Decision-Making Model

A second alternative description of real-life decision making comes from the work of Klein (1998), who has conducted numerous field studies of expert decision makers. Klein and colleagues studied experts, such as fire commanders, nurses in neonatal intensive care units, military commanders, to take a few examples, who made a variety of important decisions on their jobs. They followed these experts on the job and conducted interviews of key decision makers.

Klein and colleagues found that these experts were unlikely to structure a decision with various options. Instead, their decision makers seemed to quickly categorize a situation, even a very novel one, as an example of a pattern or proto-type. That is, they tended to recognize the kind of situation they were dealing with, and implement the appropriate solution, from memory, that applied.

Klein and colleagues collected much of their main data by asking experts to recount cases of memorable decisions. The following story presents a detailed example that will provide an illustration of their work:

The Overpass Rescue

A lieutenant is called out to rescue a woman who either fell or jumped off a highway overpass. She is drunk or on drugs and is probably trying to kill herself. Instead of falling to her death, she lands on the metal supports of a highway sign and is dangling there when the rescue team arrives.

The lieutenant recognizes the danger of the situation. The woman is semiconscious and lying bent over one of the metal struts. At any moment, she could fall to her death on the pavement below. If he orders any of his team out to help her, they will be endangered because there is no way to get a good brace against the struts, so he issues an order not to climb out to secure her.

Two of his crew ignore his order and climb out anyway. One holds onto her shoulders and the other to her legs.

A hook-and-ladder truck arrives. The lieutenant doesn't need their help in making the rescue, so he tells them to drive down to the highway below and block traffic in case the woman does fall. He does not want to chance that the young woman will fall on a moving car.

Now the question is how to pull the woman to safety.

First, the lieutenant considers using a rescue harness, the standard way of raising victims. It snaps onto a person's shoulders and thighs. In imagining its use, he realizes that it requires the person to be in a sitting position or face up. He thinks about how they would shift her to sit up and realizes that she might slide off the support.

Second, he considers attaching the rescue harness from the back. However, he imagines that by lifting the woman, they would create a large pressure on her back, almost bending her double. He does not want to risk hurting her.

Third, the lieutenant considers using a rescue strap—another way to secure victims, but making use of a strap rather than a snap-on harness. However, it creates the same problems as the rescue harness, requiring that she be sitting up or that it be attached from behind. He rejects this too.

Now he comes up with a novel idea: using a ladder belt—a strong belt that firefighters buckle on over their coats when they climb up ladders to rescue people. When they get to the top, they can snap an attachment on the belt to the top rung of the ladder. If they lose their footing during the rescue, they are still attached to the ladder so they won't plunge to their death.

The lieutenant's idea is to get a ladder belt, slide it under the woman, buckle it from behind (it needs only one buckle), tie a rope to the snap, and lift her up to the overpass. He thinks it through again and likes the idea, so he orders one of his crew to fetch the ladder belt and rope, and they tie it onto her.

In the meantime, the hook-and-ladder truck has moved to the highway below the overpass, and the truck's crew members raise the ladder. The firefighter on the platform at the top of the ladder is directly under the woman shouting, "I've got her. I've got her." The lieutenant ignores him and orders his men to lift her up.

At this time, he makes an unwanted discovery: ladder belts are built for sturdy firefighters, to be worn over their coats. This is a slender woman wearing a thin sweater. In addition, she is essentially unconscious. When they lift her up, they realize the problem. As the lieutenant put it, "She slithered through the belt like a strand of slippery spaghetti."

Fortunately, the hook-and-ladder man is right below her. He catches her and makes the rescue. There is a happy ending.

Now the lieutenant and his crew go back to the station to figure out what had gone wrong. They try the rescue harness and find that the lieutenant's instincts were right: neither [sic] is usable.

Eventually they discover how they should have made the rescue. They should have used the rope they had tied to the ladder belt. They could have tied it to the woman and lifted her up. With all the technology available to them, they had forgotten that you can use a rope to pull someone up. (Klein, 1998, pp. 18–19).

Notice a few things about this example. The first is how fast the decisions are made—by the team's estimate, the lieutenant took less than a minute to choose the ladder belt. More striking is that, although the lieutenant thought of multiple options (which in itself was unusual, according to Klein), he did not compare the different options to one another. Instead, he generated one option at a time, evaluated whether or not it was going to work and either rejected it and went on to another option or implemented it. In example after example, Klein (1998) found that experts were much less likely to consider multiple alternatives. Instead, the experts seemed to generate a workable solution as the first option they thought of.

The recognition primed decision-making model (Klein, 1998) was created to describe the findings from the observations. The model is presented schematically in Fig. 5.2. Variation 1, shown on the extreme left, presents the basic decision-making strategy Klein's experts were observed to use. Confronted with a routine or typical scenario, experts recognize the case as an example of a class of cases they have seen before. This allows them to predict which other aspects of the situation to expect and directs them in setting their priorities and goals and in implementing a solution.

Not all situations are typical, of course, as the overpass rescue example makes clear. Variation 2 deals with cases where the decision maker has to spend much more time diagnosing the situation, typically in a novel case or when a situation reminds the decision maker of multiple (and different) possibilities. Then, the decision maker will have to gather more information and devise a way to deal with inconsistencies.

Variation 3 shows how decision makers assess the likely outcomes of novel solutions, typically through mental simulation. The overpass rescue example illustrates how the lieutenant evaluates different possibilities—by thinking of likely consequences and using this information to reject or accept possible solutions.

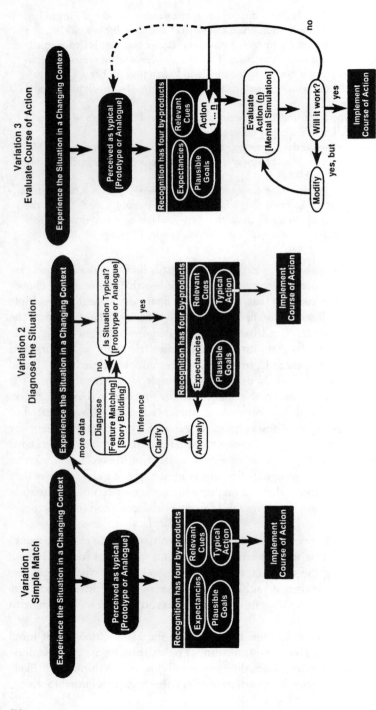

FIG. 5.2. Recognition primed decision-making model. *Note.* From *Sources of Power: How People Make Decisions* (p. 25), by G. Klein, 1998, Cambridge, MA: MIT Press. Copyright 1998 by the MIT Press. Reprinted with permission.

Klein (1998) concluded that expert decision makers satisfice—that is, they look for the first solution that will work, not necessary the optimal solution. The RPD model shares the assumption of image theory, that much of decision making takes place as people gather information and size up a situation, rather than during the final selection phase. Indeed, both IT and RPD predict that in many cases, the decision comes down to taking or leaving a single option.

Klein (1998) argued against standard advice on how to improve decision making (i.e., having people consider all their options, carefully weigh different aspects of the decision, intensively gather information about each option). Instead, Klein believes that the way to train novices to become experts is to give them many experiences in making time-pressured decisions, to teach them to detect patterns and to improve their ability to rapidly recognize and categorize new situations.

USING ANALYTIC VERSUS INTUITIVE PROCEDURES

Klein's advice suggests that people focus less on analytic procedures, such as those used in linear models, and more on developing and trusting intuition. This advice contrasts with advice typically given by psychologists on how to improve decision making (e.g., Janis & Mann, 1977). The standard advice given is to consider as large a number of options as possible, to gather as much information about each option as possible, to weigh different aspects of the options in accordance with your own values and priorities, and so on. In essence, the received wisdom on how to make optimal decisions is to follow linear models.

Wilson and colleagues have gone further to suggest that forcing people to approach decision making analytically—that is, to specify their criteria—actually lessens their satisfaction with the choices they make (Wilson & Schooler, 1991; Wilson et al., 1993).

In one study (Wilson & Schooler, 1991), college students were given five different brands of strawberry jams to taste test. Some of the students were asked to list the reasons they liked or disliked a particular jam. Other students weren't required to do such an analytical task. Later, both groups were asked to rate all of the jams. Those students who were required to list their reasons for liking or disliking a jam did not perform as well in the final ratings of the jams (as measured by how well their ratings correlated with the ratings of expert jam testers hired by *Consumer Reports* magazine).

In a follow-up study, Wilson et al. (1993) had study participants choose one of two posters—either a humorous poster or a classical art poster—that they got to keep. Once again, some participants were asked to list the reasons for their choices; other participants were not. Three weeks later, the investigators contacted study participants by phone. They were asked (among other things) how much they liked the poster they had chosen. Those who had previously listed reasons for their choice actually rated themselves as less satisfied with their poster than were people who had simply chosen a poster.

The researchers interpret this counterintuitive result as follows: People do not have direct introspective access to many of their higher order cognitive processes. That is, they don't always know why they feel or think the way that they do (Nisbett & Wilson, 1977). When pressed, people generate plausible-sounding reasons to explain their reactions. But once having announced this reason, people then use it to guide their actions, thus leading themselves astray in their future behavior. Or, as Wilson and Schooler (1991) put it, "Forming preferences is akin to riding a bicycle; we can do it easily, but cannot easily explain how. Just as automatic behaviors can be disrupted when people analyze and decompose them . . . so can preferences and decisions be disrupted when people reflect about the reasons for their feelings" (p. 182).

This view suggests that people should not be encouraged to think too much when they make decisions. This news will indeed be welcome to many of my college students, who seem to approach the task of making decisions with great dread. One of their fears, they tell me, is that they'll get so mired down in all the information and introspection that they'll never actually *do* something—they'll never actually make the decision. Wilson and Schooler's work suggests that thinking too much has another real danger. It will distort the decision-making processes itself, leading to unhappier outcomes than would be the case if people were simply asked to make a choice and not think too much about it.

However, Kmett, Arkes, and Jones (1999) reported contrary findings. They recruited high school seniors who were in the process of selecting a college. They divided students into three groups. Two were forced to use analytical decision procedures, specifically to articulate their criteria and to think about the pros and cons of different possible colleges. Contrary to the predictions from Wilson's work, students who used an analytic procedure were not less satisfied with the decisions they made when surveyed a year later (when in college).

Kmett, Arkes, and Jones (1999) disputed the generality of the claim that analytic approaches to decision making inevitably lower satisfaction. They argue that when the decision has obvious criteria that can be used, analytic procedures either help or at least do not compromise an individual's satisfaction with the decision. Notice that in the Wilson and Schooler rate-the-jam task, it is unclear what criteria there are to be applied to jams. However, high school students are easily able to articulate criteria that apply to different colleges. Put another way, the discrepancy in findings may stem from the difference in the *kinds* of decisions being made, a topic we will return to in chapter 6.

However, our intuitions often seem to sabotage our intention to make rational decisions. Anecdotally, we often seem to feel that, in life-threatening situations, the best decision is one made intuitively, rather than analytically. Consider Table 5.2, which presents three scenarios I've given to undergraduate students in my Thinking, Reasoning, and Decision Making class. I present it just after we learn

TABLE 5.2
Some Decision-Making Scenarios

---

1. Suppose you find a computerized expert system that has been shown to make better predictions than any of the individual physicians who created it. It predicts surgical outcomes with a 95% accuracy rate. The best accuracy achieved by any individual physician was 78%.

   Now you consult with one of the physician authors of the expert system, a prominent Mayo surgeon. After a thorough physical examination, he recommends you undergo a painful procedure, which he claims will save you from what looks to be a poor prognosis otherwise. However, when he plugs in the data from your specific case, the expert system suggests that you should not have the surgery. Dr. X (your physician) urges you to disregard the program's recommendation because you are a "special case." Other physicians disagree that you are a special case, although they don't examine you. Would you have the surgery or not? What would your decision depend on? Do you feel you are being rational about your decision? What constitutes rationality in this case, anyway?

2. You win the lottery, and have (after taxes) $1 million you never expected to have. You go to a well-respected and highly recommended financial planner, who recommends a particular portfolio to you. She mentions, off-handedly, that she has a computerized expert system in her office, one that she helped to create. She tells you that it has been shown to make better predictions than any of the individual planners who created it. It predicts portfolio outcomes with a 95% accuracy rate. The best accuracy achieved by any individual planner was 78%.

   Well, you guessed it. The program suggests something different than the planner originally had. She dismisses the program's recommendation, arguing that you are a special case. Other planners disagree that you are a special case, although they don't have a lengthy interview with you. Would you follow her recommended plan or not? What would your decision depend on? Do you feel you are being rational about your decision? What constitutes rationality in this case, anyway?

3. You apply to graduate school (or medical school, or law school, or business school, or ITT Technical Institute, whatever. Pretend that you really want to go this particular school). You meet with the dean of admissions. He tells you that the program is now using a new (you guessed it) computerized expert system to make admissions decisions because it has been shown to make better predictions than any of the individual educators who created it. It predicts portfolio outcomes with a 95% accuracy rate. The best accuracy achieved by any individual educator was 78%.

   The dean tells you, however, that he is prepared to veto the recommendations of the program for special cases such as you. He does NOT tell you what the program's recommendation about you is, nor what his individual recommendation would be. You find out later that other members of the admissions committee disagree that you are a special case, although they don't have a lengthy interview with you. You feel that the dean seems affable, but you can't really read him.

   Would you feel fairly treated in this situation or not? What would your feeling depend on? Do you feel you are being rational about your feeling? What constitutes rationality in this case, anyway?

---

about linear models. I've been quite surprised by the strong emotions and spirited debate these scenarios elicit. Although most of the students tell me that they "know" that "I want" them to say that they'd follow the recommendations of a computerized expert system known to have 95% reliability, they feel more comfortable following the intuitions of the human expert, even if that expert's reliability was noticeably less.

Meehl (1954, 1965) confronted this issue some years ago. He examined the relative effectiveness of holistic, clinical impressions with judgments made by statistical

models of data. A good example of this would be to compare an admissions counselor's prediction of an applicant's chances for success at a given college with the
prediction of a statistical model that weighted Scholastic Aptitude Test (SAT)
scores, high school grade point average, degree of involvement in extracurricular
activities, strength of letters of recommendation (however measured), and whatever other variables were established to be relevant to predicting success at that
college. Numerous studies of this kind have been conducted, and they overwhelmingly support the use of the nonhuman model (Dawes, 1982; Dawes &
Corrigan, 1974; Kleinmuntz, 1990). Thus, contrary to our (strong) intuitions, it is
often better, fairer, more rational, and in the long run more humane to use decision aids rather than to rely exclusively on human impressions or intuitions.

Kleinmuntz (1990) elaborated on the arguments at stake here. On the one
hand, there are many of us who feel strongly that important decisions must be
made after comprehensive assessment of all factors, including subtle nuances that
can't be easily quantified. However, note that this argument assumes that human
judges are going to be better able to accurately pick up on the nuances with their
training. In fact, there is reason to be suspicious that human cognition, with all of
its limitations and biases (such as those reviewed in chapter 3), is to be trusted
more heavily than is a formula or computer. It is probable that people, more than
computers, are likely to fall prey to selective processing of information, biased
memory or coding of information, or to inaccurately calculate information because of various cognitive limitations. Kleinmuntz suggested that heads and formulas be combined, with human experts used to *select* aspects of a decision to
focus upon, and formulas used to *combine* information from the human-made
assessments.

What we have done so far in the book is to look at the various stages or phases
of decision making. Throughout, we've glossed over the fact that decisions in different realms might be governed by different principles, or that experts and
novices might differ in predictable ways in their approaches to decision making.
We've also not thought much about whether people have distinct styles of decision making, or how these styles have come to be. We also have ignored the topic
of how individuals develop their decision-making skills and strategies. And we've
omitted discussion of how groups of people make decisions and how their culture
or climate influences these processes.

These are all important topics to consider, and we will do so in the chapters to
come. That is, we'll take the basic framework I've laid out in the first several chapters and see what impact all of the factors above have on the phases of decision
making described. Having done that, we will again come back to the issue of how
best to make a decision and how decision making can be improved.

6

Making Different Kinds of Decisions

Up until this point in the book, we've been assuming that all types of decisions are made the same way, regardless of what the decision is about. In other words, our discussion has not made distinctions among different types of decisions. But this outlook seems to contradict intuition. It seems on the face of it unlikely that when you go to a fast food restaurant and order a hamburger rather than a cheeseburger or chicken fingers that you use the same processes as when deciding, for example, whether to take a particular job offer or whether or not to put a beloved, ailing pet to sleep.

Of course, intuitions can be wrong. It could be that we use exactly the same mental processes in making all decisions, even if it doesn't feel that way. In this chapter, we'll be looking at how much the actual content of the decision—what it's a decision *about,* in other words—affects the way people approach it and the process information. First, I'll talk generally about different factors that seem to affect decision making. Then, we'll take a look at four different realms in which individuals make decisions—discussing a brief overview of consumer, legal, medical, and moral decision making in turn. Our goal will be to examine similarities and differences in decision making across these domains.

THE IDEA OF CONTENT AND CONTEXT EFFECTS

Psychologists who study people's reasoning and problem-solving skills have long known of the phenomena of content and context effects. Content effects are demonstrated when people show an inability to solve one version of a problem but solve it easily when it is described as being "about" something else.

Here's an example. Look at Fig. 6.1. It is a depiction of a task made famous by Wason (1968). It shows four cards, two with a letter and two with a digit. All four cards have a letter on one side and a digit on the other. I tell you a rule, such as "If

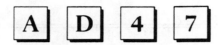

FIG. 6.1.   Depiction of the Wason (1968) selection task. *Note.* From *Cognitive Psychology In and Out of the Laboratory* (2nd ed., p. 407), by K. M. Galotti, 1999, Pacific Grove, CA: Brooks/Cole Wadsworth. Copyright 1999 by Wadsworth Publishing Company. Reprinted with permission.

a card has a vowel on one side, then it has an even number on the other side." I ask you to turn over *all* and *only* the cards that could test the rule. If you are like most people, you'll turn over the A card, which is correct, and the 4 card, which is not correct. You will fail to turn over the 7 card (as you should, to see if there is a vowel on the reverse, which would violate the rule).

People's performance improves dramatically if the four cards are labeled slightly differently: on one side, information on a person's age, and on the other, information about what a person is drinking. Then, the four cards shown say "Drinking a beer," "Drinking a Coke," "16 years of age," and "22 years of age." The rule to be investigated is "If a person is drinking a beer, then the person must be over 19 years of age." This experiment was conducted by Griggs and Cox (1982), who found that about three quarters of their college-student subjects solved the problem correctly when it was about drinking age, but none could solve the equivalent problem about letters and numbers. This is because, the authors assert, the college students' own experience with drinking-age laws (and perhaps with violations of those laws) allowed them to think of what kinds of combinations of ages and beverages would violate the rule. The same students had no comparable relevant experience to draw on when they reasoned about vowels and numbers in the other version of the task.

The general idea of a content effect, then, is that we process structurally similar information in different ways if that information is superficially about different things. Content effects are to be distinguished from context effects, the effects of information surrounding a task on the way it is performed. My favorite study demonstrating a context effect was performed by Godden and Baddeley (1975), who presented lists of 40 unrelated words to 16 scuba divers, all wearing scuba gear. Divers learned some of the lists on the shore, and the others, 20 feet under water. They were later asked to recall the words either in the same environment where they were learned or in the other environment. Results showed that recall was best when the environment was the same as the learning environment. Lists learned underwater were best recalled underwater, and lists learned on the shore were recalled best on the shore. That is, the context in which material was learned made it easier to recall that information, whether the context was underwater or on the beach.

Do context effects occur in decision making? The evidence suggests that it does. We've already talked about framing effects, which are one kind of context effect. If Gas Station A offers gasoline at $1.00 per gallon with a 5 cents per gallon discount for cash, and Gas Station B offers gasoline for $.95 per gallon with a 5 cents per gallon surcharge for credit cards, they really are offering exactly the same choices. However, many people report a preference for Station A, the one that offers a cash discount (Thaler, 1980). Tversky and Kahneman (1981) explained this as a framing effect: People evaluate outcomes as changes from a reference point, their current state. Depending on how that current state is described, they perceive certain outcomes as gains or losses. The description frames, or provides a context, for the decision.

The general importance of content and context effects is to highlight the idea that people are affected in their cognitive performance in clear ways, both by what a problem is nominally about and also by the way the problem is described or the context in which it occurs. This idea in turn suggests that the way decisions are made might likely be affected by what the decision is about, as well as by the general realm in which the decision occurs.

DECISION MAKING IN DIFFERENT DOMAINS

To examine this proposition in greater detail, we'll take a look at different kinds of decisions and look at existing literature that describes how people ordinarily seem to go about the process of making them. We'll look to see whether there are general similarities in decision-making performance in different domains, as well as at the question of whether there are important, domain-specific differences in performance.

The Adaptive Decision Maker Hypothesis

In chapter 3 we examined a decision-making task popularized by Payne (1976): an information board displaying information about different (fictitious) apartments. The board displays different pieces of information (called attributes) about different possible apartments (called alternatives) that the research participant can choose to examine, while the researcher keeps track of how many pieces of information the participant looks at and in what order.

You may recall from chapter 3 that Payne (1976) found that people's performance on this task varied a great deal as a function of the number of alternatives and the number of attributes presented. For example, when there were only two apartments to choose between, participants were more likely to examine every piece of information about both. When the number of different apartments offered increased to 6 or 12, participants examined only slightly more than half of the available information.

Moreover, the manner in which people examined information changed greatly depending on the number of alternatives. With two apartments offered, participants searched alternative by alternative, first by examining all the information available for one apartment then by looking at all the corresponding information for the other apartment. In contrast, when many apartments were offered, people switched to a strategy of looking at information attribute by attribute (e.g., examining all of the rent information for all the apartments) and quickly eliminating possible apartments.

Thus, even slight changes to the content of the problem (i.e., how many alternatives or dimensions there were to the decision) apparently influenced in a striking way the processes people used in making a decision. This study was the first of many that led Payne and other colleagues to create what has come to be called the adaptive decision maker hypothesis: the idea that people use different strategies to make decisions, depending on the specifics of the decision they are making (Payne, Bettman, & Johnson, 1993). The rationale for this hypothesis is that people want to do more than just make accurate decisions—they want also to conserve their mental energies. Thus, when faced with a task that will strain their ability to manage information (e.g., in a task with lots of available information and many different options), they will quickly cut down to a manageable size the amount of information they need to actively process to make a final selection.

Payne et al. (1993) considered the flexibility people show in decision making to be an asset. Being able to be flexible, to make decisions differently as a function of the circumstances, might mean the difference between the survival or the demise of a business organization, for example. They note that other psychologists have equated flexibility with intelligence, as well as with biological adaptivity.

But flexibility has its costs as well as benefits. If a decision maker has a variety of decision-making strategies available, how does she decide which one to use? Payne et al. (1993) assume that, in deciding how to decide, individuals attempt to balance accuracy and mental effort. Decisions that don't require a great deal of accuracy will be made with less effort than will decisions that require much effort.

Consumer Decisions

Payne's (1976) choosing an apartment task can be categorized as a type of hypothetical consumer decision. Research participants are, after all, asked to imagine themselves seeking a place to live, searching among options for an entity to rent. With another hypothetical consumer decision-making task, Abdul-Muhmin (1999) demonstrated that the kind of decision making studied in the Payne task is different in character from tasks in which people choose multiple alternatives. Some examples of such decisions include choosing a beverage, appetizer, entrée, and a dessert at a restaurant; choosing a set of cities or attractions to visit in vacation planning; choosing a set of courses to enroll in for a semester in college.

As you might imagine, selecting multiple alternatives is often a complex task. For example, in choosing a meal you might want to coordinate the various items, making sure that all parts of the meal go together. This might involve balancing—

having a lighter entrée if you want a rich dessert or vice versa. This in turn implies that your consideration of an individual item (e.g., whether or not to order the Death by Chocoloate mousse-cake for dessert) has to be considered in the context of your other selections.

Abdul-Muhmin (1999) believed that other important task variables would be the number of choices from which you had to select and the number of selections you were to make. At one extreme, consider the fictional New York sandwich shop made famous in *Saturday Night Live* comedy sketches, where the only menu items available are cheeseburgers, chips, and Pepsi drinks. (Customers who attempted to order anything else were told some variation of "No Coke—Pepsi!" or "No fries—chips!") The limited number of choices cuts down on the complexity of the decision.

At another extreme, consider a task students at my college do three times a year: choose 3 courses from the available 400 or so offered each term. There are various restrictions that have to be kept in mind, such as the fact that some courses have prerequisites and many meet during the same time period. Moreover, students need to fulfill graduations requirements, and different courses fulfill different ones. Not surprisingly, each term some students stress out over finding a set of courses that are balanced, taught by popular professors, meeting at convenient times, and that fulfill one or another of the graduation requirements.

It also matters, Abdul-Muhmin (1999) stated, what the ratio of selections to possibilities is. For example, suppose you are working with a travel agent to construct a travel itinerary of European cities you wish to visit. If you are asked to choose 9 cities from a list of 10, that's equivalent to selecting one city not to visit. For that reason, it might be easier to make that decision than it might to choose 5 of the 10 cities to visit.

Indeed, in a study where research participants were essentially asked to do this task, Abdul-Muhmin (1999) found that at first, people used different strategies when asked to make a single decision (e.g., choose one of the following 10 cities to visit) versus when they were asked to make multiple decisions (e.g., chose 3, or 5, or 7, of the following cities to visit). People in the latter three groups tended to search a higher proportion of the information made available in the task. He also reported that that Choose 3 and the Choose 7 groups showed striking similarities in their approach to the task, relative to the Choose 5 group. The Choose 5 group seemed to be minimizing their effort at the task, possibly because it seemed so difficult, because they reasoned that even a random choice would include at least some worthwhile cities to visit, or both.

The idea that people try to conserve on the effort they devote to cognitive tasks is one with a long history in the field of cognitive psychology. Neisser (1976) gave one plausible reason why: "Everyone knows that we become inefficient if we attempt too much; trying to do several things at once often ends in failure to do any of them adequately" (p. 99). In decision making, there might be good reasons for limiting the number of pieces of information sought: to stay within whatever bounds there are in our ability to process and integrate data.

In turn, this view suggests that changing the way information is presented so as to make it easier to absorb or digest (to borrow nutritional metaphors) ought to result in more information acquisition and use. Russo's (1977) work on how consumers use unit price information supports this idea. He studied the purchasing decisions of supermarket shoppers at a typical chain supermarket. He selected six products for analysis: apple juice, coffee, dish detergent, laundry detergent, peanut butter, and syrup. These products were selected because they were varied and because each one had at least 15 different combinations of brands and sizes available at the participating supermarkets.

The study took place over a period of 20 weeks. During Weeks 1–4, no unit price information was provided to consumers (the study was conducted in 1974, before the provision of unit price information was widespread). Unit prices presented on individual shelf tags were added for Weeks 5–8. During Weeks 9–16, Russo (1977) added lists of the prices, similar to the ones shown in Figure 6.2. It is easy to see from this list which individual item has the lowest and highest unit price and to see where an individual's favorite item falls relative to all other similar items. Finally, during Weeks 17–20, the store reverted to providing only shelf tags.

Russo (1977) compared people's use of unit price information when it was presented in the traditional way, on individual tags on grocery store shelves, versus as an organized lists where different brands of a product were organized by unit price. With shelf tags, the shopper needs to inspect all of the tags for a particular

Unit Prices of Consumer Goods
Listed in Order of Increasing Price/Ounce

Item	Total price	Price per ounce
Ajax Dishwashing Liquid Lemon 19 oz.	1.19	.06
Stop & Shop Ultra Dish Detergent Lemon 28 oz.	1.59	.06
Sunlight Ultra Dish Liquid Lemon 28 oz.	2.59	.09
Ivory Ultra Concentrate Dishwashing Liquid 28 oz.	2.69	.10
Dawn Dishwashing Liquid Antibacterial 25 oz.	2.59	.11
Dawn Ultra Power Plus Dish Liquid Antibacterial 25 oz.	2.79	.11
Ivory Ultra Concentrate Dishwashing Liquid 14.7 oz.	1.59	.11
Palmolive Dish Liquid Antibacterial 25 oz.	2.79	.11
Palmolive Spring Sensation Dish Liquid Botanical 25 oz.	2.79	.11
Palmolive Spring Sensation Dish Liquid Antibacterial Ocean Breeze 25 oz.	2.79	.11
Palmolive Ultra Dish Liquid Original 14.7 oz.	1.59	.11
Sunlight Ultra Dish Liquid Lemon 14.7 oz.	1.59	.11
Dawn Ultra Concentrated Dishwashing Liquid 25 oz.	2.89	.12
Palmolive Ultra Dish Liquid Dry Skin with Aloe 13 oz.	1.59	.12
Joy Ultra Dishwashing Liquid Lemon 12.6 oz.	1.59	.13

FIG. 6.2.   Example of stimuli similar to those used by Russo (1977).

product to perform the price comparisons; in the case where an ordered list is provided, the comparisons are facilitated. In fact, the mean price consumers paid dropped by 1% with unit price shelf tags (relative to prices paid at stores from the same supermarket chains that did not provide shelf tags) but dropped by 3% with the ordered lists. Essentially, providing shoppers with unit price information did, as predicted, change purchases to include cheaper brands or sizes, although the effects were small ones.

Russo and Leclerc (1991) argued that making information available to consumers (as in the shelf tag displays) is not always enough; information must be presented in ways that make it easy to process. Shelf tags tended to make consumers switch to buying larger sizes of their preferred brands, presumably because the different sizes were shelved near to one another and the unit price comparison was easy to make (Russo, 1977). Shelf tags did not cause much switching between brands, presumably because that would require a hunt all over an aisle to find how other brands compare.

On the other hand, the ordered price list did appear to cause shifts to different brands. The sales of the cheapest brands increased 6% when ordered lists were provided, but they increased only 1% when shelf tags were provided. Presumably, the ability to compare brands was facilitated when the lists gathered relevant information together in an easily processed way.

Other work on consumer decision making comes from the work of anthropologist Jean Lave and her collaborators, who followed grocery store shoppers on their shopping trips, asking them to think aloud as they made selections of products from grocery shelves (Lave, 1990; Lave, Murtaugh, & de la Rocha, 1984).

Lave and her colleagues found that shoppers, like other decision makers, could easily become overwhelmed with information. One way they cope with the potential for information overload is to ignore or screen out much of the information. Many choices are made out of habit, as shoppers appear to be replenishing supplies. In point of fact, shoppers don't often calculate unit prices nor do much mental arithmetic—in perhaps only 16% of the total items purchased did the shopper appear to engage in any calculation. As the authors describe it, "This kind of calculation [price comparison] occurs at the end of largely qualitative decision making processes which smoothly reduce numerous possibilities on the shelf to single items in the cart" (Lave et al., 1984, p. 81). When arithmetic is used, it is used to make the final selection among two or possibly three remaining alternatives that remain under consideration. All other alternatives are excluded from consideration because of other factors, such as size or brand.

Lave's description of grocery decision making fits quite well with image theory (Beach, 1998). The large set of potential alternatives is quickly pared down to one or a small handful, and only in the latter case are formal procedures employed to choose one over the other. Very little explicit decision structuring takes place, with shoppers laying out their criteria and assessing all the options on those criteria.

Legal Decisions

Let's shift our focus now from consumers to jurors—looking at how nonexperts in our legal system go about the process of rendering verdicts. Jurors in a civil or criminal trial aren't allowed to use their own gut reactions or values in making a determination; they are instead supposed to fit one or more legal standards to the specifics of a given case. For example, consider the important legal concept of liability, the central issue of most personal injury lawsuits. Liability has to do with whether or not a defendant is legally responsible for an injury to the plaintiff. Specifically, it is defined by the following characteristics: (a) whether the defendant was obliged to (or "owed a duty of care to") the plaintiff, (b) whether the defendant breached that obligation, and (c) whether the breach of obligation caused the damage. In essence, if a defendant fails to exercise reasonable care, the plaintiff can be legally liable for damages owed to the plaintiff (Kamin & Rachlinski, 1995).

To properly decide on liability, a juror must understand and apply the above definition to the circumstances of an individual case. This may require that the juror pay strict attention to legal terms and nuances, and avoid being influenced by extraneous information, prejudicial information, or both. For example, in a liability case, one extraneous piece of information in making a decision about negligence is the extent of a plaintiff's injuries.

Bornstein (1998) tested the proposition that people would judge a defendant to have more responsibility for an injury when that injury was more severe. He recruited 83 college students to serve as mock jurors and developed a trial scenario in which a woman suffering from ovarian cancer sued a drug company, alleging that the birth control pills they manufactured caused her disease. The case was based on actual lawsuits. Two alternate scenarios were constructed. They were identical in all respects except the description of the injury. In the low-severity condition, Kathy Johnson (plaintiff) was described as having discovered the ovarian cancer early, having had only one ovary removed and therefore still able to bear children, with an excellent prognosis. In the high-severity condition, Kathy Johnson was described as having detected the cancer late, having had both ovaries removed and so no longer able to have children, and having a poor prognosis.

Research participants in both conditions were given the following instructions:

> whether or not the plaintiff has suffered actual harm is not at issue—that is a given. What *is* at issue, and what determines liability, is whether . . . the defendant *caused* the harm. Legally, the plaintiff is not entitled to receive any monetary damages for the injury unless it is more likely than not that the defendant caused the injury. (Bornstein, 1998, p. 1483)

Because all participants saw the same facts of the case and received the same instructions, we might expect that they would have come to similar liability judgments. In fact, this was not the case. Mock jurors in the high-severity condition were almost twice as likely as mock jurors in the low-severity condition to find the drug company liable for Johnson's injuries. Severity alone, then, seemed to disproportionately affect the mock jurors' decision making, contrary to the instructions they were given. Interestingly, in a second study, Bornstein (1998) showed that this effect only held when jurors were able to award damages to the plaintiff. Participants in a control condition who were told that their task was not to fine the defendant nor compensate the plaintiff were much less likely to have their judgments of liability swayed by the extent of the injuries.

This study suggests that people's judgments can be inappropriately influenced by legally irrelevant information. Moreover, simple statements of legal principles were not enough to counteract these influences.

Kamin and Rachlinski (1995) provided additional evidence of this conclusion. To discuss their study, it will first be necessary to talk about hindsight bias. This is a well-documented shortcoming of human decision making, when people "consistently exaggerate what could have been anticipated in foresight" when looking back (in hindsight) on an event (Fischhoff, 1982, p. 341). Here's an example: Suppose you are faced with a choice between two jobs—one at a large company and one at a smaller one. You do your homework, researching both companies to the best of your ability; you spend hours talking with friends, mentors, and family members about the pros and cons of each choice. Eventually you decide on the job at the large company.

A few months later, you start to suspect you've made the wrong choice. Although the salary and benefits are comfortable, you increasingly feel straitjacketed by what you perceive to be rigid policies and practices. You hear that the position is still unfilled at the small company, and you talk again with them and decide to make the switch. When you announce this decision to friends, they express little surprise at your latest decision, confiding that they knew all along that your change of job would happen.

How is it that you didn't foresee this inevitable change? How is it that your friends really could see into your future when you apparently could not? In fact, one likely answer is that your friends are in error and that they are suffering from hindsight bias. The idea is that once you know how a decision has turned out, you look back on the events leading up to the outcome as being more inevitable than they really were.

It is probably easy to see how hindsight bias might affect legal decision making. Suppose, for example, that a doctor goes on trial for malpractice, being accused of misdiagnosing a serious illness. When the jury hears about the true nature of the illness, they may come to believe that it should have been more apparent all along to the physician than it actually could have been (Arkes, 1989).

Kamin and Rachlinski (1995) demonstrated hindsight bias in a legal context. They created stimuli based on a famous legal tort case. Their undergraduate research participants were divided into three groups as follows:

In the foresight condition, participants learned that a city had constructed a draw-bridge and needed to determine whether the risk of a flood warranted maintaining a bridge operator during the winter when the bridge was not in use. Hiring the operator would serve as a precaution. The operator would monitor weather conditions and raise the bridge if the river threatened to flood. The foresight condition asked participants without outcome knowledge to decide whether a flood was sufficiently probable for the city to appropriate funds for the operator.

The hindsight manipulations contained the same background facts. The story continued, however, stating that the city had decided not to hire the operator. During the first winter of the bridge's existence, debris lodged under it. This resulted in a flood that could have been prevented had an operator been hired. The flood damaged a neighboring bakery, whose owner then sued the city. Participants in the hindsight condition were instructed to hold the city liable if the flood was sufficiently probable that the city should have hired the operator to prevent it. The second hindsight condition added a debiasing manipulation in which the judge instructed participants to recognize the influential effects of hindsight and to consider alternative outcomes as had the city in foresight. (Kamin & Rachlinski, 1995, p. 93)

Kamin and Rachlinski (1995) presented participants with a slide show and audio tape depicting the case in one of the three versions of the case. Later, participants were asked to rate the likelihood that the flood would occur, to decide whether the city should (have) hire(d) the operator and whether the city should pay for damages.

Results clearly showed a difference in response as a function of whether or not participants were told that a flood had occurred—in other words, a hindsight bias. Only 24% of the foresight participants chose to hire an operator, but 56% of the hindsight and 57% of the hindsight-debiasing participants said that the operator should have been hired. Judicial instructions to guard against the hindsight bias therefore had no effect. Although this may be because those particular debiasing instructions were ineffective, other studies have similarly called into question the effectiveness of simply warning jurors not to commit a certain decision-making error.

A similar theme is sounded in the research of Ogloff (1993), on how jurors understand the legal insanity defense. The definition of insanity varies from state to state in the United States, with many states using the so-called M'Naghten rule (a defendant is not guilty by reason of insanity if, "at the time of committing the act, the defendant was laboring under such a defect of reason, from disease of the mind, so as not to know the nature and quality of the act he was doing; or, if he did know it, that he did not know what he was doing was wrong" (*Regina v. M'Naghten*, 1843; as cited in Ogloff, 1993). A second commonly used standard is the American Law Institute (ALI) standard for criminal responsibility: "A person is not responsible for criminal conduct if at the time of such conduct as a result of mental disease or defect he lacks substantial capacity either to appreciate the criminality (wrongfulness) of his conduct or to conform his conduct to the requirements of the law (ALI, 1962; section 4.01, as cited in Ogloff, 1993). Additionally, some states have adopted the GBMI (guilty but mentally ill) verdict first developed in Michigan, which holds a defendant criminally liable but recognizes his or her mental illness.

In Ogloff's (1993) first study, 255 undergraduates viewed a videotape based on a real trial in which the status of the sanity of the defendant was an issue. In the case, the fundamentalist Christian defendant killed his daughter and three of her friends after having searched for her for 3 nearly sleepless days and finding her in a known drug hangout, naked and in bed with her boyfriend. Participants, tested in groups of 10–12, watched the videotape and were given jury instructions, which varied the standard of insanity to be used—M'Naghten, ALI, GBMI, or no instructions about what constitutes insanity.

Research participants were not sensitive to the different legal definitions. In fact, regardless of the insanity standard given, about 6% of the students judged the defendant to be guilty of murder in the first degree; 17%, guilty of murder in the second degree; and 11%, not guilty by reason of insanity. These results, concluded Ogloff (1993) constituted strong evidence that mock jurors are pretty much insensitive to the distinctions and definitions drawn in instructions provided to them. Indeed, a subsequent study showed that the mock jurors were unable to remember with much precision any of the legal instructions given to them. In other words, subtleties in instructions might be lost on typical jurors.

Of course, much of this research suffers from a lack of ecological validity: The participants aren't real jurors but college students playing the role of jurors. There is no real trial, with live witnesses and several hours of testimony; there is typically a written summary of a case or a short video synopsis, which may or may not present evidence that real jurors would consider crucial (MacCoun, 1999). The students don't deliberate with other "jurors" but fill out their own individual survey. Thus, it is easy to make the argument that real jurors would make decisions differently in the context of a real trial.

On the other hand, there is no solid evidence that real jurors do escape the errors of omission or commission that the mock jurors apparently make. In many studies, the random assignment of participants to different conditions, which vary only in one or two well-controlled factors, provides enough evidence to at least bring skepticism to the idea that real jurors make decisions that are largely free from flaws.

Indeed, a posttrial survey of actual British jurors, conducted by Jackson (1995), suggested that jurors often report doing things they are not supposed to do. For example, in theory, jurors are supposed to remain open-minded to all the evidence, waiting until the deliberation phase to arrive at a final judgement. Their own view is, in general, supposed to be informed by the views of fellow jurors. Instead, Jackson found that 94% of jurors said that the discussion occurring deliberation either had no influence on their vote for a verdict or else it supported the opinion they had already come to on their own (p. 331). Jackson concludes from this that it is wrong to place too much confidence in the present British jury system (which does differ slightly from the American system, by the way).

What is it that jurors actually do during the process of serving on a case? A by-the-book juror would presumably passively and accurately record all of the information presented, be on the lookout for biases, listen carefully to instructions and legal definitions from the judge, wait until deliberation to discuss the case dispassionately with other jurors, and render a final verdict that accurately applies the relevant legal principles. We've seen evidence above that few if any jurors can be found who really do all of these things. That raises the question, what is it exactly that jurors are doing?

Hastie and Pennington (2000) argued that jurors actively construct a mental model of the case as they hear testimony about it. That model helps direct their attention, enables certain inferences to be made (and blocks others), and ultimately determines the confidence the juror will have in his or her decision. Hastie and Pennington believe that juror decision making consists of three component processes—evidence evaluation through story construction, representation of the possible verdicts, and classification of the story into the best-fitting verdict. Of these, the most influential process is the first.

Hastie and Pennington (2000) likened the juror's activity during evidence evaluation to the construction of a plausible story—a narrative that incorporates the relevant evidence. Jurors combine evidence presented at the trial with background knowledge and inferences to generate an episode schema such as that presented in Fig. 6.3. The schema enables inferences about motivations, causation, and precipitating events. The more coherent a story the juror is able to construct, the more the story will guide his or her final decision. Some stories are easier to construct than others. For example, when evidence is presented in a sequential order, mock jurors find it easier to construct coherent stories.

Given the facts of a particular case, of course, it may be possible to construct different stories that weave the facts together. Mock jurors who arrive at different verdicts have been shown to have constructed different stories. Moreover, people were more likely to falsely recall information that had not been presented but that was consistent with the story they had constructed. Stories perceived as more coherent led to perceptions of greater strength of evidence and judgments of confidence in the verdict one arrived at (Pennington & Hastie, 1988).

In evaluating evidence, jurors have also been shown to give much weight to eyewitness testimony in arriving at a verdict, even when the eyewitness testimony contradicts all of the other available evidence. Especially when a purported eyewitness is confident, jurors and other observers tend to believe the witness (Loftus, 1979).

Unfortunately, work from memory researchers throughout the world suggest that eyewitness memory is far from infallible and often subject to distortion. Loftus, Miller and Burns (1978), for example, showed research participants a series of slides that simulated an automobile accident. A red Datsun was shown coming to

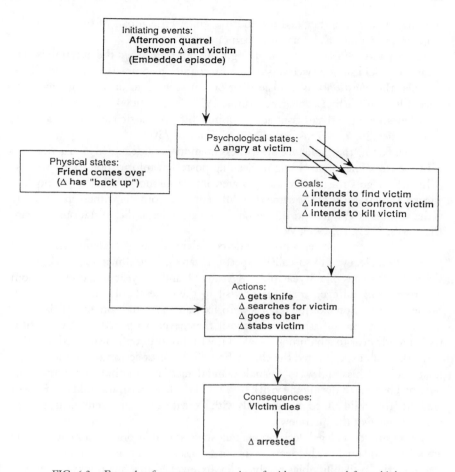

FIG. 6.3.   Example of a story representation of evidence extracted from think-aloud protocols of mock jurors rendering guilty verdicts. (Arrows represent various forms of causal influence; box labels show components of general episode schema.) *Note.* From "Explanation-Based Decision Making," by R. Hastie and N. Pennington, 2000, in T. Connolly, J. R. Arkes, and K. R. Hammond (Eds.), *Judgment and Decision Making: An Interdisciplinary Reader* (2nd ed., p. 217). New York: Cambridge University Press. Copyright 2000 by Cambridge University. Reprinted with permission.

either a stop sign or a yield sign (participants were divided into two groups, each participant saw either a stop sign or a yield sign). After viewing the slide show, participants were questioned. Embedded in the list of questions was the following item: "Did another car pass the red Datsun when it was stopped at the _____ sign?" Half the participants had the blank filled in with "stop," the other half, with "yield." Later, participants were shown a series of pairs of slides and asked to recognize which one they had previously seen. A critical pair of slides showed a red Datsun coming to either a stop sign or a yield sign.

Participants who saw a stop sign originally, but were asked the question in reference to a yield sign (or vice versa), had a recognition accuracy of only 41%. That is, when the question was a misleading one, it seemed to distort their memory trace. Other work by Loftus (see Loftus, 1979, for a review) suggests that postevent questioning reduces accuracy by quite a bit (the participants who were not asked misleading questions had overall accuracy of 75%).

Other factors that influence eyewitness memory include biased instructions for witnesses to a lineup, providing misleading postevent information to the witness (which later gets mistakenly incorporated into a memory), whether or not the alleged perpetrator is of the same or a different race from the witness, particularly if the witness is White, and the witness' own attitudes and expectations (Kassin, Ellsworth, & Smith, 1989; Wells, 1993).

Nonetheless, witnesses who provide confident, detailed accounts tend to be quite believable, even to so-called expert evaluators. Leightman and Ceci (1995) showed videotapes of a 3-year-old, a 4-year-old, and a 5-year-old, each of whom was recounting an event of a recent visit to their preschool classroom by Sam Stone, a visitor. Some of the reports were accurate ones, and some were elaborate narratives but were of aspects of the visit that never happened (e.g., the visitor took a teddy bear to a bathroom, soaked it with hot water, then smeared it with a crayon). Adult experts rated the child who told the most accurate rendition as the least credible (this child was soft-spoken and denied that anything out of the ordinary had happened during the visit); they rated the least accurate child as the most credible (this child added many details with a great deal of apparent pleasure during the course of the interview).

These studies on legal decision making suggest that jurors and potential jurors are subject to some of the decision-making biases evident in the laboratory. For example, the availability bias might easily be invoked to explain why eyewitness testimony carries such weight—the presence of a living person confidently swearing to have seen an event occur is fairly vivid and immediate and would thus be expected to have a dominant influence over peoples' judgment. Legal cases that present coherent stories also make narratives more available and salient and thus may sway potential jurors unduly.

We will return, in chapter 8, to the topic of jury decision making, in the context of how the performance of groups making decisions differs from the typical performance of individuals making decisions. To anticipate the general findings, group performance does not always (or even frequently) constitute much of an improvement over the performance of a solitary person making a decision. But for now, it suffices to say that people do not appear to spontaneously pay strict attention to legal nuances nor to always apply strict legal principles in a thoroughly dispassionate manner.

Medical Decisions

Once again in this section our focus will be on nonexpert decision making. That is, we'll examine the literature on how patients make medical decisions, deferring until chapter 8 a discussion of expert (e.g., nurse and physician) decision making.

Suppose that just after your yearly physical, your physician telephones you with the news that one of your lab results has come in and raises cause for concern. Specifically, she fears that you may be developing cancer. There are various diagnostic and treatment options for your particular condition, and several decisions will have to be made: What sorts of further tests should be run? What types of treatments should be pursued?

How involved would you want to be in making these decisions? Some individuals no doubt will want a very active role. They'll go straight from that initial telephone conversation to the nearest medical school library, the Internet, or both, to do their own research on their condition and on possible next steps. At the other end of the spectrum, some individuals will want to play an extremely passive role, following doctor's orders only. These individuals might feel it inappropriate for them to have any say in their medical care, reasoning that they don't have the medical expertise and experience to make the right choices. It may also depend on the type of medical condition as to whether or not patients want to play an active role in choosing treatment (McPherson, 1994).

Guadagnoli and Ward (1998) examined the literature on patient participation in medical decision making, reviewing over 29 previous studies of over 11,000 patients, dealing with conditions ranging from breast cancer to seizure disorders to hypertension to obesity. Also included were members of a health maintenance organization selected randomly, not necessarily receiving treatment for any condition.

Findings were often contradictory from study to study, and many variations in definitions and results were reported. For example, patient participation in decision making could mean choosing from a variety of options in one study but could mean only having a discussion with a physician in another. Thus, overall conclusions were difficult to draw. Nonetheless, the authors presented two: Patients as a rule want to be informed of treatment alternatives, and they also want to be involved in the selection of a treatment when more than one effective treatment option exists (Guadagnoli & Ward, 1998). The rub, of course, is that sometimes there is only one generally accepted treatment for a given case, so that there may not really be a decision to make.

Indeed, sometimes medical decisions don't seem like they are real decisions at all. Santalahti, Hemminki, Latikka, and Ryynänen (1998) studied the decision making of pregnant women in Finland as they chose whether or not to undergo a prenatal blood screening test to detect genetic abnormalities in the fetus. Women in Finland receive free prenatal care from government-run maternity centers, and about 99.9% of Finnish women attend them. The study was run in two Finnish towns in which all women were offered free blood serum screening. This included an assessment of the level of AFP (alfafetoprotein), a fetal product found in maternal blood serum, with high levels possibly indicative of neural tube defects, congenital nephrosis, and low levels possibly indicative of Down syndrome. Abnormal test results typically lead to further diagnostic tests, including a repeat blood screening or more invasive procedures, such as amniocentesis or chorionic villus sampling (CVS). Abnormal results here can, but do not always, lead to decisions to abort. However, it should be noted that screening tests by their nature are expected to lead to some false positive results.

The researchers invited all women who had received an abnormal screening result, as well as a control group of women with normal results matched to the experimental group in terms of age, previous number of births, and previous number of miscarriages, to participate in a study. They were particularly interested in the question, how did women make the decision to undergo the blood screening test?

Results showed that many women considered this decision to be a nondecision. Half the women considered the test to be a routine part of their prenatal care and reported that they considered it to be the "natural" thing to do. One woman said, "Of course I went to the test, it did not come to my mind that I would not go. My friends have gone and got the result. It belongs automatically to that situation. It is like that: you just go there" (Santalahti et al., 1998, p. 1070).

Only about one quarter of the women surveyed felt that they had actively made this decision (Santalahti et al., 1998). In contrast, the subsequent decision to undergo invasive diagnostic procedures, such as amniocentesis or CVS (for women receiving an abnormal screening result), was one made very actively. Presumably, for this subsequent decision, women were more able to look ahead to the next step: an abortion decision or perhaps miscarriage while undergoing the amniocentesis or CVS.

On the other hand, McPherson (1994) reported data on a study done with men with benign prostatic disease. Men who used an interactive video disk that provided extensive information about the disease and the current medical uncertainty surrounding it were significantly less likely to choose surgery than were men who made decisions without seeing the video.

Thompson, Pitts, and Schwankovsky (1994) suggested that patients prefer to be involved in decision making when the issues at stake involve lifestyle or value implications. So, patients want to be involved in decision making when faced with two possible courses of treatments, one that will result in faster improvement but involve more pain and bed rest versus one that will work more slowly but will in the end be just as successful. Patients indicate less interest in being involved when the decisions require medical knowledge (e.g., how often a nurse should wake you to check blood pressure and temperature). Arora and McHorney (2000) reported in their study of more than 2,000 patients with chronic diseases that 69% of them preferred to leave medical decisions to their physicians, especially males or older or less-educated patients.

Frosch and Kaplan (1999) discussed the concept of shared decision making, where patients and physicians review information together and arrive at a joint selection of treatment. They argued that frequently there are many treatment options, each of which has different trade-offs between benefits and risks. Physicians, they argue, cannot know how a particular patient feels about different health states and different treatment side effects and thus need to engage the patient in active discussion before making a treatment recommendation. Moreover, Frosh and Kaplan reviewed several studies that suggest that the higher patient involvement in decision making, the better the compliance with the treatment and the higher the patient satisfaction.

Another issue that may arise in making medical decisions is making trade-offs among qualitatively distinct entities. For example, consider cancer patients, who need to decide between treatment of the disease intended to cure it, which may produce severe side effects and may or may not work, and palliative therapy, which will reduce life expectancy but provide more relief from symptoms (Weeks, 1995). In essence, these patients are being asked to trade off length and quality of life.

Of course, different individuals may place different values on the quality versus the length of life. So no one set of values can be used. Moreover, asking individuals what their values are is a tricky business. We could try something along the lines of "If 0 is death and 100 is perfect health, what number would you say best describes your current state of health?" (Weeks, 1995). If your reaction is similar to mine, you don't know quite what to make of it. If you answer 50, for example, does that mean you'd be willing to trade half of your life expectancy in return for living out your remaining years in perfect health? These questions assume that people can use numerical scales meaningfully. If this assumption is not correct, then the answers people provide might be meaningless (Fishhoff, 1991). Moreover, people are likely to differ in terms of their willingness to gamble and take risks, and this may well affect their responses.

Petersen, Heesacker, and deWitt Marsh (2001) reported that patients undergoing cancer treatment used different approaches to making medical decisions. They described four different styles of medical decision making: information seeking (used by individuals who actively seek out information and think about it effortfully), information processing (used by individuals who do not seek out additional information but who do think carefully about information given to them, presumably by health care providers), advice following (used by individuals who do not spend much time thinking about information provided, but quickly place trust in an expert and follow his or her recommendations), and ruminating (used by a few individuals who avoided making a decision). The authors found that individuals who were using the first two strategies showed more and better coping strategies than did those following the last two strategies. Paradoxically, they noted, a "model" patient who follows doctor's orders without question may actually not be coping as effectively as are more active and high-maintenance patients who ask more questions.

Research by Chapman (1996; Chapman, Nelson, & Hier, 1999) has focused on whether people's decision making about health differs qualitatively from, say, their decision making about finances. Asked to make predictions about their lifetime health, people expected it to decrease over time. When asked for their preferences, they indicated that they in fact preferred this pattern to other possible patterns (e.g., ones in which health increased over time). In contrast, those same individuals expected their incomes to show a gradually increasing pattern, and they preferred this pattern to others as well.

Another issue that arises in medical decision making is competence to make decisions, particularly when a patient is refusing life-saving treatment. Searight and Hubbard (1998) pointed to several myths about decisional capacity—the ability to make competent medical decisions. For example, they argue that decisional competence is not, as widely thought, a global attribute that affects all areas of a patient's life nor is it the case that patients suffering from serious psychiatric illnesses or delirium are permanently incapable of making any informed medical decisions. Instead, these authors argue that different patients may have different capacities, depending on among other things the realm of the decision (e.g., is the decision about surgery or nursing home placement?).

Up until now I have focused only on the patient's decision making and have ignored that of the medical health professional. What effect does medical expertise have on medical decision making? We will see in chapter 7 that although a physician's knowledge base certainly improves her or his ability to make sound decisions, extensive medical education does not prevent all forms of decision-making shortcomings. Thus, patients without medical training who put themselves into the decision-making hands of their doctors are unlikely to completely prevent the introduction of biases into the decision.

Moral Decisions

Many legal and medical decisions involve moral issues. In some consumer decisions, these issues may arise as well. During my college years, for example, undergraduates across the nation organized boycotts of the products of a certain food manufacturer, alleging that the company's practice of marketing infant formula to mothers in third-world nations was morally abhorrent. It thus behooves us to consider the nature of moral decision making. As with all other topics we touch on in this chapter, the topic is vast, and we will have time to only visit one or two landmarks.

For openers, we might consider the questions, when is a decision a moral one or when does it have a moral dimension? Some cases are clear-cut: A decision to terminate life support, or to auction organs over the Internet, seems prototypical of a moral issue. Others, such as legalizing marijuana or prostitution, seem clearly to at least have major moral aspects, even if they encompass other aspects as well. And some decisions, such as what color socks to wear, don't seem to be moral ones at all.

Moshman (1999) described different distinct conceptions of what makes something a moral issue. One is that the issue involve concepts such as justice or respect for rights. A second is that the issue involve concepts such as compassion or caring. We'll take a look briefly at both.

The conception of moral reasoning as concerning justice and rights is an idea embodied in the work of the most well-known researcher of moral development, Lawrence Kohlberg. He presented older children, adolescents, and adults with hypothetical moral dilemmas and asked them to describe what decision they would make and how they would justify it. One example of the dilemmas Kohlberg presented is the now-famous *Heinz dilemma:*

> In Europe, a woman was near death from a rare form of cancer. There was one drug that the doctors thought might save her, a form of radium that a druggist in the same town had recently discovered. The druggist was charging $2,000, ten times what the drug cost him to make. The sick woman's husband, Heinz, went to everyone he knew to borrow the money, but he could only get together about half of what [the drug] cost. He told the druggist that his wife was dying and asked him to sell it cheaper or let him pay later. But the druggist said, "No." So Heinz got desperate and broke into the man's store to steal the drug for his wife. (Kohlberg, 1976, pp. 41–42).

Kohlberg (1976) proposed that people went through six different stages in the development of their moral thinking. These are outlined in Table 6.1. At each stage, a person takes a different view of how moral actions are defined. A person at Stage 1 might argue that Heinz should not steal the drug because stealing is always bad because it is against the law, and the thief would be caught and put in jail. A person at a much higher stage (say, Stage 5) might argue that certain duties (e.g., to save a human life) transcend conventional property laws or norms of social etiquette.

Different dilemmas were constructed by Kohlberg, but they all centered around issues of whose rights outweighed whose. In the Heinz dilemma, the issue is the relative priority of the wife's right to live with the druggist's right to sell his drug at a price he sets. In other dilemmas, the conflicts might be over whether an escaped prisoner who has built a new productive life of service to a new community ought to be sent back to prison or whether a doctor should help a suffering, terminally ill patient die.

Gilligan (1982) focused on the second conception of moral dilemmas: that which highlights issues of caring and compassion. She argued that another way of construing dilemmas is not in terms of who has which rights, but rather in terms of who has which responsibilities to care for one another. This view was one especially (though not exclusively) held by women:

94

TABLE 6.1
The Six Moral Stages

Level and Stage	Content of Stage		Social Perspective of Stage
	What Is Right	Reasons for Doing Right	
LEVEL I— PRECONVENTIONAL Stage 1—Heteronomous Morality.	To avoid breaking rules backed by punishment, obedience for its own sake, and avoiding physical damage to persons and property.	Avoidance of punishment, and the superior power of authorities.	*Egocentric point of view.* Doesn't consider the interests of others or recognize that they differ from the actor's; doesn't relate two points of view. Actions are considered physically rather than in terms of psychological interests of others. Confusion of authority's perspective with one's own.
Stage 2—Individualism, Instrumental Purpose, and Exchange	Following rules only when it is to someone's immediate interest; acting to meet one's own interests and needs and letting others do the same. Right is also what's fair, what's an equal exchange, a deal, an agreement.	To serve one's own needs or interests in a world where you have to recognize that other people have their interests, too.	*Concrete individualistic perspective.* Aware that everybody has his own interest to pursue and these conflict, so that right is relative (in the concrete individualistic sense).
LEVEL II— CONVENTIONAL Stage 3—Mutual Interpersonal Expectations, Relationships, and Interpersonal Conformity	Living up to what is expected by people close to you or what people generally expect of people in your role as son, brother, friend, etc. "Being good" is important and means having good motives, showing concern about others. It also means keeping mutual relationships, such as trust, loyalty, respect and gratitude.	The need to be a good person in your own eyes and those of others. Your caring for others. Belief in the Golden Rule. Desire to maintain rules and authority which support stereotypical good behavior.	*Perspective of the individual in relationships with other individuals.* Aware of shared feelings, agreements, and expectations which take primacy over individual interests. Relates points of view through the concrete Golden Rule, putting yourself in the other guy's shoes. Does not yet consider generalized system perspective.

	What Is Right	Reasons for Doing Right	Social Perspective of Stage
Stage 4—Social System and Conscience	Fulfilling the actual duties to which you have agreed. Laws are to be upheld except in extreme cases where they conflict with other fixed social duties. Right is also contributing to society, the group, or institution.	To keep the institution going as a whole, to avoid the breakdown in the system "if everyone did it," or the imperative of conscience to meet one's defined obligations (Easily confused with Stage 3 belief in rules and authority; see text.)	*Differentiates societal point of view from interpersonal agreement or motives.* Takes the point of view of the system that defines roles and rules. Considers individual relations in terms of place in the system.
LEVEL III—POST-CONVENTIONAL, or PRINCIPLED Stage 5—Social Contract or Utility and Individual Rights	Being aware that people hold a variety of values and opinions, that most values and rules are relative to your group. These relative rules should usually be upheld, however, in the interest of impartiality and because they are the social contract. Some nonrelative values and rights like *life* and *liberty*, however, must be upheld in any society and regardless of majority opinions.	A sense of obligation to law because of one's social contract to make and abide by laws for the welfare of all and for the protection of all people's rights. A feeling of contractual commitment, freely entered upon, to family, friendship, trust, and work obligations. Concern that laws and duties be based on rational calculation of overall utility, "the greatest good for the greatest number."	*Prior-to-society perspective.* Perspective of a rational individual aware of values and rights prior to social attachments and contracts. Integrates perspectives by formal mechanisms of agreement, contract, objective impartiality, and due process. Considers moral and legal points of view; recognizes that they sometimes conflict and finds it difficult to integrate them.
Stage 6—Universal Ethical Principles	Following self-chosen ethical principles. Particular laws or social agreements are usually valid because they rest on such principles. When laws violate these principles, one acts in accordance with the principle. Principles are universal principles of justice: the equality of human rights and respect for the dignity of human beings as individual persons.	The belief as a rational person in the validity of universal moral principles, and a sense of personal commitment to them.	*Perspective of a moral point of view* from which social arrangements derive. Perspective is that of any rational individual recognizing the nature of morality or the fact that persons are ends in themselves and must be treated as such.

From "Moral Stages and Moralization: The Cognitive-Developmental Approach," by L. Kohlberg, 1976, in T. Lickona (Ed.), *Moral Development and Behavior: Theory, Research, and Social Issues* (pp. 34–35). New York: Holt, Rinehart & Winston. Copyright 1976 by Holt, Rinehart & Winston. Reprinted with permission.

The moral imperative that emerges repeatedly in the women's interviews is an injunction to care, a responsibility to discern and alleviate the "real and recognizable trouble" of this world. For the men in Kohlberg's studies, the moral imperative appeared rather as an injunction to respect the rights of others and thus to protect from interference the right to life and self-fulfillment. Women's insistence on care is at first self-critical rather than self-protective, while men initially conceive obligation to others negatively in terms of noninterference. (Gilligan, 1977, p. 511)

In other words, Gilligan found some of her female interviewees using different language when thinking about moral dilemmas. Instead of focusing so much on rights, they focused on responsibilities: who was owed what by whom? The women spoke of being sensitive to others' needs, of taking care of others and themselves, and of understanding the contextual factors surrounding each relationship.

Another way to describe the distinction between the justice and care orientations was developed in a rating scale by Ford and Lowery, who worked closely with Lyons, a colleague of Gilligan. Ford and Lowery (1986) found that females were more consistent in their reported use of the care orientation than were males, and males were more consistent in their use of a justice orientation. However, when the researchers controlled for the type of moral dilemma being discussed, there were no significant gender differences, a finding also in other research investigations of moral reasoning (Galotti, 1989; Walker, de Vries, & Trevethan, 1987).

Making moral decisions might also involve issues of virtue or character (Moshman, 1999), including such things as integrity, striving for excellence, or skill in balancing competing claims. This approach to moral decision making, known as the eduaimonist approach, has not been as fully developed as the first two.

Moral decision making, then, typically involves issues that have as an important component such things as justice, care, or virtue. In this way, moral decision making is defined by content—what the decision is about. But in everyday life, people can construe the same situation in different ways. Walker, Pitts, Hennig, and Matsuba (1995) point out that, real-life, everyday dilemmas are rarely as straightforward or unambiguously moral as are the standard hypothetical dilemmas posed by Kohlberg. Reasoning about hypothetical dilemmas might inform us as to how people prioritize different moral issues but doesn't reveal very much about how people come to recognize the moral dimensions of an everyday problem.

SIMILARITIES AND DIFFERENCES ACROSS DOMAINS

In the first several chapters of the book, I described different phases or parts of the decision-making process, which are summarized in a flowchart diagram in Fig. 6.4. In my view, the various kinds of decision making all share this general structure. However, they emphasize different aspects of it.

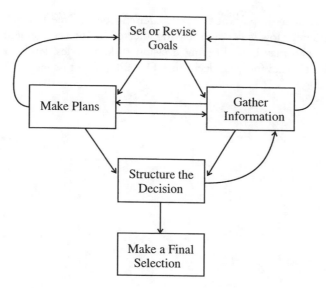

FIG. 6.4. Phases of decision making.

Moral decision making, for example, emphasizes the first component, the setting or revising of goals. The moral principles a person holds, be they about justice, care, or virtue, can all be thought of as broad and life-framing goals. Moral decision making involves recognition of the relevant ethical aspects of a decision, as well as prioritzing the goals or principles and translating these principles into a plan of action.

Legal decision making shares with moral decision making this emphasis on principles and on figuring out how to apply principles to real-life circumstances. However, legal decision making involves concepts that may or may not have to do with the ethical issues that define moral judgement. Such topics as property rights, torts, contracts, and so on, may or may not have a moral dimension to them.

Medical decision making, at least when done by a nonspecialist individual, again may or may not involve some moral decision making. But it also seems to require the acquisition and processing of a great deal of information. It may also require that an individual refine or prioritize his or her goals.

Consumer decisions can involve medical, legal, or moral issues, but they frequently don't. Consumer decisions typically seem to emphasize gathering information, structuring the decision, and making a final selection.

Of course, we have restricted our focus in this chapter to individuals and to nonexpert individuals at that. The way a doctor approaches a medical diagnosis, or a Supreme Court justice decides a case, will no doubt exhibit differences from the way these same decisions are construed by a patient or a juror. We'll explore the issue of expertise in decision making in chapter 7.

Moreover, many important decisions aren't made by lone individuals but by teams or groups. How is decision making affected by the involvement of several individuals, who may hold differing decision-making styles, levels of expertise, views on what makes for good decisions? These important issues will be explored in chapter 8.

7

Developing Decision-Making Skills, Expertise, and Style

In chapter 6, we began to explore differences in decision making, first as a function of what the decision is about. In this chapter, we'll continue that discussion, looking at differences in decision making as a function of the person making that decision.

So far, we've been assuming an adult decision maker in our discussions. But adults aren't the only ones to make decisions. Conventional wisdom holds that decision-making skills change and progress as individuals proceed through childhood and adolescence; we will examine that wisdom in this chapter.

Second, we'll look at how individuals develop expertise in a particular domain and how that expertise might affect their decision making. Some have argued that a great part of children's cognitive development is in fact the acquisition of expertise in the world, so these two topics fit together more closely than you might think.

Finally, we will turn our attention to the topic of individual differences in peoples' approaches to decision making. We'll consider the question of decision-making styles and explore some proposals for what those might be.

COGNITIVE DEVELOPMENT IN CHILDHOOD AND ADOLESCENCE: MAJOR LANDMARKS

To say that children are not miniature adults is, today, to state a truism with which no self-respecting psychologist would disagree. Children bring different skills and strategies to different developmental tasks and therefore seem to operate under different constraints. In this section, we'll take a brief look at some general developments in children's and adolescents' cognition, before turning our attention specifically to the development of decision making.

There isn't sufficient space here to review all of cognitive development, so in the sections that follow only the briefest sketch will be presented of the major cognitive achievements and challenges facing children and adults. Piaget (Piaget, 1955; Piaget & Inhelder, 1969) presented a comprehensive theory of cognitive development from infancy through adolescence. While theorists and researchers who followed did not always support Piaget's predictions or even all of his findings, it is fair to say that Piaget defined the field of cognitive development, and set many of the major questions. Therefore, our review will borrow heavily from descriptions of Piagetian stages for the three developmental periods most relevant to decision-making, while also incorporating some newer findings from non-Piagetian psychologists.

The Preschool Years

Preschoolers, children from about the age of 30 months to about 5 or 6 years, have quite a lot of cognitive skills. By the end of the period, they are fluent speakers with large vocabularies. Their language skills demonstrate a more general ability: that of representation. Preschoolers can use a spoken word to stand for, or represent, an object, person, or event.

Preschoolers are also learning a great deal about routine events. Ask your favorite 3-year-old what happens when you do X, where X is some familiar sequence of actions, such as going to McDonald's or baking cookies, or circle time (in preschool), and you are likely to hear a surprisingly knowledgeable and organized description, called a script, of the event in question (Nelson, 1986; Nelson & Gruendel, 1981). Preschoolers can also use their script knowledge to formulate plans for familiar events, such as going to the beach or grocery shopping (Hudson, Shapiro, & Sosa, 1995).

Depending on the domain, preschoolers can even be more knowledgeable than their older siblings or parents. Chi and Koeske (1983) found a 4½-year-old dinosaur expert, whose memory for dinosaur names was quite impressive when the stimuli consisted of dinosaurs he knew a great deal about.

As you might expect, preschoolers' ability to sustain their attention on a task increases as they get older, and they become more able and willing to attend to an adult giving directions (Ruff, Capozzoli, & Weissberg, 1998). However, preschool children are often described as processing information holistically, rather than analytically (Kemler, 1983). That is, children pay attention to global aspects of a stimulus and have greater difficulty focusing on details. Younger children are also less able than older children to focus their attention on certain dimensions of a stimulus while overlooking others (Strutt, Anderson, & Well, 1975).

Moreover, the preschool child is described as unable to make a distinction between what things look like and what things truly are like. Indeed, preschool children have been described as lacking the ability to distinguish appearance from reality (Flavell, Green, & Flavell, 1986; Flavell, Miller, & Miller, 2002).

Finally, preschool children are said to be egocentric. That is, they have a very difficult time taking into account any perspective other than their own. Preschoolers are notorious for giving others incomplete information, asking a stranger if they like Bobby, and unable to comprehend that the stranger has no clue who Bobby is. Recently, researchers have been turning to an examination of the development of preschoolers' theory of mind, that is, their ability to understand their own mental states (such as beliefs and desires) and those of others (Johnson, 1997; Taylor, 1996), finding a dramatic increase in understanding between the ages of 3 and 5.

Middle Childhood

Between the ages of 5 and 7, children undergo another major cognitive reorganization, as they enter the stage of *concrete operations* (Piaget & Inhelder, 1969). This means that they acquire internal mental procedures that allow them to structure and make sense of reality, to understand the distinction between how things in the world appear and how they really are. Children of this age are capable of reversible thought, recognizing that transformations of objects can be undone, at least mentally. Children's thought is also more decentered at this age, that is, it can be focused on more than one dimension at a time.

However, this does not mean that children's logical thinking is fully developed. A study by Osherson and Markman (1975) illustrated this point quite well. They gave children, adolescents, and adults a task in which they were asked to judge the truth or falsity of various statements about colored poker chips. Some of the statements were made about chips held visibly in the experimenter's hand (e.g., "The chip in my hand is red," said while holding a blue chip). Some statements were made while the chip was not visible but held in the experimenter's closed fist. Some statements had a more complicated syntax (e.g., "The chip in my hand is white or the chip in my hand is blue"). And some were tautologies, that is, always true (e.g., "Either the chip in my hand is white or it is not white"), or they were contradictions, that is, always false (e.g., "The chip in my hand is blue and the chip in my hand is not blue").

Results showed that elementary school-age children (in first through sixth grade) were unable to distinguish between statements that were empirically true or false and statements like tautologies or contradictions that were, by their logical form, automatically true or false. Tenth graders and adults, by contrast, knew that assessing the truth of a statement such as "Either the chip in my hand is white or it is not white" did not depend on the actual color of the chip.

Research suggests that much of the time of children in middle childhood is spent acquiring information and building their knowledge base (Siegler, 1998). Within a domain of knowledge, experts remember more than novices. Relative to most adults in most knowledge domains, children are novices. However, in some domains, children become experts and outperform even their very educated parents, as my (then) 5-year-old son did to me when the conversation turned to Pokémon. (Did you know there are, as of this writing, 152 different species, all with different body types, attacks, strengths, and weaknesses? I, myself, did not until so informed by my then-kindergarten son.)

Children also become more strategic during their school years. They learn about how their cognitive systems work; they learn to rehearse information that they will need to remember, instead of just hoping that they will spontaneously be able to recall it (Flavell, Beach, & Chinsky, 1966; Keeney, Cannizzo, & Flavell, 1967).

Children in the school years also acquire (not surprisingly) a great number of academic skills, including reading, writing, and basic arithmetic (Siegler, 1998). As they learn spelling-sound rules (e.g., *ph* is usually pronounced "f," at least in English), they can decode new words. As their recognition of high-frequency words (e.g., *it, the, a, and, of*) becomes automatic, mental resources are freed up to think more deeply about the meaning of other words and, later, of the text as a whole, thus increasing reading fluency. These skills lay a foundation for later acquisition of knowledge of a wide range of subjects, including social science and science.

Adolescence

Piaget describes another cognitive revolution occurring in adolescence, with the onset of formal operations. These operations enable adolescents to think more abstractly, more hypothetically, more systematically, and more reflectively.

A classic formal operational task is the combination of liquids task. Given a number of beakers containing liquids that, when mixed together properly, turn a particular color, the adolescent is asked to determine what needs to be mixed with what. This task requires, in turn, that the adolescent be able to enumerate all the possible combinations. In this example, given that there are four possible liquids to combine, there are six two-way combinations, four three-way combinations, and one combination with all four liquids. An adolescent incapable of generating all possibilities (which in turn requires some systematic thinking) is liable to over-look possibilities and risk failing at the task.

Formal thinking also involves the ability to separate whether or not a conclu-sion logically follows from whether or not it is empirically true. So, for example, in the following syllogism, all mice are larger than lions, and all lions are larger than whales; therefore, all mice are larger than whales, the conclusion is logically true, although empirically false. Adolescents are indeed much better at under-standing this distinction (Markovits, 1993; Moshman & Franks, 1986).

The actual theory of formal operations is much more complex and detailed than I've presented it here, and it has attracted perhaps the strongest criticism (see Moshman, 1999, for an overview). However, the point is that Piaget points to the fact that adolescent thinking seems qualitatively different from children's thinking, and this difference pertains to a wide variety of realms, not just academic ones.

Adolescents also face the challenge of constructing a meaningful identity, a mature sense of who they are and what their goals are (Erikson, 1968; Marcia, 1966). They need to acquire a sense of how their current experience continues their childhood experiences and foreshadows the experiences of the adulthood yet to come, that is, to have a sense of their life story (Grovetant, 1993).

Part of their identity may include the construction of a moral or value system. Included in such a system might be a notion of rights and justice (Kohlberg, 1984), a notion of responsibilities and caring (Gilligan, 1982), and a sense of how the two might be balanced. Once again there is evidence that adolescents confront moral dilemmas in more complex ways than do younger children.

Cognitive development in adolescence, then, seems to make possible a number of developments related to decision making. Sprouting cognitive skills may make it possible for adolescents to become more rational decision makers. At the same time, adolescents, at least in our society, are granted more autonomy in making important decisions—about their education, their residence, their friends, their leisure time, and consumer decisions, to name but a few—than our younger children. Thus, adolescents get much more practice at making a wider variety of important decisions.

However, the traditional picture of adolescent cognition is not a completely rosy one. Elkind (1967) described a kind of egocentrism to which adolescents are prone. Egocentrism, Elkind stated, is a failure to differentiate between perspectives. For adolescents, particularly young adolescents, this takes the following form:

> since he fails to differentiate between what others are thinking about and his own mental preoccupations, he assumes that other people are as obsessed with his behavior and appearance as he is himself . . . One consequence of adolescent egocentrism is that, in actual or impending social situations, the young person anticipates the reactions of others to himself . . . continually constructing, or reacting to, an *imaginary audience*." (p. 1030)

Second, and as a complement to this lack of differentiation, adolescents over-differentiate their own feelings from those of others, coming to see themselves as particularly special and unique:

> this belief in personal uniqueness becomes a conviction that he will not die, that death will happen to others but not to him. This complex of beliefs in the uniqueness of his feelings and of his immortality might be called a personal fable, a story which he tells himself and which is not true." (p. 1030)

Adolescent egocentrism has been advanced as a factor that can severely limit rational decision making, especially when it comes to decisions about risky behaviors, such as drinking, smoking, drug use, or sexual behavior. We'll examine this view of adolescent decision making later in the chapter.

DEVELOPMENT OF DECISION-MAKING SKILLS

We've now taken a (very) brief look at the different abilities and proclivities children of different ages and cognitive developmental stages bring to decision-making tasks. It would be wonderful to describe now precisely how these aspects of children's functioning translate into specific behaviors and attitudes relevant to making decisions. Alas, the study of how children make decisions is a fairly new area of research, so we can catch only glimpses from the literature of how children's decision making develops. To organize our discussion, I'll use the framework of the stages of decision making presented earlier in the book.

Goal Setting and Planning

In chapter 2, I made the argument that the goals people set drive and constrain their decision making. The question for us here is how the ability to set one's goals develops.

Byrnes (1998) placed the setting and pursuit of goals at the heart of his self-regulation model of decision making. Good decision making, on this view, "increases the chances that adaptive goals [e.g., those relating to personal survival, physical health, emotional well-being, and academic achievement] will be attained" (p. 30).

Table 7.1 lists the characteristics of what Byrnes called a self-regulated decision maker during the generation phase of decision making, when goals are set and

TABLE 7.1
Characteristics of Effective Decision Makers During the Goal-Setting Phase

- They give appropriate attention to informative cues
- They feel uncertain when they are confronted with ambiguous cues, and act on this uncertainty by seeking more information until a more comfortable level of certainty has been attained
- They pursue multiple adaptive goals rather than pursuing single adaptive goals, or pursuing one or more maladaptive goals
- They use strategies such as advice seeking, analogical reasoning, and causal reasoning when they lack knowledge of how to proceed in an unfamiliar situation
- They seek advice from knowledgeable and willing sources in ways that do not damage their social standing
- They appreciate the fact that it is possible to make faulty analogies and demonstrate a tendency to evaluate the appropriateness of their analogies
- They have an accurate sense of how causal outcomes depend on the interplay among actors, strategies, and contexts

Note. Based on data from *The Nature and Development of Decision Making: A Self-Regulation Model* (p. 189), by J. P. Byrnes, 1998, Mahwah, NJ: Lawrence Erlbaum Associates. Copyright 1998 by Lawrence Erlbaum Associates. Reprinted with permission.

different alternatives generated. Importantly, Byrnes (1998) noted that especially for young children, the seat of decision making may rest with a parent or teacher, such that the interpretation of cues, setting of goals, and seeking of advice falls to the adult and not to the child. Presumably, over the course of childhood and adolescence, parents, teachers, and other adults relinquish more of their decision-making authority.

Miller and Byrnes (1997) suggested that after about age 8, risk-taking behaviors show few overall age effects. In part, this may be because the degree of decision-making control exercised by parents varies idiosyncratically in different parents. Thus, the authors reported few overall age differences but great differences from context to context.

It seems plausible to speculate, however, that goal setting would change over childhood in predictable ways. First, children should become better at managing multiple goals as they become cognitively more able to deal with multiple aspects of a stimulus. In a sense, balancing one's social goals (e.g., have other kids like and respect you) with academic goals (e.g., achieve top scores on school tests) with emotional goals (e.g., feel good about one's accomplishments) probably awaits at least the development of what Piaget would call concrete operations. Certainly children closer to school age are better at planning, create more detailed plans, have more knowledge of what might go wrong, and make more attempts to remedy the possible pitfalls. Predictably, children were better planners in more familiar contexts where they had greater knowledge of events (Hudson, Sosa, & Shapiro, 1997).

Similarly, the ability to consider different options no doubt requires worldly exposure to a range of relevant information. And a child's self-efficacy and his or her own sense of how mastery of a certain skill or domain is attained have been predicted to change with development, which in turn affects the approach to decision making, although as yet in ways undocumented by research (Dweck & Leggett, 1988; Eccles, Wigfield, & Schiefele, 1998)

Information Gathering

We saw in chapter 3 that adults typically use heuristics in gathering and processing information. Although the heuristics can be useful shortcuts, when misapplied to situations, they can also make the decision maker fall prey to error. The question here is how and when these heuristics and biases are acquired.

Some work suggests that older children and adolescents rely more heavily on heuristics such as representativeness, especially when the content of the problems was social. In one study, Jacobs and Potenza (1991) gave representativeness problems to children in Grades 1, 3, and 6. Some of the problems concerned everyday objects, such as the following:

> Jim is buying a bicycle. Before buying it he gets information on different brands. A bicycle magazine says that most of their readers say the Zippo bike is best; however,

he speaks to his neighbor and she says that the Whammo bike is best. Which bike should Jim buy? (p. 169)

Other problems, formally equivalent to the previous one, involved social scenarios, such as the following:

In Juanita's class 10 girls are trying out to be cheerleaders and 20 are trying out for the band. Juanita is very popular and very pretty. She is always telling jokes and loves to be around people. Do you think Juanita is trying out to be a cheerleader or for the band? (Jacobs & Potenza, 1991, p. 169)

In both of these examples, the use of the representativeness heuristic would lead the decision maker to overlook the base rate statistical probabilities and rely more heavily, and perhaps exclusively, on the individuating information.

The use of the representativeness heuristic rose with age and appeared quite early with the social scenarios problems. Jacobs and Potenza (1991) next looked at the explanations children provided for their answers, looking to see what percentage of the time children gave representativeness explanations. The percentages of this type of explanation was 41, 61, 77, and 84, for first, third, and sixth graders as well as college students, respectively, with the social scenarios, and 13, 17, 1, and 0.4 for the object problems. Younger children were more likely to offer idiosyncratic reasons for their choices, to offer embellishments of the social scenarios to justify their responses, or both. Older children and college students were more likely to offer a textbook representativeness response.

Many of these results have been replicated in other studies of children's decision making with social scenarios (Agnoli, 1991; Davidson, 1995). Other studies (e.g., Jacobs, Greenwald, & Osgood, 1995) have demonstrated that children's ability to accurately estimate base rates of social behaviors, such as riding a bike or watching cartoons, rose from first to third to sixth grade.

Other research also documents the existence of biases in children's decision making, such as the sunk cost effect (Baron, Granato, Spranca, & Teubal, 1993), although its use is not frequent and does not seem to rise much during the years 5 to 12. These researchers also documented children's inability to realize that some decisions set precedents and to understand the implications of probabilities. Moreover, there were few significant age effects, suggesting to the authors that good decision making develops slowly in the absence of a formal curriculum on probability and decision theory.

In contrast, Reyna and Ellis (1994) reported that preschoolers showed fewer framing effects than did second graders, who in turn showed fewer framing effects than fifth graders. The authors wondered if part of the explanation is that with age, children increasingly base their decisions on the gist of the information, thus becoming more susceptible to framing effects.

Davidson (1991) examined the way children used information boards in decision-making tasks. Table 7.2 shows the kinds of information displayed on the

TABLE 7.2

Examples of 3 × 3, 3 × 6, 6 × 3 and 6 × 6 Information Boards Used in the Study

Dimensions	Size of Bike	Price of Bike	# Friends Have Bike	Special Features	Old/New	Color
3 × 3						
Bike S	Just Right	Lots of Money	None			
Bike T	Just Right	Little Money	Many Friends			
Bike W	Too Small	Little Money	Many Friends			
3 × 6						
Bike P	Too Small	Little Money	Some Friends	Some	Old	White
Bike Q	Too Big	Some Money	Many Friends	Lots	New	Blue
Bike R	Just Right	Little Money	Many Friends	Lots	New	Red
6 × 3						
Bike G	Just Right	Lots of Money	None			
Bike H	Too Small	Little Money	Some Friends			
Bike I	Too Big	Little Money	Many Friends			
Bike J	Too Big	Some Money	Some Friends			
Bike K	Too Small	Lots of Money	None			
Bike L	Just Right	Little Money	Many Friends			
6 × 6						
Bike A	Just Right	Lots of Money	Many Friends	Some	New	White
Bike B	Just Right	Little Money	Many Friends	Lots	New	Red
Bike C	Just Right	Some Money	Some Friends	Some	New	Green
Bike D	Too Big	Little Money	None	Some	Old	Black
Bike E	Too Small	Lots of Money	None	None	Old	Blue
Bike F	Too Big	Little Money	Some Friends	None	New	Yellow

Note. The identical information was used to describe combs. From "Children's Decision-Making Examined With an Information-Board Procedure," by D. Davidson, 1991, *Cognitive Development, 6,* p. 81. Copyright 1991 by Elsevier Science. Reprinted with permission.

boards in her experiment. Davidson reported that second graders examined more pieces of information than did older (fifth and eighth grade) children but in a less systematic way, jumping from one dimension on one alternative to another dimension of information with another alternative. Older children were more likely to quickly eliminate alternatives using a noncompensatory rule.

At first blush, many of the above findings seem to be suggesting that younger children fall less prey to decision-making biases, which might in turn imply that they are better decision makers. However, closer inspection of the results seems to suggest that younger children are less systematic, more idiosyncratic, and less analytic than older children and that although they do not use common adult biases, they are not making sound decisions. What changes with development seems to be the efficiency with which information is searched for and processed. Necessarily, that efficiency leads children to adopt time-saving shortcuts, such as heuristics.

A study by Klaczynski (2001a) presented many of the heuristics and biases tasks such as detecting correlations, calibrating knowledge, and statistical reasoning (i.e., comparing large sample information to anecdotal information) to adolescents. On seven of the eight tasks presented, middle adolescents (ages 15–16) had significantly higher scores than younger adolescents (ages 11–13). This suggests a change in some of the information processing of decision making by adolescents older than about 14 years of age.

Klaczynski (2001b) suggests that two different reasoning systems may be operating independently. One, a heuristic system, operates quickly and intuitively; it feels quite natural and requires little thought. This system seems to be used by adolescents and adults alike, especially when few cognitive resources are available or needed (e.g., with decisions that need to be made quickly or decisions where the need for precision is low). Analytic abilities, on the other hand, seem to develop during adolescence. These are the abilities that allow a person to calculate likelihood ratios, reason according to the rules of formal logic, or make judgments that take probabilities into account accurately. Analytic abilities operate more slowly, require more cognitive effort, and may only be available to older adolescents and adults.

A correlational study by Berzonsky and Ferrari (1996) found evidence that adolescents with different identity orientations made important decisions differently. For example, informationally oriented individuals, who actively seek out information, reported themselves to be more vigilant, less avoidant, and less likely to rationalize or pass the buck in their descriptions of how they approached decisions. Identity orientation was not correlated with intellectual ability.

Decision Structuring

Recall from chapter 4 that decision structuring consists of listing and weighing criteria, listing and evaluating alternatives on all criteria, and dealing with uncertainty.

Very little research has been done on how children create decision maps of criteria and alternatives. More has been done on how children and adolescents come to understand concepts of probability.

Kreitler and Kreitler (1986), for example, tested children ages 5 to 12 on a variety of tasks having to do with probability. In one, the experimenter put 5 white chips and 15 black chips into a small cloth bag, had the child mix the chips, and then draw chips out 1 at a time. Before each draw, the child was asked to predict which color the next chip drawn would be. After the color of the chip was announced by the child and recorded by the experimenter, it was replaced in the bag prior to the next draw. After 10 such draws, the child was given the total of white and black chips drawn and asked to say whether this distribution was as it should be and to explain his or her answer.

The authors looked to see the kind of explanations children gave and found, in line with Piagetian predictions, that 5-year-olds gave more "magical" predictions, and 12-year-olds gave more probabilistic ones. Younger children were less able to consider the fact that the chips drawn were replaced in the bag. In sum, on this and three other probabilistic tasks, older children outperformed younger ones in their understanding of, use of, and explanation of the concept of probability and chance. Interestingly, the biggest developmental gap seemed to be between the 5-year olds and the 8-year-olds, whose performance in turn did not always differ significantly from that of the 12-year-olds.

Conceptions of probability and chance certainly are (or should be!) a factor in assessing decisions of whether or not to engage in risky behaviors, such as drinking, smoking, having sex, or using drugs. It has long been believed that adolescents are less able than adults to assess risks rationally, especially given their own adolescent egocentrism (Elkind, 1967), which has been hypothesized to lead adolescents to an exaggerated sense of their own invulnerability.

However, studies that compare adolescents and adults are painting a more nuanced picture. Urberg and Rosen (1987) interviewed 100 pregnant teenagers, asking them about their decision making with regard to the pregnancy. Specifically studied were whether or not the adolescents had, prior to getting pregnant, ever thought about what they would do if they became pregnant (i.e., contingency plans), the various possible resolutions to the pregnancy they were now thinking of (i.e., number of alternatives generated), and the various consequences they foresaw for each of these alternatives (i.e., number of costs and benefits considered, ratio of costs to benefits, and future orientation).

Younger and older adolescents generated about the same number of alternatives and about the same number of positive and negative consequences. However, younger adolescents (13- to 17-year-olds) were less likely to report having had a contingency plan for pregnancy or to be thinking about future consequences of their decisions than were the older (18- and 19-year-olds) adolescents. Thus, this study provides mixed support for the proposition that decision making becomes more rational with age.

Lewis (1981) asked adolescents in grades 7, 8, 10, and 12 about hypothetical decisions, such as a decision to undergo cosmetic surgery. In this study, students listened to three tape-recorded dilemmas and were asked what the protagonist of the dilemma should do, should think about, and who if anyone might be consulted in making the decision. Older students were more likely to list risks and future consequences and to express awareness of the existence of vested interests within the dilemmas (see Mann, Harmoni, & Power, 1989, for a related discussion).

Beyth-Marom, Austin, Fischhoff, Palmgren, and Jacobs-Quadrel (1993) asked both adolescents and adults to list possible consequences, both positive and negative, of risky behaviors (e.g., drinking alcohol and driving, smoking marijuana, skipping school, driving without a license, having sex, or going to a beer party). For each of these behaviors, participants generated four to seven consequences, with more bad than good consequences listed. Response patterns were similar for adults and adolescents, however, again suggesting that adolescents show no special impediment to considering consequences. Indeed, another study (Quadrel, Fischhoff, & Davis, 1993) showed that adolescents show no more invulnerability than do adults when considering risky behaviors, contrary to the predictions from Elkind's (1967) description of adolescent egocentrism.

Making a Final Choice

Once a decision has been structured, are there developmental differences in the way final selections are made? A study by Byrnes and McClenny (1994) seems to indicate so. They compared the performance of 13-year-olds and college students playing a complex game for points. The game offered players many choice points, in which the player had to estimate the odds of certain events (i.e., hard or easy questions being asked) happening as well as his or her ability to respond to those events (i.e., answer the questions correctly). The authors hypothesized that adolescents and adults could differ in (a) the way they evaluated their options, (b) their optimism about the outcomes, (c) their beliefs about their own abilities to produce outcomes, (d) their choice of options, and (e) their memory of their performance.

Results showed that when the game offered few dimensions to be considered, adolescents and adults used similar strategies. However, adults were better able to be strategic when the game was more complex. Adults also showed greater optimism and judged themselves to have more ability to answer fact-based questions. Adolescents were also more optimistically biased in their recall of how they had performed in the game than were adults.

A later study by Byrnes, Miller, and Reynolds (1999) compared the decision making of adults to that of eighth graders using a version of the Byrnes and McClenny (1994) task. In this study, however, participants were given feedback about how best to approach this task before beginning (i.e., verbal feedback) or feedback about their own performance (i.e., outcome feedback). Adults, more than eighth graders, were able to benefit from outcome feedback and use it to enhance their performance on later trials of the game.

Ganzel (1999) conducted a study with junior high (Grades 7–8) and high school (Grades 9–12) students and adult college students, in which they were asked to choose between four hypothetical fast food restaurant jobs on a computer display. Eight dimensions of information were presented, including social factors (whether parents would approve of the job, whether friends worked at the same locations, whether the supervisor was fun or mean, whether the restaurant had a "really cool" or "really gross" reputation), as well as objective factors (whether free meals were provided, the rate of pay, the flexibility of the schedule, and the relevance to a future career). Each dimension was rated either high or low (e.g., "Your parents would be really unhappy if you took this job," vs. "Your parents would be really happy if you took this job"). Each job presented had a mixture of high and low levels across the eight dimensions so that they would have an approximately equal subjective value.

Participants could choose to look at all, some, or none of the eight dimensions for each of the four choices, and the computer kept track of how much information participants examined. Overall, the adolescents examined significantly more available information (more than 95%), relative to adults (who examined about 86%), although there were no significant age differences among the different adolescent groups. Adults were more likely to use a complex search strategy than were adolescents. Adults were also more optimistic about their chances of obtaining their preferred job than were adolescents.

Summary of Development of Decision Making

To summarize the many studies and issues discussed previously, I think the following is reasonable: All of the decision-making phases (i.e., setting goals, gathering information, structuring the decision, making the final choice) undergo some changes with age. Not enough is yet known about goal setting and how it changes with development. Regarding information gathering, the data seem to show that some older children and adolescents show more biases than do younger children. With decision structuring, fewer developmental changes have been reported. Children's understanding of probability seems to be stable by mid-childhood. Although more information is needed about a variety of decisions, it appears that older children, adolescents, and adults structure decisions similarly. More developmental differences appear when we look at making a final selection, where adults appear to look at information more strategically and in more complex ways.

A general conclusion is that many of the cognitive components of decision making seem to be pretty much in place by midadolescence (age 14 or so). In many studies with hypothetical dilemmas, such as those previously presented, differences in performance between adolescents and adults are often not very large. What does seem to differ between adolescents and adults, however, is their ability to use complex strategies and to benefit from feedback. Of course, because decision making can change with the specific decision, much more research is needed to assess the generality of this claims.

Some have argued, in fact, that the major differences between adolescent decision making and adult decision making lies not in their cognitive abilities but in their motivational and emotional proclivities (Jacobs & Ganzel, 1993; Steinberg & Cauffman, 1996). It may be that adolescents make decisions the way adults do when the adults are in a novel situation; adolescents, after all, are making many life decisions for the first time. It may also be that adolescents focus more heavily on issues related to themselves and in so doing give different weights to criteria than adults might. For example, adolescents probably care a great deal more than do adults about their social reputations. When considering risky decisions, such as the decision to smoke a cigarette or drink and drive, adolescents may be deciding rationally (with respect to their own goals) to not suffer the social consequence of being labeled a "wimp" or a "goody two-shoes," names that may simply not affect adults, who presumably have a stronger and more consolidated sense of self.

Adolescents may also weigh the sources of information differently than do adults, and this may vary as a function of the type of decision being made. When making decisions about which clubs to join, what books to read, or what hobbies to take up, adolescents rely more heavily on peers than parents. The reverse is true for future-oriented decisions, such as choosing a future occupation or spouse (Wilks, 1986), although this probably depends a great deal on the quality of communication among adolescents and parents in a family (Brown & Mann, 1990; White, 1996).

EXPERTISE

There is another way that individuals differ in the way they carry out cognitive tasks, and that is in terms of their level of expertise. In this section we'll look first generally at the effects of practice and expertise on cognitive performance, then specifically at expert decision makers and how they seem to differ from novices.

Practice and Its Effects

Psychologists and lay persons alike know the truth of the idea that practice, even if it doesn't always make perfect, certainly changes and often improves performance. My favorite real-life example of this has to do with driving a car. If you think back to your very first experience behind the wheel, you might recall your anxiety level (mine was quite high) and how hard it was to do simple things—checking your mirror, shifting, moving your foot from one pedal to the other. Your first experience driving probably happened in "slow motion," as you drove at very slow speeds (I hope), concentrating intently on the road and the car's gauges, trying not to crash or skid.

It's likely that, during that first experience, you refrained from trying to do anything other than drive—I'll wager a large sum of money that you didn't try to change radio stations, or fish out a stick of gum from your backpack, or carry on some complicated philosophical or political discussion. It's far more likely that, instead, you put all of your mental energy into gripping the wheel, holding your foot on the pedal, and scanning the world outside your windshield.

Today, if you're a seasoned driver, driving doesn't take so much of your attention. On familiar routes and under normal driving conditions, you can probably carry on an involved conversation, or tune the radio, or change a CD, or even talk on a cell phone without disrupting your driving. This change in your abilities is because of practice. As a task becomes practiced, it takes fewer mental resources, or attention, to carry out, thus freeing those resources for deployment to other tasks.

Becoming an Expert

With years of practice, some people become experts within a domain. Expertise doesn't develop overnight, of course, and some argue that true expertise comes only after a minimum of 10 years in a field (e.g., Larkin, McDermott, Simon, & Simon, 1980). And, of course, expertise is restricted to a specific domain. An expert chess player is an expert in the realm of chess but is not necessarily an expert when it comes to home repair, income tax preparation, gardening, or nuclear physics. And not just any practice will do. Ericcson and Lehman (1996) argued for the necessity of deliberate practice, "especially designed by a coach or teacher to improve specific aspects of an individual's performance through repetition and successive refinement" (p. 279). Studies of experts have suggested that they engage in deliberate practice for up to 4 hours a day.

What does it mean to be an expert in a domain? Dreyfus (1997) outlined a five-stage theory of the development of expertise. Stage 1, as you might expect, is the novice stage, in which the novice receives instruction from a teacher who attempts to break a task environment down into context-free features and rules that apply to these features. A novice driver, for example, might be told to shift gears (on a nonautomatic vehicle) when the speedometer reads 10 mph. Beginners are the ones who rely most heavily on explicit rules, according to Dreyfus (1997).

Next comes the advanced beginner stage, in which the individual starts to notice some correlation of task features that cue the application of previously learned rules. In the driving example, an advanced beginner might learn to notice that the engine sounds likes it is straining a bit when it is time to shift gears.

More situational features become noticed with practice, until the poor individual is feeling rather swamped with information. At this point, Dreyfus asserted, the individual starts to look for or create new plans for how to handle the myriad different situations that can arise. This marks Stage 3, the stage of competence. The individual relies less on rules and instead starts to develop a feel for which aspects of a situation are more urgent and which ones can be initially ignored. At the same time, their emotional involvement with the task increases, relative to the involvement of either a novice or advanced beginner.

Stage 4 is described as the stage of proficiency. Here the individual relies even more on intuition and even less on rules. Many more discriminations are made among situations, and plans tailored to specific situations seem to be more automatically evoked, requiring less deliberate intention to formulate. Working on demanding tasks becomes even less effortful, as illustrated by Dreyfuss (1997):

> The proficient driver, approaching a curve on a rainy day, may realize intuitively that the car is going dangerously fast. The driver then consciously decides whether to apply the brakes or merely to reduce pressure by some selected amount on the accelerator. Valuable moments may be lost while a decision is consciously chosen, or time pressure may lead to a less than optimal choice. However, this driver is certainly more likely to negotiate the curve safely than the competent driver who spends

additional time *deciding* based on speed, angle of curvature, and felt gravitational forces, that the car's speed is excessive. (p. 22)

In Stage 5, true expertise is achieved. This involves further travel along the path from explicit rule application to intuitive response, tailored to the specifics of a situation confronting the expert. Experts are even better than proficient individuals at making subtle discriminations among situations, as illustrated in the following:

> The expert driver, generally without any awareness, not only knows by feel and familiarity when slowing down on an off ramp is required; the foot performs the appropriate action without the driver having to calculate and compare alternatives. It seems that a beginner makes inferences using rules and facts just like a heuristically programmed computer, but that with talent and a great deal of involved experience the beginner develops into an expert who intuitively sees what to do without applying rules. (p. 23)

Dreyfus' proposals have received support from some studies of expert nurses. Tanner, Benner, Chesla, and Gordon (1993), who interviewed 130 nurses practicing in intensive care units, found that these experienced nurses spoke frequently of "knowing the patient." This in turn implied taking the general rules of nursing and applying them to a particular person experiencing a particular problem under particular circumstances. Relatedly, McKinlay, Potter, and Feldman (1996) studied physicians' diagnoses of an actor (patient) complaining of either chest pain or shortness of breath. Findings showed that the physicians differed in their diagnosis of exactly the same symptoms as a function of the age, race, or gender of the patient, the insurance status of the patient, and the type of practice the physician was in (HMO vs. private or hospital based). That is, experienced physicians were less likely to follow simple rules and more likely to take into account specifics of an individual case.

Expertise and Decision Making

Dreyfus' (1997) description of expertise fits well with Klein's (1998) descriptive studies of experts, described briefly in chapter 5. Klein's argument, you may recall, is that expert decision makers don't typically rely on formal rules, explicit comparison of multiple options, and formal decision models, such as multiattribute utility theory. Instead, they size up a situation, using intuition to pick out the important aspects and recognizing the similarity of a new situation to a previously encountered one. Experts can't always tell how they arrived at a decision and frequently make reference to intuition, or a sixth sense, as in this story from a lieutenant firefighter:

> It is a simple house fire in a one-story house in a residential neighborhood. The fire is in the back, in the kitchen area. The lieutenant leads his hose crew into the building, to the back, to spray water on the fire, but the fire just roars back at them.

"Odd," he thinks. The water should have more of an impact. They try dousing it again, and get the same results. They retreat a few steps to regroup.

Then the lieutenant starts to feel as if something is not right. He doesn't have any clues; he just doesn't feel right about being in that house, so he orders his men out of the building—a perfectly standard building with nothing out of the ordinary.

As soon as his men leave the building, the floor where they had been standing collapses. Had they still been inside, they would have plunged into the fire below. (Klein, 1988, p. 32)

Klein (1998) supported his recognition primed decision-making (RPD) model with a variety of detailed, compelling anecdotes such as these. But anecdotal evidence can only carry us so far: We don't know, for instance, how many other anecdotes there are that don't support the model.

Fortunately, some empirical work has put some of the tenets of the RPD model to a more rigorous test. Randel, Pugh, and Reed (1996), for example, studied the performance of U.S. Naval electronic warfare technicians as they worked on a simulation in front of a radar screen, identifying signals from both friendly and hostile radar systems. The operators listen to auditory signals, read computer printouts of different parameters of the signal, and communicate with others through radio contact.

The authors were able to classify 28 operators into three groups: novices, intermediates, or experts, based on their performance on a pilot simulation. In the test simulation, operators were asked at two points to pause and draw the location of different objects that had just been presented on the radar screen (a blank screen was presented and the operator had to draw from memory) and to respond to a questionnaire about tactically important information given at the end of the simulation.

Results showed that experts were superior to both intermediates and novices (and intermediates were superior to novices) at what the authors called situation awareness—having a good grasp of what is going on from moment to moment as the event unfolds. Experts drew more emitters on their blank screens than did intermediates, who in turn drew more than novices. Experts answered more questions correctly about platforms, radar, weapons, and bearings than did intermediates, who in turn performed reliably better than novices. Experts and intermediates seemed to place most of their efforts at grasping the specifics of a situation, at sizing it up, and worried less about what course of action to take. Novices did just the opposite, spending less resources to acquire information about the situation and concentrating on what action to take.

The authors take these results as support for the role of RPD in expert decision-making: "In most cases, experts do not have to spend much effort in deciding how to react to a situation: once they understand the situation, the reaction is fairly obvious. So experts concentrate on getting the situation correctly assessed" (Randel, Pugh, & Reed, 1996, p. 593).

You might think that experts pick up on and use more information than do novices, but that intuition is often incorrect. Shanteau and his colleagues (Ettenson,

Shanteau, & Krogstad, 1987; Shanteau, 1988, 1992) have studied professional auditors making decisions about auditing cases and soil judges evaluating soil texture. In both cases, experts were found to restrict the number of dimensions of information they examined to about three or four, just as students just beginning their study of the relevant field did. However, experts were better able than naive students to home in on relevant information and to filter out less relevant information.

Not all studies of experts yield a flattering picture of their decision making. In a review of previous research, Shanteau (1992) categorized domains where good and poor expert performance has been reported and described task characteristics associated with good and poor expert performance, summarized here in Table 7.3.

Notice a few things about the two columns of Table 7.3. Good expert performance has been reported with relatively static or constant stimuli (e.g., soils), as opposed to dynamic stimuli including human behavior. Experts in some domains (e.g., meteorologists) are not expected by the general public to be 100% accurate; clinicians are not allowed the same margin of error in the court of public opinion. Expertise can be more easily developed in domains with repetitive situations and a great deal of feedback.

Shanteau (1988) offered six strategies he has observed in experts in a variety of domains. First, experts are willing to make adjustments in their initial decisions, avoiding rigid adherence to rules or policies. Second, they rely on others, obtaining feedback to gain different perspectives. Third, experts learn from past decisions and adjust their future performance based on past mistakes. They avoid getting hung up on defending themselves or rationalizing their behavior.

TABLE 7.3
Task Characteristics Associated
With Good and Poor Performance in Experts

Good Performance	Poor Performance
Static stimuli	Dynamic (changeable) stimuli
Decisions about things	Decisions about behavior
Experts agree on stimuli	Experts disagree on stimuli
More predictable problems	Less predictable problems
Some errors expected	Few errors expected
Repetitive tasks	Unique tasks
Feedback available	Feedback unavailable
Objective analysis available	Subjective analysis only
Problem decomposable	Problem not decomposable
Decision aids common	Decision aids rare

Note. From "Psychological Characteristics and Strategies of Expert Decision Makers," by J. Shanteau, 1988, *Acta Psychologica, 68,* p. 259. Copyright 1998 by Academic Press. Reprinted with permission.

A fourth quality is that experts develop decision aids that allow them to escape the clutches of various decisional heuristics and biases, such as those we discussed in chapter 3. Fifth, experts might make little mistakes but not big ones. They exhibit a certain comfort level in coming to a decision that is "good enough," and don't obsess over getting everything exactly right. Finally, experts tend to break up large problems into pieces, using what Shanteau (1988) called a divide-and-conquer strategy.

INDIVIDUAL DIFFERENCES IN DECISION-MAKING STYLES

When you approach important decisions, are you likely to run to the Internet and spend hours surfing for relevant information? Or are you more likely to talk things over with friends, family members, or experts? Do you try to be systematic, thorough, objective, or rational, or do you emphasize more what feels right or seems intuitively correct? Do most of your big decisions take a while, or do you like to make them quickly, on the spur of the moment? Do you prefer to make decisions by yourself or with other people?

The fact that individuals differ in physical attributes, such as height, weight, or hair, eye, or skin color, is self-evident to just about anyone living in a community. It is also no news flash that people differ intellectually—with some more capable of difficult cognitive tasks than others. We use terms such as *smart* or *bright* or *sharp* to describe such people. And there are a variety of intellectual abilities in which people differ. To give just a few examples, consider verbal abilities, mathematical abilities, spatial abilities, musical abilities, and interpersonal abilities. A person good in one or two of these abilities isn't necessarily good at all of them (Gardner, 1983).

But more than in intellectual abilities, people also seem to differ in the way they use their intellectual abilities, that is, the way they approach situations or problems. These approaches may relate more to personality differences than to ability differences and have come to be called cognitive, thinking, or learning styles (Rayner & Riding, 1997; Sternberg, 1997).

Cognitive Styles

Much work on individual differences in psychology has centered on the idea of cognitive styles, a description of different people's ways of processing information. Different proposals have been offered for dimensions along which people differ. One of these is the dimension of impulsivity/reflectivity; it is discussed here as an example.

Consider Fig. 7.1, which presents five pairs of abstract designs. Individuals within a pair are highly similar. But are they, or are they not, exactly alike? It's your

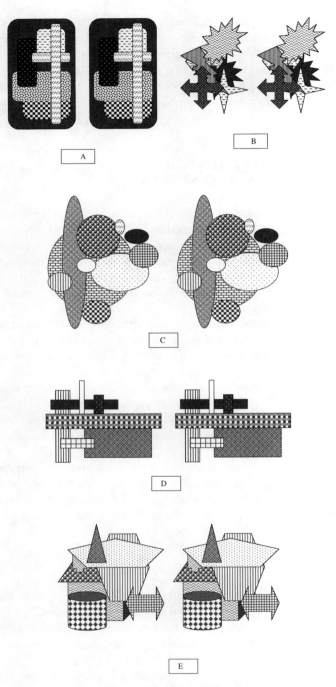

FIG. 7.1. Pairs of similar (and sometimes identical) figures.

task to figure out which ones are exactly alike and which ones have a small, subtle difference. Notice and try to describe your reaction to this task.

Some people approach this kind of task in a careful, deliberate, painstaking fashion. They systematically scan from one to the other looking intently for differences that may be quite minute. They take quite a bit of time before they conclude that the paired designs are identical (i.e., to conclude that they have searched exhaustively before concluding that there are no differences to find). These individuals are described as having a reflective cognitive style, or a slow cognitive tempo (Kagan, 1966). They take their time and make few mistakes. They may not finish a task, but the work they do complete is likely to have few errors. On the task in Figure 7.1, reflective individuals would be likely to spend much more time on it and to be more accurate. (They would correctly choose B and E as displaying figures that differ slightly.)

Impulsive individuals, by contrast, work much faster and make more errors. They are the ones likely to make quicker decisions and be less concerned about the possibility of errors. Impulsive individuals often feel that when confronting a cognitive task there is some kind of clock running. They feel "under the gun," needing to make a response, almost any response, just to have the task completed.

There are other proposals for cognitive style dimensions. Table 7.4 provides additional examples and brief descriptions of each. The specifics of the different proposals need not concern us too much here. Instead, the general point to be taken from this is that psychologists have been interested for quite some time in the proposition that people have different characteristic ways of processing information. Some work even suggests that some cognitive style differences are associated with (and may even stem from) different brain organizations, such as frontal lobe activity (Waber, 1989) or different EEG patterns of activity (Riding, Glass, Butler, & Pleydell-Pearce, 1997).

One individual difference that may impact decision making greatly is something called need for cognition (NFC; Cacioppo & Petty, 1982). Individuals with greater need for cognition are those who have stronger motivation to engage in cognitive tasks. That is, they enjoy more activities such as researching, gathering information, and thinking, relative to low-NFC individuals. High-NFC individuals are also more likely to make decisions based on aspects of the situation relevant to the issues at hand, whereas low-NFC individuals are more likely to become sidetracked by peripheral issues.

In Verplanken's (1993) study, high- and low-NFC individuals worked at an information display board task similar to those we discussed in chapter 3. Participants were asked to select one of four refrigerators, and five pieces of information were potentially available on each: price, size, energy use, life span, and judgment of a consumer organization. Some participants were asked to make their decision in a restricted amount of time—5 minutes or fewer. This was about half the time taken by participants doing the same task when not under time pressure.

TABLE 7.4
Descriptions and Fundamental Dimensions of Cognitive Style

Label	Description	References
Key Dimension: Wholist–Analytic		
Constricted-flexible control	Tendency for distraction or resistance to interference.	Klein (1954)
Broad-narrow	Preference for broad categories containing many items rather than narrow categories containing few items	Pettigrew (1958); Kogan and Wallach (1964)
Analytical-nonanalytic	A conceptual response which differentiates attributes or qualities conceptualizing rather than a theme or total effect.	Kagan et al. (1964); Messick and Kogan (1963)
Levelling-sharpening	Tendency to assimilate detail rapidly and lose detail or emphasize detail and changes in new information.	Klein (1954); Gardner et al. (1959)
Field-dependence/ field independence	Individual dependency on a perceptual field when analyzing a structure or form which is part of the field.	Witkin and Asch (1948a, 1948b); Witkin (1961); Witkin (1971); Witkin et al. (1977)
Impulsivity-reflectiveness	Tendency for quick as against a deliberate response	Kagan et al. (1964); Kagan (1966)
Cognitive-complexity	A tendency for the multidimensional or simplicity or unidimensional processing of information.	Harvey et al. (1961); Gardner and Schoen (1962)
Automization-restructuring	Preference for simple repetitive tasks rather than restructuring tasks	Tiedemann (1989)
Converging-diverging	Narrow, focused, logical, deductive thinking rather than broad, open-ended, associational thinking to solve problems.	Hudson (1966, 1968); Guilford (1967)
Serialist-holist	The tendency to work through learning tasks or problem solving incrementally or globally and assimilate detail.	Pask and Scott (1972); Pask (1976)
Splitters-lumpers	A response to information and interpretation which is either analytical and methodical or global.	Cohen (1967)
Adaptors-innovators	Adaptors prefer conventional, established procedures and innovators restructuring or new perspectives in problem solving	Kirton (1976, 1994)
Concrete sequential concrete random/ abstract sequential abstract random	The learner learns through concrete experience and abstraction either randomly or sequentially	Gregorc (1982)
Reasoning-intuitive active-contemplative	Preference for developing understanding through reasoning and/or by spontaneity or insight and learning activity which allows active participation or passive reflection	Allison and Hayes (1996)

(Continued)

TABLE 7.4 (*Continued*)

Label	Description	References
Key Dimension: Verbal–Imagery		
Abstract versus concrete	Preferred level and capacity of abstraction.	Harvey et al. (1961)
Tolerance for unrealistic experiences	Individual readiness to accept perceptual variance with conventional reality or "truth."	Klein et al. (1962)
Verbalizer-visualizer	The extent to which verbal or visual strategies are used when processing information.	Paivio (1971); Riding and Taylor (1976); Richardson (1977)
Key Dimensions: Wholist–Analytic and Verbal–Imagery		
Analytic-Wholist and Verbal-Imager	Tendency for the individual to process information in parts as a whole and think in words or pictures	Riding (1991, 1994); Riding and Cheema (1991); Riding and Rayner (1995)

Note. From "Towards a Categorisation of Cognitive Styles and Learning Styles," by S. Rayner and R. Riding, 1997, *Educational Psychology, 17,* pp. 8–9. http://www.tandf.co.uk/journals. Copyright 1997 by Taylor & Francis Ltd. Reprinted with permission.

Time pressure had little effect on the behavior of high-NFC participants, who tended to search for about the same amount of information on each alternative, regardless of whether they were under time pressure or not. However, time pressure had a large effect on low-NFC participants, who drastically changed their approach to the task when working under time constraints.

Verplanken (1993) interpreted these results as follows: If low-NFC participants normally allocate less mental energy to cognitive tasks, including decision making tasks, then they will have fewer resources to devote to them. When time pressures are introduced, these pressures will disproportionately cause the low-NFC participants to need to switch strategies to ones that are easier to implement but possibly less accurate. In turn, they will give up searching for much information and will respond more impulsively. In contrast, high-NFC individuals will have a more vested interest in making good decisions and will find ways to maintain the quality of their information searches, even when pressured.

Klaczynski and Fauth (1996) demonstrated differences as a function of need for cognition on a more real-world task. First, the authors demonstrated no significant relationship between NFC and cognitive ability, suggesting that NFC really is a stylistic dimension and not one derived from intellectual power. Second, the authors showed that low-NFC individuals were those more likely to drop out of college, suggesting that styles do affect important life outcomes for people.

Undergraduate students were asked to estimate their chances of experiencing both positive and negative life events (e.g., achieving occupational success, having happy children, traveling to Europe vs. developing a chronic disease, being fired from a job, and getting divorced). Most participants showed an optimistic bias, believing that they would experience more positive and fewer negative life events than would their peers. Interestingly, those individuals high in NFC were the most optimistically biased, particularly in the domain of academic or career events.

In related work, Stanovich and West (1997, 1998) investigated the effects of both cognitive ability and thinking dispositions (styles) on performance on a variety of reasoning and decision-making tasks. Cognitive ability was assessed by Scholastic Aptitude Test scores; scores on the Raven's Matrices, a measure of general problem solving and analytic intelligence; and reading comprehension scores. These researchers also measured peoples' thinking dispositions—their tendency to value reflectiveness more than impulsivity, their willingness to be open to new ways of thinking, their tolerance for ambiguity, and their ability to be skeptical of claims.

Stanovich and West (1998) had their participants also engage in a number of thinking, reasoning, and decision-making tasks. They found that the cognitive ability measures correlated significantly and moderately with all of these tasks. That result suggests that people with more cognitive capacity (e.g., larger memory or faster processing speed) are able to execute all of these higher order cognitive tasks more accurately.

More surprising, Stanovich and West (1998) found that thinking dispositions—the more stylistic variables—also correlated significantly (though not as strongly as the cognitive ability measures) with all the thinking, reasoning, and decision-making task performances. Stanovich and West measured a person's tendency to be open-minded, cognitively flexible, and skeptical (as opposed to rigid and lacking skepticism); this variable correlated significantly with people's ability to reason statistically, with heuristics tasks similar to those presented in chapter 3, and to evaluate the quality of arguments. Thus, the authors concluded that people's thinking style, in addition to their cognitive ability, does make a difference in their capacity to successfully complete a task.

Decision-Making Styles

Some work has attempted to identify and describe different decision-making styles specifically. Blustein and Phillips (1990), for example, described a variety of decision-making styles: rational, involving systematic thinking and a clear orientation to the future; intuitive, involving relying on inner experience and dispensing with information gathering or deliberation; and dependent, in which the decision maker looks to other authorities to make the decisions.

Niles, Erford, Hunt, and Watts (1997) identified clusters of decision-making styles among college students. One dimension they described was that of systematicity versus spontaneity—the tendency to deliberate and gather much information versus the tendency to rely on instinct or gut impressions. Another dimension they discovered was internal versus external decision making—the tendency to be autonomous versus to solicit input from others (Johnson, 1978).

Dollinger and Danis (1998) reported on a cross-cultural investigation of decision-making styles, investigating two modes they called adaptors (i.e., people who improve on existing procedures or methods) versus innovators (i.e., people who invent new procedures or methods), finding Chinese respondents to outscore both American and Japanese repondents in adaptor scores, whereas U.S. students showed higher innovator scores than the Asian students.

Finally, Scott and Bruce (1995) updated some of these earlier attempts to describe styles. To the rational, intuitive, dependent, and spontaneous styles already described, they added a fifth: avoidant. They created a survey instrument to assess these styles and tested it not only with undergraduates but also with military officers and graduate (MBA) students.

Investigations of how much styles matter in making important real-life decisions awaits further investigation, although some work has begun. Friedrich (1987) found that college students who perceived little internal control over their vocations sought less information, generated fewer alternatives, and considered fewer pros and cons of each alternative in their search for a summer job, relative to students who perceived themselves to have more control over their occupations and careers.

Niles et al. (1997) found that their college students who had a systematic (rather than spontaneous) decision-making style were more likely to report themselves as having stronger career self-efficacy beliefs and to have accomplished more of the preliminary career decision-making work (e.g., assessing their values and their skills). Especially interesting was the finding that students who used an external decision-making style (e.g., relying on others as sounding boards and sources of information), showed stronger confidence in their career decision making than did students with a more internal or autonomous style.

We have so far seen a number of different proposals for different styles with which people approach either decision-making tasks specifically or any cognitive task more generally. Every theorist, it seems, has her or his own taxonomy of ways in which individuals differ. Is there a way to tie them together?

One dimension of difference that seems to crop up in many of the learning style, thinking style, and decision-making style investigations is the contrast between rational and intuitive approaches. The former connotes approaching a task objectively, unemotionally, analytically, and thoroughly; the latter, personally, emotionally, drawing on one's feelings, and wholistically.

One proposal, made by Stanovich and West (Stanovich, 1999; Stanovich & West, 2000), explores this distinction. Stanovich proposed that there may be two different cognitive systems at work when people approach complex cognitive tasks, such as reasoning and decision making. System 1 is used automatically, implicitly, and tacitly; it takes relatively little effort to operate and indeed it may be hard to inhibit it from functioning when something in the environment triggers or cues it. It fits well with the idea of an intuitive approach. Any automatic thinking would fall under System 1; it's the kind of thinking that seems to come naturally to us, even if it results in a wrong answer. According to Stanovich, many of the errors committed by research participants in many of the standard heuristics and biases laboratory tasks (such as those discussed in chapter 3, including availability, representativeness, sunk cost, and illusory correlation) result from the use of System 1 processes.

Stanovich (1999) contrasted System 1 with System 2, described as being comprised of harder, slower, more deliberate, intentional, and analytic processes, such as formal reasoning. System 2 captures the essence of what most people mean by *rational*—something that is analytic, explicit, rule based, and objective. System 2 processes operate more slowly than do System 1 processes, but they are more flexible and more able to be applied across more situations, regardless of the specific context.

Stanovich's proposal has generated much controversy (see responses to Stanovich & West, 2000, published along with their article), and some see it as making System 2 processes more important or more valuable than System 1 processes. Frish (2000), for example, made an analogy between System 1 and System 2 on the one hand and the Chinese concepts of yin and yang on the other, regarding each half as complementary to the other. Kahneman (2000) offered the possibility that "System 1 may have its own kind of intuitive intelligence. For example, some people may have particularly nuanced and subtle representations of persons and social categories. These people will make better judgments by representativeness than others, and may consequently achieve greater predictive accuracy than others" (p. 683).

The rational/intuitive dimension is not the only one common to several proposals for individual differences, however. Others include extraversion/introversion and spontaneous versus deliberate. It remains to be seen how much people's differences along any of these dimensions are associated with differences in decision making and how large and frequent such differences are.

We have seen a number of proposals throughout this section for categorizing the ways people differ in their approach to complex cognitive tasks. Some of the issues have revolved around how stable a person's classification into one type or another is, that is, how likely it is that a person characterized with one style on, for example, Tuesday will also be characterized as having that style on Wednesday. There are also disagreements over how best to characterize differences: Is it in terms of the way people acquire information? The way they think about or process information already acquired? Do the differences stem from variation in biological aspects of the brain or to global personality differences? Do the variations show up consistently in different situations?

More work needs to be done to follow individuals who have different decision-making styles as they confront real-life decisions, to see where the behavior, cognition, or emotional reactions start to diverge. Are there systematic differences in the decision-making behaviors different people exhibit (e.g., in goal setting, information gathering, decision structuring?) Are the differences more emotional in nature, in people's reactions to the process, either during the process or in retrospect? How malleable are people's decision-making styles, and what kinds of experiences help foster change? All of these are crucial questions, very much under active investigation in the study of real-life decision making.

SUMMARY

We've seen in this chapter more ways that individuals can differ in the ways they approach a decision. Developmentally, there are differences in a child's or an adult's ability to focus, to behave consistently, and to reason about the future. Although the use of heuristics and biases increases over childhood, it appears that this leads to an overall decrease in idiosyncratic responding. However, it appears to be the case that by late childhood or early adolescence, decision-making performance starts to approximate adultlike behavior.

A second individual difference in decision making has to do with one's level of previous practice or knowledge within a domain. The existence of these differences causes us to be cautious in making overly general claims about decision making.

Third, there may be stable differences in people's approach to the task of decision making. These may stem from personality differences, neurological differences, or some combination. Just as performance can depend on the type of decision being made, as we saw from chapter 6, it can also be affected by the relevant characteristics of the decision maker, as we have seen in this chapter.

Our focus so far has been on the individual decision maker, working alone. Indeed, many decisions are made by individuals. However, many others are not made by any one person but by groups of people. There is reason to wonder how these kinds of decision making will differ from the kind of individual decision making we have discussed so far. I'll discuss that issue in chapter 8.

8

Group and Organizational Decision Making

The preceding seven chapters have focused on decisions made by individuals. We've examined the goal setting, decision structuring, and selections made by people, acting as if the individual people have sole responsibility for the entire task. But in many cases, this simply isn't true.

Many decisions are made by pairs of people, such as a couple deciding on purchasing a house, a car, or making an investment. Parents choose day care and, later, schools or school programs for their young children. Siblings make decisions about health care for aging parents. In some cases, the number of people involved in a decision grows even larger: Work groups develop a marketing plan; juries decide the fate of accused criminals.

In this chapter, we'll look at group decision making, starting with small, dyadic groups, next looking at larger groups, such as teams, committees, or juries. We'll next consider organizational and cultural effects on the process of decision making. Our focus here will be on how group decision making differs from individual decision making, both in terms of the processes involved (e.g., negotiation) and the outcome. For example, are several heads better than one; that is, do groups typically make better decisions than individuals? We'll begin by looking at how two people make decisions together.

DYADIC DECISION MAKING

Couples obviously make many decisions together. Married couples or couples living together might decide whether or not to change residence, build or buy a house or car or other major consumer good, have or adopt a child, place a child in an educational or day-care setting, to name just a few. Friends or business partners might decide to take a trip together, to launch a new venture, or to merge their operations. In this section, we'll look at how two people make decisions.

Two-person decision making has often been studied by both psychologists and economists by means of a task known as the *prisoner's dilemma* (Rapoport &

Chammah, 1965). A version of the task is as follows: Imagine two friends, call them Becky and Dave. Becky and Dave together rob a bank and are later apprehended by a vigilant and aggressive police detective. He immediately sequesters Becky and Dave in separate interrogation rooms and offers each the following deal: If they each refuse to confess to the robbery, they will be convicted of a lesser charge, namely, possession of stolen goods (to wit: marked bills taken from the bank), and they will each serve 1 year in prison. If one confesses and the other doesn't, the confessor would get no time in prison (in exchange for their testimony against the other); the one who didn't confess would serve a 10-year sentence for robbery. If both confess, they will each serve an 8-year sentence.

We can think of the choices confronting Becky and Dave in terms of a payoff matrix, such as the one shown in Fig. 8.1, which shows the various outcomes as a function of what Becky decides to do and what Dave decides to do. Notice that if Becky and Dave could talk to each other directly and negotiate, or if Becky and Dave have full faith and confidence in one another, they would be best off not confessing and serving the 1-year sentence. However, if they aren't absolutely sure

	If Becky	
	Confesses	**Doesn't confess**
If Dave — Confesses	Becky serves 8 years Dave serves 8 years	Becky serves 10 years Dave serves 0 years
If Dave — Doesn't confess	Becky serves 0 years Dave serves 10 years	Becky serves 1 year Dave serves 1 year

FIG. 8.1.   Depiction of a *prisoner's dilemma* payoff matrix.

of what the other one is going to do, then they are best off confessing. The name of the task derives from the fact that if both Becky and Dave act in their own short-term best interest (by confessing), then they undercut their own long-run best interest (Ajzen, 1996).

Research on people's performance in prisoner dilemma situations reveals that people typically choose a competitive (confess) strategy, although if task instructions emphasize cooperating, this tendency can be reduced. When the payoffs are large for cooperating relative to those for confessing, cooperation increases. Prior communication increases cooperation, as you might expect. When the task is run for several trials, partners tend to reciprocate cooperation or defection. Finally, women are more likely than males to act competitively (i.e., choosing to confess; Ajzen, 1996).

Despite the extensive research done on this task, no one thinks it's a terribly helpful model of what people do in everyday life. After all, a husband and wife trying to decide whether to buy a Honda Accord or a Toyota Camry don't typically sequester themselves in separate rooms, nor are the payoffs they face so devilishly devised.

However, some research has demonstrated that when two people make decisions, they often settle on less than optimal outcomes for both of them. Thompson and Hrebec (1996) called this situation a lose–lose agreement. They offer the following as just some examples where a settlement that appears beneficial to both parties is not the settlement that those two parties achieve:

Situation 1. A man and a woman have been married for many years. They are both experiencing stresses from career development, adolescent children, and middle age. Both want their union to become stronger and more committed. Instead, it dissolves into animosity, recrimination, and litigation.

Situation 2. A hard-charging entrepreneur wishes her partner would show more initiative and shoulder more of the increasing workload. The easy-going partner would prefer to be more involved but believes that the hard-charging partner wants to retain control of all aspects of the enterprise. As the business grows, each becomes more frustrated.

Situation 3. Two countries have been in conflict for decades. Each would benefit from peaceful coexistence. But their attempts at peace talks never achieve substantive progress, and the conflict rages on. (Thompson & Hrebec, 1996, p. 396)

Thompson and Hrebec (1996) regarded the following as critical elements for a lose–lose agreement to occur. First, the decision making must be interdependent —unilateral decisions made by one party don't count. Relatedly, the decision must be made cooperatively—that is, voluntarily agreed to by both parties. Lose–lose agreements pertain to conflicts of interest, typically the allocation of scarce resources. Lose-lose agreements require that there be more than one feasible outcome and that the two parties' preferences be compatible but that, because of incomplete information, the parties don't realize it, despite the availability of open communication.

A study by Thompson and Hrbec (1996), performed as a laboratory experiment in negotiation, revealed that almost 25% of the negotiating dyads fail to agree on the outcome that would have benefited both. In a later meta-analysis examining the results of 32 experiments involving more than 5,000 participants, Thompson and Hrebec (1996) reported that on average, lose–lose agreements emerged 20% of the time. Even when incentives were high, and the participants had practice at negotiating, lose–lose agreements still emerged.

But what about dyadic decision making in real life? Kirchler (1995) has argued that social scientists will need to develop new methods to investigate such decision making:

> [There is] . . . little doubt that decision-making in everyday situations deviates markedly from the images found in normative models. People in a household solve their problems when they are still tired in the morning, or tired again, in the evening after work. Economic decisions are embedded in everyday family life, which in turn is interlaced with a variety of different problems. These problems often do not occur in neat sequential order, but must be solved concurrently. Under these circumstances, it is not surprising that household members jump from one problem to the next without first solving the previous one. (Kirchler, 1995, p. 395)

Kirchler (1995) argued that in order to understand a couple's decision making, one first must understand the dynamics of the relationship between the husband and wife. He presents a schematic representation, reproduced in Fig. 8.2. In harmonious relationships, Kirchler predicted, the feelings, thoughts, and actions of the two partners will be more intertwined, and the decision is more likely to be made in such a way that it optimizes the outcomes for the good of both the husband and wife. In such relationships, Kirchler said, both partners bring diverse resources to each other, feel responsible for satisfying each other's needs, therefore making fewer demands on the other. In all, partners in harmonious relationships act altruistically quite spontaneously.

If the spouses have a less harmonious relationship, then the governing "love principle" mutates into a "credit" principle. When this principle reigns, the two spouses make efforts to do favors for each other but wait for and expect eventual payback. As Kirchler (1995) described it, "the accounts of mutual favors must be balanced" (p. 397), at least over the long term.

In less harmonious relationships, decisions are governed by the "equity principle," meaning that they behave more like business partners (or even rivals), bartering to achieve fair and balanced outcomes. And, as the relationship quality deteriorates, power differences between the spouses become more influential, with the more powerful spouse having greater influence over decisions regardless of the desires of the other spouse. Such decision making is governed by the "egoism principle."

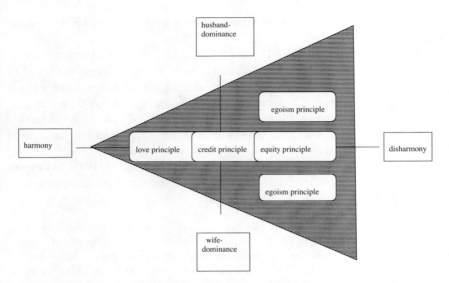

FIG. 8.2.   Interaction principles as dependent on the structure of the relationship. From "Studying economic decisions within private households: A critical review and design for a 'couple experiences diary,'" by E. Kirchler, 1995, *Journal of Economic Psychology, 16*, p. 396. Copyright 1995 by Elsevier Science. Reprinted with permission.

The process of decision making also depends on the particular decision, of course. Some habitual decisions are made by the use of cognitive scripts, that is, without much thought and following previous decisions. However, "the more expensive, social prestigious, and relevant a good is for all, the more likely it will be that the members of a household will participate in the decision and try to get their way" (Kirchler, 1995, p. 397).

To date, little systematic research has been done to test Kirchler's (1995) predictions, although some preliminary supportive evidence is offered in his article. He has argued that in-depth studies of household decision making will need to assess not only the particular decision being made but also the frequency and importance to household members, the quality of the relationship between family members, the spheres of influence each individual has in making certain types of decisions (e.g., if the wife makes grocery decisions and the husband makes appliance decisions), as well as the decision-making styles of all parties.

GROUP DECISION MAKING

The layperson's theory of group decision making goes something like this: Many heads are better than one. Different individuals in the group presumably bring different idiosyncratic views to the decision, and through vigorous discussion, the idiosyncracies ought to cancel each other out until what remains is a more rational and high-quality decision than would have been made by any of the individuals in the group.

Indeed, a now-classic study by Shaw (1932) seemed to bear out this view. College students were given a number of items on a problem-solving test; some worked on the problems individually and some in groups of four. Fewer than 8% of the solutions arrived at by individuals were correct, compared with 53% of the solutions given by groups. Shaw attributed the group superiority to the group members checking errors and rejecting incorrect suggestions. Clearly, in this instance, many heads were better than one.

However, other research by social psychologists on other kinds of decision making does not paint such an optimistic picture of the validity of group decision making:

> Groups, like individuals, have shortcomings. Groups can bring out the worst as well as the best in man. Nietzsche went so far as to say that madness is the exception in individuals but the rule in groups. A considerable amount of social science literature shows that in circumstances of extreme crisis, group contagion occasionally gives rise to collective panic, violent acts of scapegoating, and other forms of what could be called group madness. Much more frequent, however, are instances of mindless conformity and collective misjudgment of serious risks, which are collectively laughed off in a clubby atmosphere of relaxed conviviality. (Janis, 1982, p. 3)

Indeed, a review article by Kerr, MacCoun, and Kramer (1996) argues that there is no simple answer to the question, which are more biased, individuals or groups?

Groupthink

Janis (1982) described several foreign policy fiascoes that resulted from decisions made by United States presidents, among them, the invasion of the Bay of Pigs, the decision not to take steps to prepare for an attack on Pearl Harbor, and the decision to try to cover up the Watergate break-in. In each case, Janis found that very bright cabinet-level advisors to the President convinced themselves that a particular course of action was the right one, even though many, many clear signs of warning of impending disaster were in evidence.

Janis (1982) used the term *groupthink* to describe group decision making gone wrong in a particular way. Essentially, what often happens is that members of the group are trying so hard to preserve harmony within the group and to come to consensus that they adopt courses of action that are very flawed. Sabini (1992) has defined groupthink to mean "a deterioration of mental efficiency, reality testing, and moral judgement that results from ingroup pressures to seek consensus" (p. 98).

Here's a brief example of the phenomenon of groupthink:

Consider what happened a few days before disaster struck the small mining town of Pitcher, Oklahoma, in 1950. The local mining engineer had warned the inhabitants to leave at once because the town had been accidentally undermined and might cave in at any moment. At a Lion's Club meeting of leading citizens, the day after the warning was issued, the members joked about the warning and laughed uproariously when someone arrived wearing a parachute. What the club members were communicating to each other by their collective laughter was that "sensible people like us know better than to take seriously those disaster warnings; we know it can't happen here, to our fine little town." Within a few days, this collective complacency cost some of these men and their families their lives." (Janis, 1982, p. 3)

Some of the factors that seem to lead to groupthink have to do with group cohesiveness. To the degree that members of a group feel a sense of shared purpose and values, the group becomes more able to exert power over its members to conform to group norms. In close-knit groups, it may very difficult for an individual to express and maintain a dissenting point of view, especially if the dissenter is the only one advocating a particular position. Even if the rest of the group tries to listen politely, there is still strong pressure for a dissenting member to accede to the judgements of the rest of the group.

Janis (1982) listed eight symptoms of groupthink, divided into three categories. The first category pertains to overestimating the group, either in terms of its power or morality. The second category has to do with closed-mindedness—dismissing ideas or information that runs contrary to the group's take on a situation. The third category is concerned with pressures toward uniformity. The list of symptoms is presented in Table 8.1.

Janis (1982) argued that when many of the symptoms of groupthink are present, certain specifiable consequences are likely to result. Groups suffering from groupthink are likely to perform incomplete surveys of alternatives and of objectives. They are inclined to fail to examine risks of their preferred choice and also to fail to reexamine initially rejected alternatives. Their information search is likely to be poor, and the processing of information biased. Finally, groupthink groups are very unlikely to develop necessary contingency plans.

Janis believes that several antecedent conditions must be present for groupthink to occur. The first, of course, is the existence of a cohesive group. The second has to do with insulation of the group from other nongroup members who might possess important information. This insulation prevents groups from getting other opinions and information that could conflict with their own thinking.

The third ingredient, Janis (1982) asserted, is a lack of a tradition of impartial leadership: "In the absence of appropriate leadership traditions, the leader of a policy-making group will find it all too easy to use his or her power and prestige to influence the members of the group to approve of the policy alternative he or she prefers instead of encouraging them to engage in open inquiry or critical evaluation" (p. 176). Last, Janis pointed to the lack of norms requiring methodical procedures for decision making as an antecedent condition for groupthink. Such

TABLE 8.1
Symptoms of Groupthink

Type I: Overestimations of the group—Its power and morality

1. An illusion of invulnerability, shared by most or all members, which creates excessive optimism and encourages taking extreme risks.
2. An unquestioned belief in the group's inherent morality, inclining the members to ignore the ethical or moral consequences of the decision.

Type II: Closed-mindedness

3. Collective efforts to rationalize in order to discount warnings or other information that might lead the members to reconsider their assumptions before they recommit themselves to their past policy decisions.
4. Stereotyped views of enemy leaders as too evil to warrant genuine attempts to negotiate, or as too weak and stupid to counter whatever risky attempts are made to defeat their purposes.

Type III: Pressures toward uniformity

5. Self-censorship of deviations from the apparent group consensus, reflecting each member's inclination to minimize to himself the importance of his doubts and counterarguments.
6. A shared illusion of unanimity concerning judgments conforming to the majority view (partly resulting from self-censorship of deviations, augmented by the false assumption that silence means consent).
7. Direct pressure on any member who expresses strong arguments against any of the group's stereotypes, illusions, or commitments, making clear that this type of dissent is contrary to what is expected of all loyal members.
8. The emergence of self-appointed mindguards—members who protect the group from adverse information that might shatter their shared complacency about the effectiveness and morality of their decisions.

Note. From *Groupthink: Psychological Studies of Policy Decisions and Fiascoes* (2nd ed., pp. 174–175), by I. L. Janis, 1982, Boston, MA: Houghton Mifflin. Copyright 1982 by Houghton Mifflin Company. Reprinted with permission.

norms might require that people gather evidence using a particular system that presumably would work against biases.

Janis (1982) also noted that certain situational factors make groupthink more likely. High stress, extreme time pressure, and low feelings of self-esteem each might contribute to a tendency for groups to fall prey to groupthink.

Esser and Lindoerfer (1989) applied Janis' groupthink model to a governmental report issued following the space shuttle *Challenger* disaster in 1986. The authors identified 88 statements in the *Report of the Presidential Commission on the Space Shuttle Challenger Accident* that represented either positive or negative instances of the antecedents and consequences of the groupthink phenomenon as outlined by Janis (1982). They found twice as many positive as negative groupthink statements. Moreover, when they analyzed the number of instances relevant to groupthink as a function of time before the actual launch, they found that as the launch time grew closer, the ratio of positive to negative groupthink instances grew. The authors conclude that the evidence is "consistent with the notion that the decision to launch the *Challenger* involved groupthink" (p. 167).

However, other investigators have offered a less enthusiastic appraisal of the groupthink concept. Most of the evidence cited to support it comes from retrospective case studies of decision disasters, and the few experimental attempts to test the theory have rarely included all of the antecedent conditions Janis discussed. Aldag and Fuller (1993) suggested that more rigorous, impartial, and empirical testing is needed of the groupthink assumptions and predictions, and they present a more complex version of the model, known as the general group problem-solving model.

Accuracy of Group Versus Individual Decision Making

Janis' (1982) model of groupthink was derived from post hoc examination of political crises. One might make the argument that groupthink is confined to such types of decision-making contexts and that in other, noncrisis situations group decision making is superior to individual decision making. Of course, a test of this claim requires that we define what it means for one decision to be better or worse than another decision. Decisions can vary in creativity, in accuracy, in efficiency, in the degree to which those affected by the decision buy in to the solution, and all of these could be used as indices of decision quality.

Gigone and Hastie (1997) performed a meta-analysis comparing group to individual decision making, using the measure of accuracy. They found that in most of the studies they reviewed, groups' judgments were more accurate than the judgments of typical individuals, equally accurate with judgments of the mean group member's accuracy, and less accurate than the judgments of the most accurate group member. Research participants in these studies ranged from college students to expert loan officers; group size ranged from 3 to 8 members; and the types of decisions made ranged from prediction of course grades, prediction of which firms would go into bankruptcy, judging teacher salaries, or forecasting sales or weather.

By what mechanisms are group decisions made? Presumably individual group members first use their knowledge and background information to come to individual judgments. They bring these initial judgments to a group discussion, where information is shared and possibly critiqued or debated. During that discussion, members have the chance to revise their own judgments. After discussion, members presumably have a richer set of shared information from which to make a more informed decision. But this model makes several assumptions, among which is the important idea that different members of the group actually do share their information.

Information Sharing

Larson, Christensen, Abbot, and Franz (1996) carried out a series of studies examining the ways groups of decision makers share information. Three-person teams, each comprised of one resident (physicians with almost 3 years of postdoctoral clinical training), one intern (physicians nearing the end of their 1st year of post-doctoral clinical training), and one medical student (in the 3rd of 4 years of study) were formed. The team was given two hypothetical cases to diagnose. One concerned a 45-year-old woman brought to the emergency room after she fainted in her kitchen; the other concerned a 44-year-old man with blood in his urine.

These cases were constructed because the presenting symptoms could potentially have multiple causes, are fairly common, but do not have what the authors call "scripted diagnostic routines that every physician is taught" (Larson et al., 1996, p. 318). Moreover, the authors used a computerized medical expert system to generate other information and symptoms to make the cases realistically complex. Each member of the team viewed (separately) one 6-minute videotape showing the patient (portrayed by an actor) being interviewed by a male physician in an examining room in as realistic a depiction as possible.

Each case had three different videotapes made, and a different team member viewed each videotape. Some of the information conveyed by the patient was conveyed in all three videotapes; therefore, each team member shared that information. However, some information (unshared information) was unique to a particular videotape and thus to a particular team member. This was done to mimic the real-life situation that different group members typically bring different information to a decision-making task.

After team members viewed their videotapes individually, they met in a conference room to discuss the cases and come to a diagnosis. These conferences were videotaped, and coders took note of which pieces of information about the case were discussed and in which order.

Results showed that teams were much more likely to discuss the shared information than the unshared information. Seventy-six percent of the shared information (that is, information presented in all three videos of the same case) was raised in the conference, compared with only 64% of the unshared information (information presented in only one of the videos). Moreover, shared information was discussed earlier than unshared information, on average. The authors concluded that "open group discussion is a less than optimal means of pooling members' unshared information, even in teams of professional decision makers. Groups apparently have difficulty accessing the very information that discussion is presumed to elicit" (Larson et al., 1996, p. 327), namely, the unshared information.

Winquist and Larson (1998) noted that any time shared information points to a suboptimal alternative, there is a threat to rational decision making. In their study, the shared information given to all team members (in this case, undergraduate students asked to select a professor for a teaching award) pointed to one alternative, whereas unshared information (i.e., information given to only one team member) actually revealed another alternative as the most deserving of the award. These authors showed that those groups who pooled more of their unshared information made better decisions, a result replicated by Larson, Christensen, Franz, and Abbott (1998).

Coming to a Group Decision

When different individuals in a group favor different options, some process of coming to a final decision must be reached. Various means of doing this are possible, of course, depending on the procedure the group adopts, known as the decision rule (Barron, Kerr, & Miller, 1992). For example, juries typically must reach a unanimous decision to convict; the decision rule there is unanimity. Other groups might use a majority rules decision rule, or a two-thirds majority rules decision. Of course, if multiple decisions are on the agenda, then the order in which decisions get made plausibly could affect any particular decision's outcome. And the way in which individuals express their preference (e.g., voting for one alternative vs. rank ordering all alternatives) will also affect outcomes.

Most of the research done on decision rules, however, has focused on the relatively simple case of a group of people making a single decision with a finite number of outcomes. Consider, for example, the case of a six-person jury that needs to come to a unanimous decision of guilty or not guilty (or else be hung, or unable to come to consensus). Their initial individual views of the case—before group discussion—are called the initial splits, and the seven possibilities are presented in the leftmost columns of Table 8.2. All six jurors could believe the defendant to be guilty, in which case the initial split would be 6–0. Or five of them could believe the defendant guilty and one of them believe the defendant to be innocent, in which case the initial split would be 5–1.

A model originally formulated by Davis (1973) called the social decision scheme, or SDS model, attempted to show a link between these initial splits and final outcomes, given different decision rules (Stasser, 1999). Two possible decision rules are illustrated in Table 8.2. The first shows the probability of a particu-

TABLE 8.2
Some Social Decision Schemes

Initial Splits		Final Verdict				
		Majority Rules/Hung Otherwise			Proportionality	
Guilty	Not Guilty	Guilty	Not Guilty	Hung	Guilty	Not Guilty
6	0	1.00	0.00	0.00	1.00	0.00
5	1	1.00	0.00	0.00	0.83	0.17
4	2	1.00	0.00	0.00	0.67	0.33
3	3	0.00	0.00	1.00	0.50	0.50
2	4	0.00	1.00	0.00	0.33	0.67
1	5	0.00	1.00	0.00	0.17	0.83
0	6	0.00	1.00	0.00	0.00	1.00

Note. From *Group Process, Group Decision, Group Action* (p. 96), by R. S. Baron et al., 1992, Pacific Grove, CA: Brooks/Cole. Copyright 1992 by Open University Press. Adapted with permission.

lar verdict (i.e., guilty, not guilty, or hung jury) given the initial splits under a "majority rules" decision rule. Under this rule, the group always comes to a decision in line with the majority opinion of individuals under the initial split; only when individual opinion is evenly split does the jury hang.

A second possible decision rule is the proportionality rule, which says that the eventual group decision tracks the proportion of individuals who initially hold that view. Thus, if 83% of the jury members (five out of six) initially lean a certain way, then the eventual group decision will follow that leaning 83% of the time. Data from real juries has been reported that support both models (Barron, Kerr, & Miller, 1992; Kerr, 1981). Data from other studies also indicate that initial individual preferences are major determinants of group decisions (Kelly & Karau, 1999).

Kerr (1981) also studied the intermediate steps taken by groups, in this case mock juries of six-person groups asked to read and decide on one-page summaries of armed robbery cases. A group in which, at any point in the deliberations, four people were inclined to vote guilty, and two, not guilty, was somewhat more likely to move to a state in which the inclinations were 5–1 (guilty vs. not guilty) than to move to a state in which opinions were evenly divided. Said another way: "Group members were more likely to join a majority than to defect from one . . . and this drawing power increases with the size of the majority" (p. 690). Moreover, groups were more likely to shift toward acquitting a defendant than they were to shift toward convicting a defendant. As groups gained experience making decisions together, they were more able to shift individual views toward a group consensus.

The type of decision made also affects group outcomes. Laughlin, Kerr, Davis, Halff, and Marciniak (1975) had undergraduate participants perform a challenging intellectual test, the Terman Concept Mastery Test. After they finished the test alone, they were put into groups, ranging in size from 2 to 5, and asked to retake the test (participants in the control group retook the test alone). Results showed that the most commonly observed pattern of group decision making was one the authors called truth supported wins, wherein groups chose the correct answer if and only if one member advocated it and another member supported the first. A later study by Kirchler and Davis (1986) suggested that a truth wins model applies mostly to problems where a correct answer exists, and its correctness is manifest once it is seen. However, this model is less likely to occur on judgment decisions, such as selecting one of two candidates for a job, where no such obviously correct option exists. Power differences among individuals (e.g., differences in perceived expertise relative to the decision) also affect judgment decisions more than they affect intellective decisions.

The Role of Group Leaders

Although some groups are simply ad hoc, other groups, particularly those in continuing organizations such as workplaces, elect or appoint leaders to manage the work of the group. Social psychologists have tried to identify characteristics that would make a person a good leader but have often found that those characteristics depend on the task the group is undertaking and the circumstances surrounding them in facing that task (Sabini, 1992).

Conventional wisdom, and some psychological research, however, suggests that directive leadership can result in poor group process and poor decision-making outcomes for groups (Peterson, 1997). The term *directive leadership* refers to authoritarian leadership, wherein the leader exerts a lot of power and direction and manages the group with the proverbial iron fist. However, Peterson made a distinction between two types of directive leadership: outcome directiveness, in which a leader strongly advocates one particular option or alternative, and process directiveness, in which a leader does not advocate a position of her or his own but instead firmly pushes for discussion of all alternative ideas. His research showed that process directiveness was correlated with group members' rating the leader as effective (whether or not the leader was liked) and greater feelings of group confidence, better group process, and higher quality decisions. Outcome directiveness, in contrast, was unrelated to perceived leader effectiveness, was correlated with less group confidence, and was unrelated to the quality of the final decision reached.

Peterson (1997) gathered data from the laboratory, with groups of undergraduates engaging in a simulation of an international crisis, working with a confederate leader who adopted either a high or low level of outcome directiveness and either a high or low level of process directiveness. In a follow-up study, Peterson observed decision making of actual city council members from 11 cities throughout the San Francisco Bay area and replicated the laboratory results. He concludes that leaders can most beneficially affect group decision making by showing commitment to good process—that is, by encouraging all points of view to be heard and paying more attention to how decisions are made rather than what particular decisions are made.

ORGANIZATIONAL AND CULTURAL CONTEXTS FOR DECISIONS

Most research on decision making treats a decision as a "critical moment of final choice" (Langley, Mintzberg, Pitcher, Posada, & Saint-Macary, 1995). We tend to think of single decisions in isolation, made as a discrete and discernable series of steps. As psychologists, we adopt this framework as we interview research participants about their decision making.

However, especially in the context of organizational decision making, Langley et al. (1995) make the following point:

> "decision" and decision processes as decomposable elements tend to become mere figments of the researchers' conceptions, or artifacts of their methods. Or to use an even more graphic metaphor, if a decision is like a wave breaking over the shore—

that is, perhaps identifiable at some sort of climax—then tracing a decision process back into an organization becomes much like tracing the origin of a wave back into the ocean.

Langley et al. (1995) questioned the idea that organizations frequently or typically make decisions—that is, clear choices of actions. It may be more frequent, they offered, that individuals in organizations take little steps and make small commitments that coalesce into a policy, without any series of smaller explicit decisions being made.

Langley et al. (1995) noted that in organizations, decisions can be linked in multiple ways. One way is sequentially—a decision to adopt one policy may require a later decision about how best to implement it. Various types of sequential linkages among decisions exist. A *nesting* linkage, for example, is when a major decision involves one or more minor decisions. For example, your decision to buy a new car might necessitate a decision on where to obtain financing, which might further entail a decision about how much money you wish to have financed. A *snowballing* linkage occurs when you make a series of decisions, the first relatively minor, but each succeeding one more important that the last. A *recurrence* linkage occurs when the same type of decision is repeatedly encountered.

Decisions can also be linked precursively: where one decision changes the array of future decisions. Thus, a decision to locate a manufacturing facility in one locale rather than another potentially opens up and closes off other sets of decisions. So, for example, an *evoking* linkage may introduce new problems or opportunities; a *preempting* linkage means that one decision makes other decisions moot or irrelevant; a *learning* linkage means that experience with one set of decisions causes the decision maker to draw on his learning in making future decisions, both in that domain as well as others. Finally, decisions can be linked laterally, if they share resources or a common context. A manager allocating 50% of his budget to one project will have fewer resources to allocate to other projects.

Instead of talking about and focusing on single decisions, Langley et al. (1995) wondered if it would be more productive to think about issue streams—that is, related series of decisions that address a common issue. Organizations deal with webs of issues, they argued, that can be represented as networks of interconnected issues that evolve dynamically over time.

The approach that a group takes to decision making may also be influenced by cultural factors. Many of the models previously presented in this book probably apply best to Western cultures, with an emphasis on individuals and individual activity, great freedom of choice, and ideological values emphasizing short-term as opposed to long-term gains, the preference for risk and adventure over caution, and the need to appeal to the majority of people within the decision-making group (Mann et al., 1998).

Mann and his colleagues have examined differences in decision making between Western, individualistic cultures (e.g., the United States, Australia, New

Zealand) and East Asian, group-oriented cultures (Mann et al., 1998; Radford, Mann, Ohta, & Nakene, 1991; Radford, Mann, Ohta, & Nakane, 1993). As expected, Japanese students were more likely to report involving others in making decisions, whereas Australian students were more likely to be self-reliant (Radford et al., 1991). However, these studies relied on students' responses to a questionnaire about how they typically made decisions, not to studies of actual decision-making behavior. Thus, although the results are suggestive, their applicability to real-life decisions awaits further tests.

In this chapter, we have seen that groups making decisions encounter challenges in this activity that individual decision makers do not. We have also seen that simply having a group make a decision does not guarantee improvement in decision quality. Thus, many heads are not always better than one and may in some instances be worse. Conversely, under certain circumstances (e.g., a group leader committed to process directiveness, a group norm encouraging open expression of diverse views—processes that work specifically against groupthink), better decision making may be possible. Once again, the challenge for researchers will be to identify what types of decisions and what types of groups can lead to improvement.

Groups are influenced, of course, by the cultural values in which they are embedded. We need to understand much more about how local and global cultures have an impact on decision making, and these questions are beginning to be asked.

Improving
Decision Making

Several months ago, I was teaching the final class of my sophomore level Thinking, Reasoning, and Decision Making psychology class. Our topic was improving these cognitive skills. David, an outspoken student, raised his hand at the beginning of the class. "So," he asked, "since you study all this stuff, does that mean you never make any bad decisions? Or have you given up hope that anyone can ever make a good decision?"

I'd like the first answer to be "yes" (i.e., it's true that I no longer make any bad decisions). Alas, many of the ways decision making go wrong, I am convinced, are built into our habitual ways of processing information. Without constant vigilance, these sources of error creep in. And constant vigilance is tiring. So, yes, I make my share of bad decisions, too.

Happily, the answer to the second question is also "no." Although not all my decisions are good, many of them are better, I think, than they would have been if I did not know about the literature in decision making. I think, perhaps optimistically, that education and training can help people make some better decisions, and in this chapter I'll describe some things that I think help.

IMPEDIMENTS TO GOOD
DECISION MAKING

Throughout the book, we've seen examples of decision making that don't go well. We've also seen, in chapters 2–5, that the process of decision making can be decomposed into several components: setting goals, gathering information, structuring information, and making a final choice. Although many laboratory studies of decision making have focused exclusively on the final component, there is reason to believe that the first three components are at least as, and possibly more, important in understanding real-life decision making.

Along the way in the book, we have seen several different proposals for what specific biases or problems account for decision-making shortcomings. Here, I classify these different proposals into three major categories: having unclear values and goals, biased information processing, and affective reactions to the state of doubt.

Unclear Values, Goals, and Priorities

In chapter 1, I reviewed various definitions of what makes a decision good or rational. Most of those definitions had to do with making choices that further one's own goals and objectives. This assumes, of course, that people are clear on what their own values and goals are.

However, educators and counselors would be quick to point out that people are not always in touch with what they really want. In fact, many popular self-help books (e.g., Covey et al., 1994; McGraw, 1999) are aimed at helping people discover just what their core values and goals really are. Without this knowledge, decisions made will not be guided by one's values. Covey et al. (1994) explained it this way:

> Our struggle to put first things first can be characterized by the contrast between two powerful tools that direct us: the clock and the compass. The clock represents our commitments, appointments, schedules, goals, activities—what we do with, and how we *manage* our time. The compass represents our vision, values, principles, mission, conscience, direction—what we feel is important and how we *lead* our time.
>
> The struggle comes when we sense a gap between the clock and the compass—when what we do doesn't contribute to what is most important in our lives.
>
> For some of us, the pain of the gap is intense. We can't seem to walk our talk. We feel trapped, controlled by other people or situations. We're always responding to crises . . . putting out fires and never making the time to know what would make a difference. We feel our lives are being lived for us. . . .
>
> Some of us feel empty. We've defined happiness solely in terms of professional or financial achievement, and we find that our "success" did not bring us the satisfaction we thought it would. We've painstakingly climbed the "ladder of success" rung by rung—the diploma, the late nights, the promotions—only to discover as we reached the top rung that the ladder is leaning against the wrong wall. (Covey et al., 1994, pp. 19–20).

How could we not be clear on our own goals? To understand this, it is worth reflecting on the fact that goals can and do vary in many dimensions, as we saw in chapter 2. For our current purposes, Gollwitzer (1996) made an important distinction, between a wish and a binding goal. A wish is some sort of desire that may or may not be feasible, may or may not conflict with other wishes or goals, and may or may not, ultimately, be desirable. For example, I may have a fleeting wish to be a daredevil skier, even though such an occupation doesn't fit well with my current one, which I very much enjoy, nor with my own desire for thrills, adventure, and danger, which my friends would tell you is relatively quite low.

A binding goal is a wish to which a person has made a commitment and has some sort of plan for implementing. In one study, Gollwitzer (1996) found that people who were asked to think about a specific means of implementing a goal made much more progress toward it than did people merely asked to reflect on the goal's desirability or to think about alternative ways to implement it. He explains that having implementation plans helps people keep from being distracted from the goal, makes them more able to mobilize effort toward a goal, and allows them to resume pursuit of a goal even when temporarily sidetracked.

If people are not clear about whether something is merely a wish or a binding goal, then there will be difficulty in rationally figuring out how much effort ought to be devoted to the pursuit of that goal. Prioritization of goals becomes very difficult and, perhaps, impossible. In turn, this allows for less important goals to overwhelm more important ones. For example, if you are dieting, the goal of losing weight and the goal of eating something high in calories and fat (and therefore yummy) often are in conflict. If you want to fulfill the first goal, you'll have to resist the second.

Another way that having clear goals in mind can affect decision making has to do with habitual choices. Behaviors that are repeated frequently become habitual, meaning that they require less effort and thought to be carried out (Aarts, Verplanken, & Van Knippenberg, 1998). Such practice with making a particular choice can lead to that selection becoming ingrained. Habitual choices involve cognitive shortcuts, and it tends to be easier just to continue the habit than to think through whether or not that choice continues to serve one's needs.

So, for example, a worker who is unhappy (but not desperately so) in his or her current job might continue to work at it, out of habit, rather than seriously contemplating alternatives, such as changing jobs or restructuring the current one. Having a clear goal in mind, such as "Find a position that gives me satisfaction and enjoyment," might provide the incentive to the worker to not settle for less than what he or she really wants.

Finally, having clear goals in mind might help decision makers avoid always making what Janis and Mann (1977) called "incremental" decision making: making a series of small changes that constitute improvements over the status quo but may never quite achieve a desired objective. For example, these authors assert that many occupational choices are not made with a clear career goal in mind but rather in incremental steps:

> A man or woman starts off getting a certain type of job training and then finds it more and more difficult to switch to another type of career. The person anticipates social disapproval for "wasting" his training, which tends to increase with each increment of training or advancement. And, of course, he is also deterred from changing by his own sense of prior investment of time, effort, and money in the direction he has already moved. (p. 35)

A person with a clear sense of her own goals would be more able to resist the pull of sunk costs and more able to realize that the path she is traveling on is not one destined to help her fulfill her life plans and dreams.

Biased Information Processing

A second major way that things go wrong in decision making has to do with our cognitive architecture, the way we as human beings appear to be wired to process information. Many times our ability to take in and interpret information stands us in very good stead. However, as the work of so many researchers has shown, there are a long list of ways that our natural way of approaching decisions isn't sufficient to make rational decisions.

Let us quickly review some of the heuristics and biases presented in chapter 3: First, people frequently judge the frequency or probability of an event by the ease with which examples can be constructed or brought to mind (availability heuristic). They expect random processes to always generate results that appear random, and they pay more attention to vivid case studies than they do to base rate statistical information representing large numbers of cases (representativeness heuristic). The way a question or problem is phrased often dramatically affects people's choices or preferences (framing effect). People perceive, interpret, and remember data that supports their initial ideas (confirmation bias) and see patterns of associations that may not truly be there, if the association makes sense in terms of their current thinking (illusory correlation). People are also reluctant to abandon a plan or course of action once they have invested resources in it (sunk cost effect).

Another aspect of decision making found in many research studies concerns overconfidence—that is, a tendency to place too much trust in one's own ability to gather enough information or to think of enough consequences. People are much more likely to have inappropriately high regard for their performance than they are to be inappropriately critical of it. The problem with overconfidence, of course, is that it keeps people from adopting strategies or tactics that might combat or address common decisional biases.

What explains all these biases? Why aren't people better at information processing? Cognitive psychologists from diverse theoretical camps agree: People have a limited capacity for doing cognitive tasks. There's only so much information we can attend to at one time, perceive and interpret, hold onto in short-term memory (Miller, 1956).

Given these capacity limits, people need to adopt techniques to manage information—to be able to focus, to whittle down the potentially overwhelming amount of incoming information to some manageable level. That often means using shortcuts, quick-and-dirty rules of thumb, rather than always engaging in complicated methods of analysis.

Arkes (1991) made this point very clearly:

> Suppose a person adopts a quick and dirty strategy to solve a problem. Because it is quick, it is easy to execute. This is a benefit. Because it is dirty, it results in more errors than a more meticulous strategy. This is a cost. Although the choice of this

strategy may result in fewer correct answers compared with the other strategy, this cost may be outweighed by the benefit of time and effort saved. (p. 487)

Arkes (1991) also asserted that many biases in judgment stem from the nature of the way our memory systems work. To explain this idea, I will first need to talk a little bit about semantic memory, that is, stored memories of our knowledge, such as addition and subtraction facts, definitions of words, geographic and historical facts, and the like.

Research on semantic memory has repeatedly demonstrated the existence of a phenomenon known as semantic priming (Neely, 1990). The idea is this: If you are shown the word *bread* very quickly, you will be primed, or made ready, to recognize or see words that are semantically related, such as *butter* or *wheat*. The effects are small, on the order of a few hundred milliseconds, but very reliable. The effects are also automatic—they don't depend on your conscious participation or willful efforts. The theoretical explanation is that semantic memory operates according to the principle of spreading activation—that is, when one node in semantic memory is activated, that activation spreads to other related nodes.

Arkes (1991) believes that these principles help to explain the existence of several decision-making biases. For example, consider overconfidence and confirmation bias:

> For example, suppose I am asked whether Oslo or Leningrad is further north, and I answer, "Oslo." Now I am asked to assign a confidence level to my answer. To complete this task, I search my semantic memory for the information that made Oslo seem like the correct answer. Items pertaining to Oslo's nearby glaciers and fjords are much more strongly cued than information concerning Oslo's summer warmth. The evidence I am most likely to retrieve thus is an unrepresentative sample of all available evidence, and my confidence is thereby inappropriately inflated. (p. 489)

Arkes (1991) also listed another feature of our cognitive architecture he believes underlies the use of other heuristics. This is the fact that we have nonlinear responses to stimuli. This rather abstract concept is depicted in Fig. 9.1. Specifically, when two stimuli are in the middle range of our experience, we see the differences between them as slightly bigger than they actually are. However, at the extreme ends of our experience, we are undersensitive to differences between stimuli.

Arkes (1991) related this law of psychophysics to the sunk cost effect as follows:

> Persons who have already invested substantial amounts and who have not yet realized compensatory returns are at Point B in [Fig. 9.1]. Persons in that situation are not very sensitive for further losses; a small subsequent expenditure of funds will therefore cause negligible psychological disutility. Hence, such persons are willing to "throw good money after bad" in a desperate attempt to recoup their sunk cost, even though such behavior may be irrational. If a particular project is a poor idea, the fact that it has already wasted a lot of money does not make it a better idea. (p. 490)

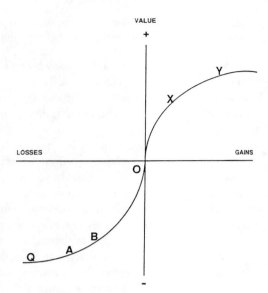

FIG. 9.1.   The value function of prospect theory. From "Costs and Benefits
of Judgment Errors: Implications for
Debiasing," by H. R. Arkes, 1991, *Psychological Bulletin, 110,* p. 490. Copyright 1991 by the Econometric Society.
Reprinted with permission.

Affective Reactions to the State of Doubt

John Dewey, a famous American philosopher of education, distinguished any ordinary kind of thinking (including daydreaming, mind wandering, idle navel gazing)
from a particularly important kind of thinking called reflective thinking, which he
defined as "active, persistent, and careful consideration of any belief or supposed
form of knowledge in the light of the grounds that support it and the further conclusions to which it tends" (1933, p. 9). He believed that such thinking had two
stages: first, "a state of doubt, hesitation, perplexity, mental difficulty, in which
thinking originates," and second, "an act of searching, hunting, inquiring, to find
the material that will resolve the doubt, settle and dispose of the perplexity" (p. 12.)

In theory, the state of doubt is an important one not to rush out of. To make
good decisions, it seems likely that we may need to stay in doubt for longer than
might feel comfortable, while we gather information, entertain different possibilities, revise our thinking, integrate various opinions, structure the decision, and
come to a choice. Said another way, rushing impulsively to a premature decision
can lead to irrationality and poor outcomes (Baron, 1985).

The problem is, for many, that the state of doubt can be a quite unpleasant one.
I've seen this most regularly with undergraduate students I advise. They are asked
to declare a college major the final term of their sophomore year and in fact are not
allowed to do so earlier (the theory being that if they aren't allowed to declare a
major, they will stay more open-minded). You would think that my college's policy would take a lot of the pressure off of making this decision for incoming 1st-
year students. But you would be very wrong.

Many entering 1st-year students that I advise either announce with great confidence that they already know their major—biology or English, for example—or their career path—premed or prelaw, for example. Despite the fact that statistically probably only about half end up with the major or program they announce, these students project an air of confidence about them, however misplaced.

A second set of students, and perhaps most of those I advise, do not have the luxury of feeling so settled (and so smug). These are the students that ask if they can close my office door while we talk and "admit" (often while looking at their shoes) that they don't yet have a major finally selected. It seems that a few are hoping that I'll just announce one to them ("Hmmm. Well, having known you for all of 10 minutes, I declare you to be an economics major.") or that some other simple method for selection can be found.

As the students progress to their sophomore year, the decision becomes more frantic, and the undecided students become more ashamed. Why can't they just pick? Students from the first, confident group can experience more stress when they find out that their intended major doesn't interest them or doesn't fit with their career goals or their self-image. And then they feel they have to scramble to find a correct choice (as if only one major would be correct, and all the others would be incorrect).

Some percentage of students, and I can't be sure how large it is, seems to grab at majors, just to have the decision over with. The choice seems to be driven less by careful reflection, information integration, and selection, and more by a frantic need to feel the relief that comes from completing a difficult chore.

Staying in the state of doubt doesn't feel very good. People in it feel indecisive, as if they are waffling and not making progress. It may be that we need more explicit support for the idea that being an effective decision maker doesn't mean making rapid decisions with great certainty, but rather, the slow, careful, deliberate gathering and processing of information.

DECISION-MAKING AIDS AND TRAINING

In previous chapters, I've talked a bit about possible ways of addressing some decision-making shortcomings and biases. Here, we'll consider some of these and other ideas in more detail.

The Balance-Sheet Method

Janis and Mann (1977), in a classic work on decision making, offered seven criteria by which the effectiveness of decision making can be assessed. These criteria are presented in Table 9.1. Failure to meet any single criteria exposes a decision maker to risks of unanticipated setbacks and later regret. The more criteria that are unfulfilled, the greater the risks of making decisions irrationally or ineffectively.

TABLE 9.1
Seven Criteria of Effective Decision Making

The decision maker, to the best of his ability and within his information processing capabilities:
1. Thoroughly canvasses a wide range of alternative courses of action;
2. Surveys the full range of objectives to be fulfilled and the values implicated by the choice;
3. Carefully weighs whatever he knows about the costs and risks of negative consequences, as well as the positive consequences, that could flow from each alternative;
4. Intensively searches for new information relevant to further evaluation of the alternatives;
5. Correctly assimilates and takes account of any new information or expert judgment to which he is exposed, even when the information or judgment does not support the course of action he initially prefers;
6. Reexamines the positive and negative consequences of all known alternatives, including those originally regarded as unacceptable, before making a final choice;
7. Makes detailed provisions for implementing or executing the chosen course of action, with special attention to contingency plans that might be required if various known risks were to materialize.

Note. From *Decision Making: A Psychological Analysis of Conflict, Choice, and Commitment* (p. 11), by I. L. Janis and L. Mann, 1977, New York: The Free Press. Copyright 1977 by Simon & Schuster. Reprinted with permission.

Many of these criteria address the idea of thinking of a variety of possible consequences of different alternatives. Given what we know about information processing limitations, however, it is clear that some method is needed to help a person avoid being swamped by too many pieces of information. The balance-sheet procedure advocated by Janis and Mann (1977) provides just such a method.

Fig. 9.2 depicts a blank balance sheet. A decision maker is asked to consider, for each alternative under consideration, the possible gains and losses to himself or herself, as well as to others, both tangible and intangible (the latter having to do with social approval).

The balance-sheet technique has no special magic; it works (to the degree that it does) to slow people down, to get them to avoid making fast, unexamined decisions, and to focus them on the wide variety of consequences different alternatives have. By writing the information down, this technique also helps them to manage information overload and to keep track of more information than could be handled simultaneously by our limited-capacity processor. Thus, a balance-sheet procedure may help people keep alive more than one or two alternatives at a time (Janis & Mann, 1977).

We've seen examples of other kinds of decision aids that are structurally similar to the balance sheet. Consider Fig. 4.1 or Table 4.1. Both present specifically tailored formats for structuring a specific decision. The first presents a decision maker with a ready list of factors to consider; the second is more open-ended. However, both of these methods share with the balance-sheet method the feature that the number of alternatives considered is left open to the decision maker.

The more open-ended the procedure, the more that is left up to the decision maker's thoroughness in imagining alternatives, costs, benefits, consequences, and the likelihood of occurrence. Thus, although such procedures encourage more reflective thought, they don't guarantee it. A very impulsive decision maker will be expected to fill out the sheet less thoroughly than a very reflective decision maker, although this prediction, and the magnitude of the difference, remains to be empirically tested.

	Positive Anticipations +	Negative Anticipations −
1. Tangible gains + and losses − for SELF		
2. Tangible gains + and losses − for OTHERS		
3. Self-approval + or self-disapproval −		
4. Social approval + or disapproval −		

FIG. 9.2. The balance sheet grid. From *Decision Making: A Psychological Analysis of Conflict, Choice, and Commitment* (p. 407), by I. L. Janis and L. Mann, 1977, New York: The Free Press. Copyright 1977 by Simon & Schuster. Reprinted with permission.

Koriat, Lichentstein, and Fischhoff (1980) asked participants in a laboratory study to do a very similar thing: list reasons for and against each alternative prior to making a decision. This had the effect of markedly diminishing their overconfidence. Apparently, taking the time to imagine alternatives brings to mind reasons why one's first impulse might not be correct.

A related technique is to have people imagine their construal of an alternative —that is, to explicitly consider the details of a situation in which they imagine an alternative being chosen, then to explicitly consider alternative construals (Griffin, Dunning, & Ross, 1990). Even having people imagine any plausible alternative for an event will be sufficient to debias them against overconfidence (Hirt & Markman, 1995). So, for example, a doctor diagnosing a disease is likely to be less overconfident if she imagines not just the likely consequences of the first diagnosis but those of any other alternative, even a remotely possible one. As the doctor imagines even remotely plausible possibilities, she becomes more able to detach from seeing the first choice as the only choice.

Training in the Use of Specific Procedures

What about specific training? Can specific, formal instruction on some of the theories of decision making actually take hold and influence people's decision making in their everyday lives? Although research into this question is just beginning, there is growing evidence that at least sometimes the answer is yes.

Larrick, Morgan, and Nisbett (1990) reported on two studies that addressed this question. In both cases, they were focused on whether the teaching of cost–benefit rules would influence people's later self-reported behaviors when they made decisions. They concentrated on three specific principles: The first was the *greatest net benefit* principle, which states that "the action with the greatest positive difference between the total benefit and the total cost of its outcome should be chosen from the set of possible actions." The second, which the authors called the *sunk cost* principle, stated that "only future benefits and costs (not those already purchased) should be considered when making a choice." Finally, the *opportunity cost* principle reminds people that "A cost of undertaking a given course of action is foregoing the expected net benefits associated with other courses of action" (Larrick et al., 1990, p. 280).

All of these principles are ones well articulated in the field of economics. So, in a first study, Larrick et al. (1990) compared professors of economics with professors of biology, art history, and romance languages at the University of Michigan. All groups were highly educated, but only the first had specific training in these three principles.

Larrick et al. (1990) gave the professors a questionnaire concerning issues relevant to the University of Michigan that embodied the three principles. They also asked them to describe whether, in their own lives, they had discontinued activities after paying a sunk cost, dropped a pursuit (e.g., a research project) that was not working out, realized the opportunity costs of their own time use, and so on. Results showed that on almost all questions, economists were much more likely to reason, and report personal decisions, in line with the three principles than were all other groups of professors. The authors concluded: "Economics thus is a system of rules of choice that is practiced by its adherents as well as preached" (p. 366).

Of course, this study doesn't prove that it is the training in economics that affected the choices. An alternative explanation is that people who naturally make decisions this way are drawn to study economics in the first place. So Larrick et al. (1990) performed two other studies in which they trained undergraduate students in the use of the principles, then followed up later to see whether the effects persisted.

In the first study, participants were trained on the sunk cost principle, then tested. Results showed that training made people reason more normatively, even when the test problems differed in content from the training examples. In a follow-up study, a group of participants were first trained on principles including the sunk cost principle. They were contacted by telephone 4 to 6 weeks later, purportedly from an independent consumer opinion survey firm. Questions in the survey addressed whether or not participants made use of the sunk cost principle in their own decisions, as well as their ability to reason about campus issues involving sunk costs. Results showed an effect of training: Participants who had received training were more likely than those who had not to reason in accordance with normative principles and to report the use of the principles in their own decision making.

Other research has shown that training can help people identify and use other decision-making principles. For example, Fong, Krantz, and Nisbett (1986) showed that people can be trained to use the law of large numbers (i.e., the idea that large samples will be less likely to yield discrepant results from a population than will small samples). This research was replicated and extended with samples of children from high school and middle school (Kosonen & Winne, 1995) and with other samples of undergraduates (Nisbett, 1993). Nisbett et al. (1983), in fact, asserted that people have intuitive and abstract versions of some statistical rules, such as the law of large numbers, and that they use these rules correctly when the problem they are facing cues them to do so.

Obtaining Feedback

Another way to improve decision making is to give people feedback on their performance when they make decisions (Arkes, 2001). Too often, we don't have accurate information about how well our decision making works. Some decisions that are made poorly turn out just fine—I chose my undergraduate college, for example, because the campus was so pretty and lucked out that it just so happened to be a wonderful institution. At the same time, some very good decisions turn out poorly because of chance factors. One can do a great deal of research on great vacation spots, for example, but have the idyllic resort setting you've chosen just happen to be hit by a hurricane the week you happen to be there.

The point here is that the outcome of a decision isn't always a good measure of whether the decision was made well. We don't often have good feedback on whether or not our decisions were made rationally as opposed to whether or not they turned out to our liking. And our memories for our performances are quite likely to be distorted, just the way our memories are for other information. Moreover, we have a vested interest in seeing ourselves as good decision makers, and thus memories of good decisions might be more available than are memories of poor decisions. In turn, this is likely to make us more confident in our decision-making abilities than we have a rational right to be.

Arkes (in press) notes that weather forecasters and expert bridge players have both been found to show excellent correspondence between the accuracy of their predictions (or bids) and their confidence in those predictions (Keren, 1987; Murphy & Winkler, 1984). This result is in stark contrast to the typical finding that people's confidence is unrelated to, and usually far above, their accuracy. Arkes believes that the reason for these two groups' superior performance is twofold: One, they make explicit, public predictions, and two, they receive immediate feedback on those predictions.

In everyday life, we are seldom put in the position of having to make what Arkes (in press) calls an official prediction. We make a decision, and after the outcome is known, we tell others something like "I was pretty sure that would happen." However, much of the time our recall of our predictions is very likely to be wrong and tainted by hindsight bias. Thus, our intuitions frequently tell us that most of our predictions come true, when it is far more likely that far fewer of our predictions are in fact accurate. We just don't keep formal track.

Moreover, few everyday life decisions provide immediate feedback or crystal clear feedback. For example, suppose that you choose a college that isn't the absolutely best choice you could make. In such a situation, you may well find yourself scouting out an appropriate niche in that setting and finding the resources you need to make the best of the situation—and that best might be quite good.

A third problem with feedback is that, unless it is glowingly positive, few of us really welcome it. I've worked for people who, when told of morale problems in the organization, greet the news with ranting and yelling and pouting and sulking. Pretty soon, everyone else in the organization gets the message that no feedback is preferable to negative feedback. In the long run, however, the organizational leader misses out on important information.

The implication of all of this is that feedback is important. To improve on decision making, people should keep explicit, written track of their performance, making explicit (written) predictions before the fact, then comparing outcomes to predictions and explicitly analyzing what makes decisions go right and go wrong.

QUESTIONS AND ISSUES FOR FURTHER RESEARCH

In this book, I have covered a lot of ground. I hope I have convinced you that researchers have much of use to say about how people make decisions and how those decisions can be improved. The last few decades have yielded hundreds of studies that have addressed these issues in substantive and practical ways.

At the same time, existing research has raised several other issues and questions that are left for future exploration. To fully understand everyday decision making (a prerequisite for trying to improve it), we will need to have these inquiries undertaken.

First, the field needs to develop research methods that allow the study of actual decision making in the field, the office, the home, the school, the store, the hospital, the courtroom, or whatever the natural habitat of the decision is. Investigators need to know how to elicit the thinking that people engage in "on line"—that is, while they are actually undertaking the process.

Most of the remaining pressing questions in the field, in my opinion, are the ones we covered in chapters 6 through 8: the ways in which the basic decision-making processes are affected by individual differences in the decision maker(s).

We need to understand much more about the making of different kinds of decisions. I believe the field needs more in-depth case studies of people making actual decisions that are important to them so that psychologists can create a taxonomy of types of decisions.

We also need to understand more about how different people approach decision-making tasks. Specifically, do people with different decision-making styles set different goals? Or set similar goals but in different ways? How does style affect the way that they acquire information or evaluate it? Do years of education or type of education (e.g., field of specialization) have strong effects, and if so, what are these? Are there differences in decision making as a function of broader personality traits, as a function of ability differences, or both? Do these individual differences arise as a function of different developmental stages or phases? Are experts likely or able to perform different aspects of decision making differently, and if so, what aspects of practice allow these differences to emerge? These important questions are just beginning to receive attention.

Much more research is needed on group decision making to discover how it is similar to, and different from, individual decision making. How important are individual styles or traits or abilities when a decision is made by a group? How similar are the processes involved? Because many important decisions are made (at least nominally) by groups—school boards, city councils, or trustees, for example —we need to know more about these processes.

Finally, we need more information about how decision making as a cognitive process is shaped by the cultural context in which it occurs. Are basic components

of the process different from one culture to the next? How much of a contribu-
tion does cultural setting make to the way a decision is formulated, structured,
and made?

Decision making is a crucially important cognitive process. I hope this book
has convinced you of that assertion and provided motivation for you to examine
your own decision making more carefully, critically, and thoroughly. I hope it has
also awakened your interest and excitement in following developments in a very
active research field. Much is known about human decision making and much
remains to explore.

References

Aarts, H., Verplanken, B., & Van Knippenberg, A. (1998). Predicting behavior from actions in the past: Repeated decision making or a matter of habit? *Journal of Applied Social Psychology, 28,* 1355–1374.

Abdul-Muhmin, A. G. (1999). Contingent decision behavior: Effect of number of alternatives to be selected on consumers' decision processes. *Journal of Consumer Psychology, 8,* 91–111.

Agnoli, F. (1991). Development of judgmental heuristics and logical reasoning: Training counteracts the representativeness heuristic. *Cognitive Development, 6,* 195–217.

Ajzen, I. (1996). The social psychology of decision making. In E. T. Higgins & A. W. Kruglanski (Eds.), *Social psychology: Handbook of basic principles* (pp. 297–325). New York: Guilford.

Aldag, R. J., & Fuller, S. R. (1993). Beyond fiasco: A reappraisal of the groupthink phenomenon and a new model of group decision processes. *Psychological Bulletin, 113,* 533–552.

Arkes, H. R. (1989). Principles in judgment/decision making research pertinent to legal proceedings. *Behaviors Sciences and the Law, 7,* 429–456.

Arkes, H. R. (1991). Costs and benefits of judgment errors: Implications for debiasing. *Psychological Bulletin, 110,* 486–498.

Arkes, H. R. (1996). The psychology of waste. *Journal of Behavioral Decision Making, 9,* 213–224.

Arkes, H. R. (2001). Overconfidence in judgmental forecasting. In J. S. Armstrong (Ed.), *Principles of forecasting handbook* (pp. 495–516). Boston: Kluwer.

Arkes, H. R., & Ayton, P. (1999). The sunk cost and Concorde effects: Are humans less rational than lower animals? *Psychological Bulletin, 125,* 591–600.

Arkes, H. R., & Blumer, C. (1985). The psychology of sunk cost. *Organizational Behavior and Human Decision Processes, 35,* 124–140.

Arora, N. K., & McHorney, C. A. (2000). Patient preference for medical decision making: Who really wants to participate? *Medical Care, 38,* 335–341.

Austin, J. T., & Vancouver, J. B. (1996). Goal constructs in psychology: Structure, process, and content. *Psychological Bulletin, 120,* 338–375.

Baddeley, A. (1993). Working memory and conscious awareness. In A. F. Collins, S. E. Gathercole, M. A. Morris, & P. E. Morris (Eds.), *Theories of memory* (pp. 11–28). Hillsdale, NJ: Lawrence Erlbaum Associates.

Bandura, A. (1989). Human agency in social cognitive theory. *American Psychologist, 44,* 1175–1184.

Baron, J. (1985). *Rationality and intelligence.* Cambridge, UK: Cambridge University Press.

Baron, J. (1994). *Thinking and deciding* (2nd ed.). Cambridge, UK: Cambridge University Press.

Baron, J., Granato, L., Spranca, M., & Teubal, E. (1993). Decision-making biases in children and early adolescents: Exploratory studies. *Merrill-Palmer Quarterly, 39,* 22–46.

Baron, R. S., Kerr, N. L., & Miller, N. (1992). *Group process, group decision, group action.* Pacific Grove, CA: Brooks/Cole.

Bastardi, A., & Shafir, E. (1998). On the pursuit and misuse of useless information. *Journal of Personality and Social Psychology, 75,* 19–32.

155

Bastardi, A., & Shafir, E. (2001). Nonconsequential reasoning and its consequences. *Current Directions in Psychological Science, 9,* 216–219.

Beach, L. R. (1993). Broadening the definition of decision making: The role of prechoice screening of options. *Psychological Science, 4,* 215–220.

Beach, L. R. (Ed.). (1998). *Image theory: Theoretical and empirical foundations.* Mahwah, NJ: Lawrence Erlbaum Associates.

Beach, L. R., & Mitchell, T. R. (1987). Image theory: Principles, goals, and plans in decision making. *Acta Psychologica, 66,* 201–220.

Beach, L. R., & Mitchell, T. R. (1998). The basics of image theory. In L. R. Beach (Ed.), *Image theory: Theoretical and empirical foundations* (pp. 3–18). Mahwah, NJ: Lawrence Erlbaum Associates.

Beach, L. R., & Potter, R. E. (1992). The pre-choice screening of options. *Acta Psychologica, 81,* 115–126.

Berzonsky, M. D., & Ferrari, J. R. (1996). Identity orientation and decisional strategies. *Personality and Individual Differences, 20,* 597–606.

Beyth-Marom, R., Austin, L., Fischhoff, B., Palmgren, C., & Jacobs-Quadrel, M. (1993). Perceived consequences of risky behaviors: Adults and adolescents. *Developmental Psychology, 29,* 549–563.

Blustein, D. L., & Phillips, S. D. (1990). Relation between ego identity statuses and decision-making styles. *Journal of Counseling Psychology, 37,* 160–168.

Bornstein, B. H. (1998). From compassion to compensation: The effect of injury severity on mock jurors' liability judgments. *Journal of Applied Social Psychology, 28,* 1477–1502.

Brown, J. E., & Mann, L. (1990). The relationship between family structure and process variables and adolescent decision making. *Journal of Adolescence, 13,* 25–37.

Buehler, R., Griffin, D., & Ross, M. (1994). Exploring the "planning fallacy": Why people underestimate their task completion times. *Journal of Personality and Social Psychology, 67,* 366–381.

Byrnes, J. P. (1998). *The nature and development of decision making: A self-regulation model.* Mahwah, NJ: Lawrence Erlbaum Associates.

Byrnes, J. P., & McClenny, B. (1994). Decision-making in young adolescents and adults. *Journal of Experimental Child Psychology, 58,* 359–388.

Byrnes, J. P., Miller, D. C., & Reynolds, M. (1999). Learning to make good decisions: A self-regulation perspective. *Child Development, 70,* 1121–1140.

Cacioppo, J. T., & Petty, R. E. (1982). The need for cognition. *Journal of Personality and Social Psychology, 42,* 116–131.

Carroll, A., Durkin, K., Hattie, J., & Houghton, S. (1997). Goal setting among adolescents: A comparison of delinquent, at-risk, and not-at-risk youth. *Journal of Educational Psychology, 89,* 441–450.

Carver, C. S. (1996). Some ways in which goals differ and some implications of those differences. In P. M. Gollwitzer & J. A. Bargh (Eds.), *The psychology of action* (pp. 645–672). New York: Guilford.

Chapman, G. B. (1996). Expectations and preferences for sequences of health and money. *Organizational Behavior and Human Decision Processes, 67,* 59–75.

Chapman, G. B., Nelson, N., & Hier, D. B. (1999). Familiarity and time preferences: Decision making about treatments for migraine headaches and Crohn's disease. *Journal of Experimental Psychology: Applied, 5,* 17–34.

Chapman, L. J. (1967). Illusory correlation in observational report. *Journal of Verbal Learning and Verbal Behavior, 6,* 151–155.

Chapman, L. J., & Chapman, J. P. (1967). Genesis of popular but erroneous psychodiagnostic observations. *Journal of Abnormal Psychology, 72,* 193–204.

Chapman, L. J., & Chapman, J. P. (1969). Illusory correlation as an obstacle to the use of valid psychodiagnostic signs. *Journal of Abnormal Psychology, 74,* 271–280.

Chi, M.T.H., & Koeske, R. D. (1983). Network representation of a child's dinosaur knowledge. *Developmental Psychology, 19,* 29–39.

Covey, S. R. (1989). *The 7 habits of highly effective people: Restoring the character ethic.* New York: Simon & Schuster.

Covey, S. R., Merrill, A. R., & Merrill, R. R. (1994). *First things first: To live, to love, to learn, to leave a legacy.* New York: Simon & Schuster.

Davidson, D. (1991). Children's decision-making examined with an information-board procedure. *Cognitive Development, 6,* 77–90.

Davidson, D. (1995). The representativeness heuristic and the conjunction fallacy effect in children's decision making. *Merrill-Palmer Quarterly, 41,* 328–346.

Davis, J. H. (1973). Group decision and social interaction: A theory of social decision schemes. *Psychological Review, 80,* 97–125.

Dawes, R. M. (1982). The robust beauty of improper linear models in decision-making. In D. Kahneman, P. Slovic, & A. Tversky (Eds.), *Judgment under uncertainty: Heuristics and biases* (pp. 391–407). New York: Cambridge University Press.

Dawes, R. M., & Corrigan, B. (1974). Linear models in decision-making. *Psychological Bulletin, 81,* 95–106.

Dewey, J. (1933). *How we think: A restatement of the relation of reflective thinking to the educative process.* Boston: D. C. Heath.

Dollinger, M. J., & Danis, W. (1998). Preferred decision-making styles: A cross-cultural comparison. *Psychological Reports, 82,* 755–761.

Donovan, J. J., & Radosevich, D. J. (1998). The moderating role of goal commitment on the goal difficulty-performance relationship: A meta-analytic review and critical reanalysis. *Journal of Applied Psychology, 83,* 308–315.

Dreyfus, H. L. (1997). Intuitive, deliberative, and calculative models of expert performance. In C. E. Zsambok & G. Klein (Eds.), *Naturalistic decision making* (pp. 17–35). Mahwah, NJ: Lawrence Erlbaum Associates.

Dunegan, K. J. (1993). Framing, cognitive modes, and image theory: Toward an understanding of a glass half full. *Journal of Applied Psychology, 78,* 491–503.

Dweck, C. S. (1996). Implicit theories as organizers of goals and behaviors. In P. M. Gollwitzer & J. E. Garth (Eds.), *The psychology of action* (pp. 69–90). New York: Guilford.

Dweck, C. S. (2000). *Self theories: Their role in motivation, personality, and development.* Philadelphia: Psychology Press.

Dweck, C. S., Chiu, C., & Hong, Y. (1995). Implicit theories: Elaboration and extension of the model. *Psychological Inquiry, 6,* 332–333.

Dweck, C. S., & Leggett, E. L. (1988). A social-cognitive approach to motivation and personality. *Psychological Review, 95,* 256–273.

Eccles, J. S., Wigfield, A., & Schiefele, U. (1998). Motivation to succeed. In W. Damon (Series Ed.) & N. Eisenberg (Vol. Ed.), *Handbook of child psychology: Social, emotional, and personality development* (5th ed., pp. 1017–1095). New York: Wiley.

Edwards, W., & von Winterfeldt, D. (1986). On cognitive illusions and their implications. In H. R. Arkes & K. R. Hammond (Eds.), *Judgment and decision making: An interdisciplinary reader* (pp. 642–679). Cambridge, UK: Cambridge University Press.

Eich, E. (1995). Searching for mood dependent memory. *Psychological Science, 6,* 67–75.

Elkind, D. (1967). Egocentrism in adolescence. *Child Development, 38,* 1025–1034.

Elliott, E. S., & Dweck, C. S. (1988). Goals: An approach to motivation and achievement. *Journal of Personality and Social Psychology, 54,* 5–12.

Emmons, R. A. (1996). Striving and feeling: Personal goals and subjective well-being. In P. M. Gollwitzer & J. E. Garth (Eds.), *The psychology of action: Linking cognition and motivation to behavior* (pp. 313–337). New York: Guilford.

Ericsson, K. A., & Lehman, A. C. (1996). Expert and exceptional performance: Evidence of maximal adaptation to task constraints. *Annual Review of Psychology, 47,* 273–305.

Erikson, E. H. (1968). *Identity: Youth and crisis.* New York: Norton.

Esser, J. K., & Lindoerfer, J. S. (1989). Groupthink and the space shuttle *Challenger* accident: Toward a quantitative case analysis. *Journal of Behavioral Decision Making, 2,* 167–177.

Ettenson, R., Shanteau, J., & Krogstad, J. (1987). Expert judgment: Is more information better? *Psychological Reports, 60,* 227–238.

Fagley, N. S., & Miller, P. M. (1997). Framing effects and arenas of choice: Your money or your life? *Organizational Behavior and Human Decision Processes, 71,* 355–373.

Fischhoff, B. (1982). For those condemned to study the past: Heuristics and biases in hindsight. In D. Kahneman, P. Slovic, & A. Tversky (Eds.), *Judgment under uncertainty: Heuristics and biases* (pp. 330–344). New York: Cambridge University Press.

Fischhoff, B. (1991). Value elicitation: Is there anything in there? *American Psychologist, 46,* 835–847.

Flavell, J. H., Beach, D. R., & Chinsky, J. M. (1966). Spontaneous verbal rehearsal in memory task as a function of age. *Child Development, 37,* 283–299.

Flavell, J. H., Green, F. L., & Flavell, E. R. (1986). Development of knowledge about the appearance-reality distinction. *Monographs of the Society for Research in Child Development, 51,* 1–87.

Flavell, J. H., Miller, P. H., & Miller, S. A. (2002). *Cognitive development* (4th edition). Upper Saddle River, NJ: Prentice-Hall.

Ford, M. R., & Lowery, C. R. (1986). Gender differences in moral reasoning: A comparison of the use of justice and care orientations. *Journal of Personality and Social Psychology, 50,* 777–783.

Friedrich, J. (1987). Perceived control and decision making in a job hunting context. *Basic and Applied Social Psychology, 8,* 163–176.

Frisch, D. (2000). The tao of thinking. *Behavioral and Brain Sciences, 23,* 672–673.

Frisch, D., & Clemen, R. T. (1994). Beyond expected utility: Rethinking behavioral decision research. *Psychological Bulletin, 116,* 46–54.

Frosch, D. L., & Kaplan, R. M. (1999). Shared decision making in clinical medicine: Past research and future directions. *American Journal of Preventive Medicine, 17,* 285–294.

Galotti, K. M. (1989). Gender differences in self-reported moral reasoning: A review and new evidence. *Journal of Youth and Adolescence, 18,* 475–488.

Galotti, K. M. (1995a). A longitudinal study of real-life decision making: Choosing a college. *Applied Cognitive Psychology, 9,* 459–484.

Galotti, K. M. (1995b). Memories of a "decision-map": Recall of a real-life decision. *Applied Cognitive Psychology, 9,* 307–319.

Galotti, K. M. (1998, November). *Real-life decision making: Pregnancy and birthing decisions.* Presentation made at the Psychonomic Society Meetings, Dallas, TX.

Galotti, K. M. (1999a). Making a "major" real-life decision: College students choosing an academic major. *Journal of Educational Psychology, 91,* 379–387.

Galotti, K. M. (1999b). *Cognitive psychology in and out of the laboratory* (2nd ed.). Pacific Grove, CA: Brooks/Cole Wadsworth.

Galotti, K. M., & Mark, M. C. (1994). How do high school students structure an important life decision? A short-term longitudinal study of the college decision-making process. *Research in Higher Education, 35,* 589–607.

Ganzel, A. K. (1999). Adolescent decision making: The influence of mood, age, and gender on the consideration of information. *Journal of Adolescent Research, 14,* 289–318.

Gardner, H. (1983). *Frames of mind: The theory of multiple intelligences.* New York: Basic Books.

Gigone, D., & Hastie, R. (1997). Proper analysis of the accuracy of group judgments. *Psychological Bulletin, 121,* 149–167.

Gilligan, C. (1977). In a different voice: Women's conceptions of self and morality. *Harvard Educational Review, 47,* 481–517.

Gilligan, C. (1982). *In a different voice: Psychological theory and women's development.* Cambridge, MA: Harvard University Press.

Gleitman, H., Fridlund, A. J., & Reisberg, D. (1999). *Psychology* (5th ed.). New York: W. W. Norton.

Godden, D. R., & Baddeley, A. D. (1975). Context-dependent memory in two natural environments: On land and underwater. *British Journal of Psychology, 66,* 325–331.

Gollwitzer, P. M. (1996). The volitional benefits of planning. In P. M. Gollwitzer & J. E. Garth (Eds.), *The psychology of action.* New York: Guilford.

Griffin, D. W., Dunning, D., & Ross, L. (1990). The role of construal processes in overconfident predictions about the self and others. *Journal of Personality and Social Psychology, 59,* 1128–1139.

Griggs, R. A., & Cox, J. R. (1982). The elusive thematic-materials effect in Wason's selection task. *British Journal of Psychology, 73,* 407–420.

Grotevant, H. D. (1993). The integrative nature of identity: Bringing the soloists to sing in the choir. In J. Kroger (Ed.), *Discussions on ego identity* (pp. 121–146). Hillsdale, NJ: Lawrence Erlbaum Associates.

Guadagnoli, E., & Ward, P. (1998). Patient participation in decision-making. *Social Science and Medicine, 47,* 329–339.

Hastie, R., & Pennington, N. (2000). Explanation-based decision making. T. Connolly, H. R. Arkes, & K. R. Hammond (Eds.), *Judgement and decision making: An interdisciplinary reader* (2nd ed., pp. 212–228). New York: Cambridge University Press.

Hirt, E. R., & Markman, K. D. (1995). Multiple explanation: A consider-an-alternative strategy for debiasing judgments. *Journal of Personality and Social Psychology, 69,* 1069–1086.

Hogarth, R. (1980). *Judgment and choice: The psychology of decisions.* Chichester, UK: Wiley.

Hollenbeck, J. R., Williams, C. R., & Klein, H. J. (1989). An empirical examination of the antecedents of commitment to difficult goals. *Journal of Applied Psychology, 74,* 18–23.

Hudson, J. A., Shapiro, L. R., & Sosa, B. B. (1995). Planning in the real world: Preschool children's scripts and plans for familiar events. *Child Development, 66,* 984–998.

Hudson, J. A., Sosa, B. B., & Shapiro, L. R. (1997). Scripts and plans: The development of preschool children's event knowledge and event planning. In S. L. Friedman & E. K. Scholnick (Eds.), *The developmental psychology of planning: Why, how, and when do we plan?* (pp. 77–102). Mahwah, NJ: Lawrence Erlbaum Associates.

Jackson, J. (1995). Juror decision-making and the trial process. In G. Davies, S. Lloyd-Bostok, M. McMurray, & C. Wilson (Eds.), *Psychology, law, and criminal justice: International developments in research and practices* (pp. 327–336). Berlin, DE: Walter de Gryter.

Jacobs, J. E., & Ganzel, A. K. (1993). Decision-making in adolescence: Are we asking the wrong question? *Advances in motivation and achievement, 8,* 1–31.

Jacobs, J. E., Greenwald, J. P., & Osgood, D. W. (1995). Developmental differences in base rate estimates of social behaviors and attitudes. *Social Development, 4,* 165–181.

Jacobs, J. E., & Potenza, M. (1991). The use of judgment heuristics to make social and object decisions: A developmental perspective. *Child Development, 62,* 166–178.

James, W. (1983). *The principles of psychology.* Cambridge, MA: Harvard University Press. (Original work published 1890)

Janis, I. L. (1982). *Groupthink: Psychological studies of policy decisions and fiascoes* (2nd ed.). Boston, MA: Houghton Mifflin.

Janis, I. L., & Mann, L. (1977). *Decision making: A psychological analysis of conflict, choice, and commitment.* New York: The Free Press.

Johnson, E. A. (1997). Children's understanding of epistemic conduct in self-deception and other false belief stories. *Child Development, 68,* 1117–1132.

Johnson, R. H. (1978). Individual styles of decision making: A theoretical model for counseling. *Personnel and Guidance Journal, 56,* 530–536.

Kagan, J. (1966). Reflection-impulsivity: The generality and dynamics of conceptual tempo. *Journal of Abnormal Psychology, 71,* 17–24.

Kahneman, D. (2000). A psychological point of view: Violations of rational rules as a diagnostic of mental processes. *Behavioral and Brain Sciences, 23,* 681–683.

Kahneman, D., & Tversky, A. (1973). On the psychology of prediction. *Psychological Review, 80,* 237–251.

Kahneman, D., & Tversky, A. (1979). Prospect theory: An analysis of decision under risk. *Economet-rica, 47,* 263–291.

Kahneman, D., & Tversky, A. (1984). Choices, values, and frames. *American Psychologist, 39,* 341–350.

Kamin, K. A., & Rachlinski, J. J. (1995). Ex post = ex ante: Determining liability in hindsight. *Law and Human Behavior, 19,* 89–104.

Kassin, S. M., Ellsworth, P. C., & Smith, V. L. (1989). The "general acceptance" of psychological research on eyewitness testimony. *American Psychologist, 44,* 1089–1098.

Keeney, T. J., Cannizzo, S. R., & Flavell, J. H. (1967). Spontaneous and induced verbal rehearsal in a recall task. *Child Development, 38,* 953–966.

Kelly, J. R., & Karau, S. J. (1999). Group decision making: The effects of initial preferences and time pressure. *Personality and Social Psychology Bulletin, 25,* 1342–1354.

Kemler, D. G. (1983). Holistic and analytic modes in perceptual and cognitive development. In T. J. Tighe & B. E. Shepp (Eds.), *Perception, cognition, and development: Interactional analyses* (pp. 77–102). Hillsdale, NJ: Lawrence Erlbaum Associates.

Keren, G. (1987). Facing uncertainty in the game of bridge: A calibration study. *Organizational Behavior and Human Decision Processes, 39,* 98–114.

Kerr, N. L. (1981). Social transition schemes: Charting the group's road to agreement. *Journal of Personality and Social Psychology, 41,* 684–702.

Kerr, N. L., MacCoun, R. J., & Kramer, G. P. (1996). Bias in judgment: Comparing individuals and groups. *Psychological Review, 103,* 687–719.

Kirchler, E. (1995). Studying economic decisions within private households: A critical review and design for a "couple experiences diary." *Journal of Economic Psychology, 16,* 393–419.

Kirchler, E., & Davis, J. H. (1986). The influence of member status differences and task type of group consensus and member position change. *Journal of Personality and Social Psychology, 51,* 83–91.

Klaczynski, P. A. (2001a). Analytic and heuristic processing influences on adolescent reasoning and decision-making. *Child Development, 72,* 844–861.

Klaczynski, P. A. (2001b). Framing effects on adolescent task representations, analytic and heuristic processing, and decision making: Implications for the normative-descriptive gap. *Journal of Applied Development, 22,* 289–309.

Klaczynski, P. A., & Fauth, J. M. (1996). Intellectual ability, rationality, and intuitiveness as predictors of warranted and unwarranted optimism for future life events. *Journal of Youth and Adolescence, 25,* 755–773.

Klein, G. (1998). *Sources of power: How people make decisions.* Cambridge, MA: MIT Press.

Klein, H. J., Wesson, M. J., Hollenbeck, J. R., & Alge, B. J. (1999). Goal commitment and the goal-setting process: Conceptual clarification and empirical synthesis. *Journal of Applied Psychology, 84,* 885–896.

Kleinmuntz, B. (1990). Why we still use our heads instead of formulas: Toward an integrative approach. *Psychological Bulletin, 107,* 296–310.

Kmett, C. M., Arkes, H. R., & Jones, S. K. (1999). The influence of decision aids on high school students' satisfaction with their college choice decision. *Personality and Social Psychology Bulletin, 25* 1293–1301.

Kohlberg, L. (1976). Moral stages and moralization: The cognitive-developmental approach. In T. Lickona (Ed.), *Moral development and behavior: Theory, research, and social issues* (pp. 31–53). New York: Holt, Rinehart & Winston.

Kohlberg, L. (1984). *Essays in moral development. Volume II: The psychology of moral development.* San Francisco: Harper & Row.

Koriat, A., Lichtenstein, S., & Fischhoff, B. (1980). Reasons for confidence. *Journal of Experimental Psychology: Human Learning and Memory, 6,* 107–118.

Kosonen, P., & Winne, P. H. (1995). Effects of teaching statistical laws on reasoning about everyday problems. *Journal of Educational Psychology, 87,* 33–46.

Kreitler, S., & Kreitler, H. (1986). Development of probability thinking in children 5 to 12 years old. *Cognitive Development, 1,* 365–390.

Langley, A., Mintzberg, H., Pitcher, P., Posada, E., & Saint-Macary, J. (1995). Opening up decision making: The view from the black stool. *Organization Science, 6,* 260–279.

Larkin, J., McDermott, J., Simon, D. P., & Simon, H. A. (1980). Expert and novice performance in solving physics problems. *Science, 208,* 1335–1342.

Larrick, R. P., Morgan, J. N., & Nisbett, R. E. (1990). Teaching the use of cost-benefit reasoning in everyday life. *Psychological Science, 1,* 362–370.

Larson, J. R., Jr., Christensen, C., Abbott, A. S., & Franz, T. M. (1996). Diagnosing groups: Charting the flow of information in medical decision-making teams. *Journal of Personality and Social Psychology, 71,* 315–330.

Larson, J. R., Jr., Christensen, C., Franz, T. M., & Abbott, A. S. (1998). Diagnosing groups: The pooling, management, and impact of shared and unshared case information in team-based medical decision making. *Journal of Personality and Social Psychology, 75,* 93–108.

Laughlin, P. R., Kerr, N. L., Davis, J. H., Halff, H. M., & Marciniak, K. A. (1975). Group size, member ability, and social decision schemes on an intellective task. *Journal of Personality and Social Psychology, 31,* 522–535.

Lave, J. (1990). The culture of acquisition and the practice of understanding. In J. W. Stigler & R. A. Shweder (Eds.), *Cultural psychology: Essays on comparative human development* (pp. 309–328). New York: Cambridge University Press.

Lave, J., Murtaugh, M., & de la Rocha, O. (1984). The dialectic of arithmetic in grocery shopping. In B. Rogoff & J. Lave (Eds.), *Everyday cognition: Its development in social context* (pp. 67–94). Cambridge, MA: Harvard University Press.

Leichtman, M. D., & Ceci, S. J. (1995). The effects of stereotypes and suggestions on preschoolers' reports. *Developmental Psychology, 31,* 568–578.

Lewis, C. C. (1981). How adolescents approach decisions: Changes over grades seven to twelve and policy implications. *Child Development, 52,* 538–544.

Lichtenstein, S., Fischhoff, B., & Phillips, D. (1982). Calibration of probabilities: The state of the art to 1980. In D. Kahneman, P. Slovic, & A. Tversky (Eds.), *Judgement under uncertainty: Heuristics and biases* (pp. 306–344). Cambridge, UK: Cambridge University Press.

Little, B. R. (1983). Personal projects: A rationale and method for investigation. *Environment and Behavior, 15,* 273–309.

Little, B. R. (1998). Personal project pursuit: Dimensions and dynamics of personal meaning. In P.T.P. Wong & P. S. Fry (Eds.), *The human quest for meaning: A handbook for research and clinical applications* (pp. 193–212). Mahwah, NJ: Lawrence Erlbaum Associates.

Locke, E. A., & Latham, G. P. (1990). *A theory of goal setting and task performance.* Englewood Cliffs, NJ: Prentice Hall.

Loftus, E. F. (1979). *Eyewitness testimony.* Cambridge, MA: Harvard University Press.

Loftus, E. F., Miller, D. G., & Burns, H. J. (1978). Semantic integration of verbal information into a visual memory. *Journal of Experimental Psychology: Human Learning and Memory, 4,* 19–31.

MacCoun, R. J. (1999). Epistemological dilemmas in the assessment of legal decision making. *Law and Human Behavior, 23,* 723–730.

Mann, L., Harmoni, R., & Power, C. (1989). Adolescent decision-making: The development of competence. *Journal of Adolescence, 12,* 265–278.

Mann, L., Radford, M., Burnett, P., Ford, S., Bond, M., Leung, K., Nakamura, H., Vaughan, G., & Yang, K. (1998). Cross-cultural differences in self-reported decision-making style and confidence. *International Journal of Psychology, 33,* 325–335.

Marcia, J. E. (1966). Development and validation of ego identity status. *Journal of Personality and Social Psychology, 3,* 551–558.

Markovits, H. (1993). The development of conditional reasoning: A Piagetian reformulation of mental models theory. *Merrill-Palmer Quarterly, 39,* 131–158.

Maslow, A. H. (1954). *Motivation and personality (2nd ed.)*. New York: Harper & Row.

McGraw, P. C. (1999). *Life strategies: Doing what works, doing what matters*. New York: Hyperion.

McGregor, I., & Little, B. R. (1998). Personal projects, happiness, and meaning: On doing well and being yourself. *Journal of Personality and Social Psychology, 74*, 494–512.

McKinlay, J. B., Potter, D. A., & Feldman, H. A. (1996). Non-medical influences on medical decision-making. *Social Science and Medicine, 42*, 769–776.

McPherson, K. (1994). The best and the enemy of the good: Randomised controlled trials, uncertainty, and assessing the role of patient choice in medical decision making. *Journal of Epidemiology and Community Health, 48*, 6–15.

Meece, J. L., Blumenfeld, P. C., & Hoyle, R. H. (1988). Students' goal orientations and cognitive engagement in classroom activities. *Journal of Educational Psychology, 80*, 514–523.

Meehl, P. E. (1954). *Clinical versus statistical prediction: A theoretical analysis and a review of the evidence*. Minneapolis: University of Minnesota Press.

Meehl, P. E. (1965). Seer over sign: The first good example. *Journal of Experimental Research in Personality, 1*, 27–32.

Miller, D. C., & Byrnes, J. P. (1997). The role of contextual and personal factors in children's risk taking. *Developmental Psychology, 33*, 814–823.

Miller, G. A. (1956). The magical number seven, plus or minus two: Some limits on our capacity for processing information. *Psychological Review, 63*, 81–97.

Miller, G. A., Galanter, E., & Pribram, K. H. (1960). *Plans and the structure of behavior*. New York: Henry Holt.

Mitchell, T. R., & Beach, L. R. (1990). ". . . Do I love thee? Let me count . . ." Toward an understanding of intuitive and automatic decision making. *Organizational Behavior and Human Decision Processes, 47*, 1–20.

Moshman, D. (1999). *Adolescent psychological development: Rationality, morality, and identity*. Mahwah, NJ: Lawrence Erlbaum Associates.

Moshman, D., & Franks, B. A. (1986). Development of the concept of inferential validity. *Child Development, 57*, 153–165.

Murphy, A. H., & Winkler, R. L. (1984). Probability forecasting in meterorology. *Journal of the American Statistical Association, 79*, 489–500.

Neely, J. H. (1990). Semantic priming effects in visual word recognition: A selective review of current findings and theories. In D. Besner & G. W. Humphreys (Eds.), *Basic processes in reading: Visual word recognition* (pp. 264–336). Hillsdale, NJ: Lawrence Erlbaum Associates.

Neisser, U. (1976). *Cognition and reality: Principles and implications of cognitive psychology*. San Francisco: W. H. Freeman.

Nelson, K. (1986). Event knowledge and cognitive development. In K. Nelson (Ed.), *Event knowledge: Structure and function in development* (pp. 1–20). Hillsdale, NJ: Lawrence Erlbaum Associates.

Nelson, K., & Gruendel, J. M. (1981). Generalized event representation: Basic building blocks of cognitive development. In A. Brown & M. Lamb (Eds.), *Advances in developmental psychology* (Vol. 1, pp. 131–158). Hillsdale, NJ: Lawrence Erlbaum Associates.

Nichols-Hoppe, K. T., & Beach, L. R. (1990). The effects of test anxiety and task variables on predecisional information search. *Journal of Research in Personality, 24*, 163–172.

Niles, S. G., Erford, B. T., Hunt, B., & Watts, R. H., Jr. (1997). Decision-making styles and career development in college students. *Journal of College Student Development, 38*, 479–488.

Nisbett, R., & Ross, L. (1980). *Human inference: Strategies and shortcomings of social judgment*. Englewood Cliffs, NJ: Prentice-Hall.

Nisbett, R. E. (1993). Reasoning, abstraction, and the principles of 20th century psychology. In R. E. Nisbett (Ed.), *Rules for reasoning* (pp. 1–12). Hillsdale, NJ: Lawrence Erlbaum Associates.

Nisbett, R. E., Krantz, D. H., Jepson, C., & Kunda, Z. (1983). The use of statistical heuristics in everyday inductive reasoning. *Psychological Review, 90*, 339–363.

Nisbett, R. E., & Wilson, T. D. (1977). Telling more than we can know: Verbal reports on mental processes. *Psychological Review, 84,* 231–259.

Novacek, J., & Lazarus, R. S. (1990). The structure of personal commitments. *Journal of Personality, 58,* 693–715.

Nurmi, J. (1991). How do adolescents see their future? A review of the development of future orientation and planning. *Developmental Review, 11,* 1–59.

Ogloff, J.R.P. (1993). Jury decision making and the insanity defense. In N. J. Castellan, Jr. (Ed.), *Individual and group decision making: Current issues* (pp. 167–201). Hillsdale, NJ: Lawrence Erlbaum Associates.

Osherson, D. N., & Markman, E. (1975). Language and the ability to evaluate contradictions and tautologies. *Cognition, 3,* 213–226.

Payne, J. W. (1976). Task complexity and contingent processing in decision making: An information search and protocol analysis. *Organizational Behavior and Human Decision Processes, 16,* 366–387.

Payne, J. W., Bettman, J. R., & Johnson, E. J. (1993). *The adaptive decision maker.* Cambridge, UK: Cambridge University Press.

Pennington, N., & Hastie, R. (1988). Explanation-based decision making: The effects of memory structure on judgement. *Journal of Experimental Psychology: Learning, Memory, and Cognition, 14,* 521–533.

Perkins, D. N. (1985). Postprimary education has little impact on informal reasoning. *Journal of Educational Psychology, 77,* 562–571.

Perkins, D. N., Allen, R., & Hafner, J. (1983). Difficulties in everyday reasoning. In W. Maxwell (Ed.), *Thinking: The expanding frontier* (pp. 177–189). Philadelphia: Franklin Institute.

Peterson, R. S. (1997). A directive leadership style in group decision making can be both virtue and vice: Evidence from elite and experimental groups. *Journal of Personality and Social Psychology, 72,* 1107–1121.

Phillips, J. M., & Gully, S. M. (1997). Role of goal orientation, ability, need for achievement, and locus of control in the self-efficacy and goal-setting process. *Journal of Applied Psychology, 82,* 792–802.

Piaget, J. (1955). *The language and thought of the child* (M. Gabain, Trans.). New York: World Publishing Co.

Piaget, J., & Inhelder, B. (1969). *The psychology of the child.* New York: Basic Books.

Pinker, S. (1997). *How the mind works.* New York: W. W. Norton.

Plous, S. (1993). *The psychology of judgment and decision making.* Philadelphia: Temple University Press.

Potter, R. E., & Beach, L. R. (1994a). Decision making when the acceptable options become unavailable. *Organizational Behavior and Human Decision Processes, 57,* 468–483.

Potter, R. E., & Beach, L. R. (1994b). Imperfect information in pre-choice screening of options. *Organizational Behavior and Human Decision Processes, 59,* 313–329.

Quadrel, M. J., Fischhoff, B., & Davis, W. (1993). Adolescent (in)vulnerability. *American Psychologist, 48,* 102–116.

Rachlin, H. (1989). *Judgment, decision, and choice: A cognitive/behavioral synthesis.* New York: Freeman.

Radford, M.H.B., Mann, L., Ohta, Y., & Nakane, Y. (1991). Differences between Australian and Japanese students in reported use of a decision process. *International Journal of Psychology, 26,* 35–52.

Radford, M.H.B., Mann, L., Ohta, Y., & Nakane, Y. (1993). Differences between Australilian and Japanese students in decisional self-esteem, decisional stress, and coping styles. *Journal of Cross-Cultural Psychology, 24,* 284–297.

Randel, J. M., Pugh, H. L., & Reed, S. K. (1996). Differences in expert and novice situation awareness in naturalistic decision making. *International Journal of Human–Computer Studies, 45,* 579–597.

Rapoport, A., & Chammah, A. M. (1965). *Prisoner's dilemma: A study in conflict and cooperation.* Ann Arbor: The University of Michigan Press.

Rayner, S. & Riding, R. (1997). Towards a categorisation of cognitive styles and learning styles. *Educational Psychology, 17,* 5–27.

Reilly, B. A., & Doherty, M. E. (1989). A note on the assessment of self-insight in judgment research. *Organizational Behavior and Human Decision Processes, 44,* 121–131.

Reyna, V. F., & Ellis, S. C. (1994). Fuzzy-trace theory and framing effects in children's risky decision making. *Psychological Science, 5,* 275–279.

Riding, R. J., Glass, A., Butler, S. R., & Pleydell-Pearce, C. W. (1997). Cognitive style and individual differences in EEG alpha during information processing. *Educational Psychology, 17,* 219–234.

Roediger, H. L., III, & Guynn, M. J. (1996). Retrieval processes. In E. L. Bjork & R. A. Bjork (Eds.), *Memory* (pp. 197–236). San Diego, CA: Academic Press.

Ruff, H. A., Copozzoli, M., & Weissberg, R. (1998). Age, individuality, and context as factors in sustained visual attention during the preschool years. *Developmental Psychology, 34,* 454–464.

Russo, J. E. (1977). The value of unit price information. *Journal of Marketing Research, 14,* 193–201.

Russo, J. E., & Leclerc, F. (1991). Characteristics of successful product information programs. *Journal of Social Issues, 47,* 73–92.

Sabini, J. (1992). *Social psychology.* New York: W. W. Norton.

Santalahti, P., Hemminki, E., Latikka, A., & Ryynänen, M. (1998). Women's decision-making in prenatal screening. *Social Science and Medicine, 46,* 1067–1076.

Scholnick, E. K., & Friedman, S. L. (1987). The planning construct in the psychological literature. In S. L. Friedman, E. S. Scholnick, & R. R. Cocking (Eds.), *Blueprints for thinking: The role of planning in cognitive development* (pp. 3–38). Cambridge, UK: Cambridge University Press.

Scholnick, E. K., Friedman, S. L., & Wallner-Allen, K. E. (1997). What do they really measure? A comparative analysis of planning tasks. In S. L. Friedman & E. K. Scholnick (Eds.), *The developmental psychology of planning: Why, how, and when do we plan?* (pp. 127–156). Mahwah, NJ: Lawrence Erlbaum Associates.

Scott, S. G., & Bruce, R. A. (1995). Decision-making style: The development and assessment of a new measure. *Educational and Psychological Measurement, 55,* 818–831.

Searight, H. R. (1992). Assessing patient competence for medical decision making. *American Family Physician, 45,* 751–759.

Searight, H. R., & Hubbard, S. L. (1998). Evaluating patient capacity for medical decision making: Individual and interpersonal dimensions. *Families, Systems, and Health, 16,* 41–54.

Seidl, C., & Traub, S. (1998). A new test of image theory. *Organizational Behavior and Human Decision Processes, 75,* 93–116.

Senter, S. M., & Wedell, D. H. (1999). Information presentation constraints and the adaptive decision maker hypothesis. *Journal of Experimental Psychology: Learning, Memory, and Cognition, 25,* 428–446.

Shanteau, J. (1988). Psychological characteristics and strategies of expert decision makers. *Acta Psychologica, 68,* 203–215.

Shanteau, J. (1992). Competence in experts: The role of task characteristics. *Organizational Behavior and Human Decision Processes, 53,* 252–266.

Shaw, M. E. (1932). A comparison of individuals and small groups in the rational solution of complex problems. *American Journal of Psychology, 44,* 491–504.

Sheldon, K. M., & Elliot, A. J. (1998). Not all personal goals are personal: Comparing autonomous and controlled reasons for goals as predictors of effort and attainment. *Personality and Social Psychology Bulletin, 24,* 546–557.

Siegler, R. S. (1998). *Children's thinking* (3rd ed.). Upper Saddle River, NJ: Prentice Hall.

Silverman, K. (Ed.). (1986). *Benjamin Franklin: Autobiography and other writings.* New York: Penguin Books.

Simon, H. A. (1955). A behavioral model of rational choice. *Quarterly Journal of Economics, 69,* 99–118.

Simon, H. A. (1956). Rational choice and the structure of the environment. *Psychological Review, 63,* 129–138.

Simons, D. J., & Galotti, K. M. (1992). Everyday planning: An analysis of daily time management. *Bulletin of the Psychonomic Society, 30,* 61–64.

Slovic, P., Lichtenstein, S., & Fischhoff, B. (1988). Decision making. In R. C. Atkinson, R. J. Herrnstein, G. Lindzey, & R. D. Luce (Eds.), *Steven's handbook of experimental psychology: Vol. 2: Learning and cognition* (2nd ed., pp. 673–738). New York: Wiley.

South Central Builders Association. (1999). *A checklist for home buyers.* Owatonna, MN: Author.

Stanovich, K. E., (1999). *Who is rational? Studies of individual differences in reasoning.* Mahwah, NJ: Lawrence Erlbaum Associates.

Stanovich, K. E., & West, R. F. (1997). Reasoning independently of prior belief and individual differences in actively open-minded thinking. *Journal of Educational Psychology, 89,* 342–357.

Stanovich, K. E., & West, R. F. (1998). Individual differences in rational thought. *Journal of Experimental Psychology: General, 127,* 161–188.

Stanovich, K. E., & West, R. F. (2000). Individual differences in reasoning: Implications for the rationality debate? *Behavioral and Brain Sciences, 23,* 645–726.

Stasser, G. (1999). A primer of social decision scheme theory: Models of group influence, competitive model-testing, and prospective modeling. *Organizational Behavior and Human Decision Processes, 80,* 3–20.

Staw, B. M., Barsade, S. G., & Koput, K. W. (1997). Escalation at the credit window: A longitudinal study of bank executives' recognition and write-off of problem loans. *Journal of Applied Psychology, 82,* 130–142.

Steinberg, L., & Cauffman, E. (1996). Maturity of judgment in adolescence: Psychosocial factors in adolescent decision making. *Law and Human Behavior, 20,* 249–272.

Sternberg, R. J. (1997). *Thinking styles.* Cambridge, UK: Cambridge University Press.

Strutt, G. F., Anderson, D. R., & Well, A. D. (1975). A developmental study of the effects of irrelevant information on speeded classification. *Journal of Experimental Child Psychology, 20,* 127–135.

Tanner, C. A., Benner, P., Chesla, C., & Gordon, D. R. (1993). The phenomenology of knowing the patient. *Image: Journal of Nursing Scholarship, 25,* 273–280.

Taylor, M. (1996). A theory of mind perspective on social cognitive development. In R. Gelman & T. K. Au (Eds.), *Perceptual and cognitive development* (pp. 283–329). San Diego, CA: Academic Press.

Thaler, R. H. (1980). Toward a positive theory of consumer choice. *Journal of Economic Behavior and Organization, 1,* 39–60.

Thompson, L., & Hastie, R. (1990). Social perception in negotiation. *Organizational Behavior and Human Decision Processes, 47,* 98–123.

Thompson, L., & Hrebec, D. (1996). Lose-lose agreements in interdependent decision making. *Psychological Bulletin, 120,* 396–409.

Thompson, S. C., Pitts, J. S., & Schwankovsky, L. (1994). Preferences for involvement in medical decision-making: Situational and demographic influences. *Patient Education and Counseling, 22,* 133–140.

Tversky, A. (1972). Elimination by aspects: A theory of choice. *Psychological Review, 79,* 281–299.

Tversky, A., & Kahneman, D. (1971). Belief in the law of small numbers. *Psychological Bulletin, 76,* 105–110.

Tversky, A., & Kahneman, D. (1973). Availability: A heuristic for judging frequency and probability. *Cognitive Psychology, 5,* 207–232.

Tversky, A., & Kahneman, D. (1974). Judgment under uncertainty: Heuristics and biases. *Science, 185,* 1124–1131.

Tversky, A., & Kahneman, D. (1981). The framing of decisions and the psychology of choice. *Science, 211,* 453–458.

Tversky, A., & Kahneman, D. (2000). Judgment under uncertainty: Heuristics and biases. In T. Connolly, H. R. Arkes, & K. R. Hammond (Eds.), *Judgement and decision making* (2nd ed., pp. 35–52). New York: Cambridge University Press.

Urberg, K. A., & Rosen, R. A. (1987). Age differences in adolescent decision-making: Pregnancy resolution. *Journal of Adolescent Research, 2,* 447–454.

Verplanken, B. (1993). Need for cognition and external information search: Responses to time pressure during decision-making. *Journal of Research in Personality, 27,* 238–252.

von Winterfeldt, D., & Edwards, W. (1986). *Decision analysis and behavioral research.* Cambridge, UK: Cambridge University Press.

Waber, D. (1989). The biological boundaries of cognitive styles: A neuropsychological analysis. In T. Globerson & T. Zelnicker (Eds.), S. Strauss (Series Ed.), *Cognitive style and cognitive development:* Vol. 3. *Human Development* (pp. 11–35). Norwood, NJ: Ablex.

Wadsworth, M., & Ford, D. H. (1983). Assessment of personal goal hierarchies. *Journal of Counseling Psychology, 30,* 514–526.

Walker, L. J., de Vries, B., & Trevethan, S. D. (1987). Moral stages and moral orientations in real-life and hypothetical dilemmas. *Child Development, 58,* 842–858.

Walker, L. J., Pitts, R. C., Hennig, K. H., & Matsuba, M. K. (1995). Reasoning about morality and real-life moral problems. In M. Killen & D. Hart (Eds.), *Morality in everyday life: Developmental perspectives* (pp. 371–407). Cambridge, UK: Cambridge University Press.

Wason, P. C. (1960). On the failure to eliminate hypotheses in a conceptual task. *Quarterly Journal of Experimental Psychology, 12,* 129–140.

Wason, P. C. (1968). Reasoning about a rule. *Quarterly Journal of Experimental Psychology, 20,* 273–281.

Wason, P. C. (1977). "On the failure to eliminate hypotheses . . ."—A second look. In P. N. Johnson-Laird & P. C. Wason (Eds.), *Thinking: Readings in cognitive science* (pp. 307–314). Cambridge, UK: Cambridge University Press.

Weeks, J. (1995). Measurement of utilities and quality-adjusted survival. *Oncology, 9,* 67–70.

Wells, G. L. (1993). What do we know about eyewitness identification. *American Psychologist, 48,* 553–571.

Wilks, J. (1986). The relative importance of parents and friends in adolescent decision making. *Journal of Youth and Adolescence, 15,* 323–334.

Williams, R. L., & Long, J. D. (1991). *Manage your life* (4th ed). Dallas, TX: Houghton Mifflin.

Wilson. T. D., Lisle, D. J., Schooler, J. W., Hodges, S. D., Klaaren, K. J., & LaFleur, S. J. (1993). Introspecting about reasons can reduce post-choice satisfaction. *Personality and Social Psychology Bulletin, 19,* 331–339.

Wilson, T. D., & Schooler, J. W. (1991). Thinking too much: Introspection can reduce the quality of preferences and decisions. *Journal of Personality and Social Psychology, 60,* 181–192.

Winquist, J. R., & Larson, J. R., Jr. (1998). Information pooling: When it impacts group decision making. *Journal of Personality and Social Psychology, 74,* 371–377.

Zaleski, Z. (1987). Behavioral effects of self-set goals for different time ranges. *International Journal of Psychology, 22,* 17–38.

Zaleski, Z. (1988). Attributions and emotions related to future goal attainment. *Journal of Educational Psychology, 80,* 563–568.

Author Index

Subject Index

About the Author

Kathleen Marie Galotti received a BA degree (with a double major in Psychology and Economics) from Wellesley College, an MA and a PhD in Psychology, and an MSE in Computer and Information Sciences at the University of Pennsylvania. She joined the faculty of Carleton College in 1983, and currently holds the titles Professor of Psychology and Cognitive Studies, and Director of the Cognitive Studies Concentration. She teaches courses in her specialities, developmental and cognitive psychology, as well as courses in introductory psychology and statistics. She is the author of *Cognitive Psychology in and out of the Laboratory*, a textbook, and more than two dozen journal articles. Her research, focusing on reasoning and decision making and the development of these skills, has been supported by the National Institutes of Health, the National Science Foundation, and the Spencer Foundation. She is a parent to Timmy (age 8), and Kimberlynn (age 4 months) and trains and exhibits Bernese Mountain dogs in obedience in her spare time.